Aaron

Aaron

Revised Edition

by Henry Aaron

with

Furman Bisher

THOMAS Y. CROWELL COMPANY
New York / *Established 1834*

First published in 1968 under the title *"Aaron, r.f."*.
Copyright © 1974, 1968 by Henry Aaron and Furman Bisher

Manufactured in the United States of America

1 2 3 4 5 6 7 8 9 10

Library of Congress Cataloging in Publication Data

Aaron, Henry, 1934-
    Aaron.

    1. Aaron, Henry, 1934-   2. Baseball.
I. Bisher, Furman.   II. Title.
GV865.A25A3   1974   796.357′092′4 [B]   74-566
ISBN 0-690-00509-1

1

IT WAS PRETTY CLOSE TO MIDNIGHT, and I was in Chicago. I can't remember the name of the hotel. I think it was the Sherman, but I'm not sure. I never was one for remembering names and dates and statistics. I can tell you how it happened, but I have to leave the fine details to the record books.

Anyway, this was after the 1957 baseball season. I had had a big one. The Milwaukee Braves had won the pennant and the World Series, and Miller Brewing Company had hired me to do some promotional work. That's what I was doing in Chicago.

I was supposed to have gone home that day, but the weather was real bad—a lot of snow and ice, and so bad you couldn't even get from Chicago to Milwaukee. Besides, a boy from south Alabama hasn't had a lot of experience driving on ice.

I had bought a newspaper and was reading in bed when the telephone rang. I hesitated, then picked it up. (Tell you the truth, a baseball player never knows what's going to be on the other end of the line when he answers a telephone. A lot of times I don't answer. I just let it ring.)

I said hello, and a man said, "Is this Hank Aaron?"

"Yeah, this is me. Who's this?"

He never did tell me who he was. Or if he did, it wasn't a name I remembered. He said he was calling from one of the newspaper offices in Chicago, and to this day I don't know how he found out where I was.

"Have you heard the news?" he said.

"What news?" I said.

"Well, then, let me be the first to congratulate you. You've been voted the Most Valuable Player in the National League."

Now, if I had had to lie there and tell that fellow I was surprised, I'd have been a liar. I thought I had a good shot at it. I'd led the National League in home runs, runs batted in, and runs scored, and had made 198 hits and batted .322, and we had won everything in sight. But you are never sure that the livestock is all in until the barn door is shut.

There were some pretty big players around the National League in 1957: Stan Musial, Ernie Banks, Warren Spahn, Willie Mays and Ed Mathews, just to name a few. And among all these, this fellow had told me that I was the Most Valuable.

"You don't say!" I said. "You really mean it?"

"That's right, Most Valuable Player," he said. "I'd like to send a photographer around and get a picture, okay?"

"Sure," I said, "send him on."

I put the phone back on the cradle and I dropped that newspaper to the floor and I just put my head back and stared at the ceiling. I ran it back and forth through my mind, "Henry Aaron, Most Valuable Player. Henry Aaron, Most Valuable Player."

I even imagined how the line of type would look in the record book where they list all the batting champions and pitching champions and Most Valuable Players.

"1957—Henry Aaron, Milwaukee Braves," right after the name of Don Newcombe, all the way back to Frank Frisch, and in between, Stan Musial, Willie Mays, Jackie Robinson, Roy Campanella and great players I'd read about when I was a little boy living "Down the Bay" in Mobile, Alabama.

I didn't see much of that photographer after he got there. He got the usual kind of poses. Hold up two fingers like V for victory, and smile big and read the newspaper for him, like I was reading the news. But I wasn't hearing him or seeing him. My mind was in a world all its own.

I looked out the window after he left and it was still snowing. I felt cozy there. I felt so good I never thought I'd ever want to go to bed again.

"Most Valuable Player," I said out loud. Not bad for a kid who left home with two dollars in his pocket, two pairs of pants and two sandwiches in a brown paper bag. My mother cried and my sisters cried, and I thought back to that day at the railroad station in Mobile, a little black kid—because I was little and not too fleshy—taking his first train ride to be a baseball player at the age of seventeen. My mother had made me take the sandwiches.

"They may not serve you on the train, son," she said. "You take these sandwiches. I don't want you going hungry."

They would have served me on the train, all right, but the two dollars would have just about made the tip. I didn't go to the dining car planning to eat. I just passed through looking around to see what the inside of a train was like. I didn't know that people really sat down and ate their dinner off a table while the train was moving.

I was on my way to Winston-Salem, North Carolina, to become an Indianapolis Clown. That's no circus act. It's a baseball team, probably the most famous barnstorming team in the world. I'm not certain. Maybe the Kansas City Monarchs team is, because of Satchel Paige and Jackie Robinson and Josh Gibson, the old catcher who used to play for them. At least, they're the two most famous black barnstorming teams in baseball.

It seems like I've been doing nothing but catching trains or planes or something ever since. It didn't take me long to learn how to sleep sitting up. It was either sleep that way with the Clowns, or not sleep at all. We lived in a bus so much that the guy sitting in the seat next to you was known as your roommate. These guys who complain about meal money and conditions in the big leagues today ought to have had dinner with the Clowns.

Our bus would stop at a store some place out in the

country, and you'd buy a can of sardines or pork-and-beans or some bologna and a big bottle of pop, or some crackers and cheese, and that was dinner.

One day we had stopped at this little store in some little town in North or South Carolina. I never knew what state we were in. We'd play our games at night and load up and drive until the next afternoon. All I'd do was sleep.

Anyway, we stopped at this little store and I got some bread and bologna and milk. Just about the time I started to take a swig of my milk, a bug flew into it. What I said wasn't printable.

My roommate was a pitcher named Jenkins, an older fellow who was some kind of preacher. At least he was always spouting off some kind of sermon to you. Not a bad guy; in fact, a nice guy, but always preaching.

"What's your trouble, Aaron?" he said.

"Darn bug flew in my drink," I said. "If he's thirstier than I am, let him have it." And I poured it on the ground.

"That's waste, boy!" Jenkins said. He tried to stop me. "That's a sin, Aaron, waste like that. Somewhere in the world somebody would have a treat with that milk. Don't forget, Aaron, waste is a sin."

I looked at him kind of funny. He was tall and bony, with big eyes set back in his head and real short hair. When our bus stopped for us to eat, you could always bet that Jenkins would eat a few slices of bologna and half a loaf of bread. You want to know what he did with the other half a loaf? He'd sell it.

Well, that night after the bug flew into my milk, I found out why Jenkins was so dead set against waste. When we got our meal money, which was all of two dollars a day, he put a dollar of it in an envelope and sealed it.

"What are you doing with that?" I asked him.

"Mailing it to my wife," he said. "I send her half my meal money every day."

I've thought about old, tall, bony "Preacher" Jenkins a lot of times since then, like when I'd be sitting in the Edgewater Beach Hotel in Chicago having breakfast, or at Ernie's in San Francisco having dinner, or riding up there in a plane, 30,000 feet high, having one of those luxury meals the airlines serve. Him sending half his meal money home every day and living on bologna and beans and sardines. If I sent half my meal money home today, I'd be sending home more than Jenkins was making.

Never did I recall Jenkins any more clearly, though, than on February 23, 1967. That was another big day in my life. There have been two real big moments in my career in baseball outside of something that actually took place on the field. I mean the kind of moments that sports writers call "milestones."

On that date I signed a contract with the Braves for $100,000 a year for two years. You may think this makes me sound mercenary, like money means everything. It does mean a lot, especially if you haven't got any, but baseball is economics, and baseball economics says you haven't "arrived" until you hit the $100,000 class. You saw how Juan Marichal held out with San Francisco that same spring because he wanted to be the highest-paid pitcher in baseball. (Sandy Koufax had just retired.) It means that much to a player. I don't know how Marichal made out as far as being the highest-paid pitcher in the game is concerned, but the newspapers said the Giants gave him $110,000, and he seemed satisfied.

I'll just plain have to admit that getting into the $100,000 class gave me a feeling I'd never had before. Ted Williams had made it, Joe DiMaggio had made it, Stan Musial had made it, Willie Mays had made it, Mickey Mantle had made it, and Sandy Koufax had made it—and now I had made it.

I could have hit 62 home runs, batted .400 and driven in 150 runs and I wouldn't have felt any more like I "belonged" than I did when I signed that contract for $100,000.

Let me tell you about that day.

It took place in Atlanta. By that time the Braves had moved from Milwaukee, and unless you've been hiding under a rock or on a long business trip, you've read about all that noise. (We'll take that up later.)

My ex-wife, Barbara, and I were going to visit my folks in Mobile and her folks in Jacksonville before spring training. Before I left home, I got a call from Bill Bartholomay, the president of the Braves. We were still living in Mequon, Wisconsin, which is a suburb of Milwaukee.

"Hank, can you stop over in Atlanta on your way down?" he said. "We'll have the signing and a press conference and make it official."

I had talked over salary with Bill in January when I was in Atlanta on some other business, and then I had met him in Chicago a little later and worked out all the other details. It was not an average, run-of-the-mill contract, as you will see later, and it took some extra figuring. There weren't any disagreements or haggling involved. They knew what I wanted and were willing to pay. It was a matter of spreading it out the way my lawyer advised me to have it spread out.

I told Bill Bartholomay I'd be there, and on the morning of February 23, Barbara and Dorinda, the baby—she was five then—caught a plane to Atlanta. We couldn't take the other three children with us because they were in school.

The *Atlanta Journal* had already printed a story that we had agreed to terms and that my salary would be $100,000 a year. What it didn't say was that I was signing for two years, the first time the Braves had ever signed a player for more than one season.

The press conference was at five o'clock in the afternoon in Bill Bartholomay's office in Atlanta Stadium. I was a little more excited than usual about it, and I wore my Sunday best. I had on a gray silk suit, one of those that shines back at you. Barbara had on a new mustard-colored coat I'd just bought her, with a fur collar and fur on the cuffs. If I was going to sign for $100,000 a year, I thought we ought to do our best to look like we were worth the price.

The press conference drew a big crowd for a kid who left home with two dollars, two pairs of pants and two sandwiches. There were guys with tape recorders, television cameras, and ballpoint pens and paper, and for a fellow who's known as the quiet type, I talked my head off for an hour or so.

Bill opened up by saying something I'll never forget.

"The Braves recognize Hank Aaron as a great ball player, and have for several years," he said. "I am happy now that we can make it official for him in salary."

Now, this may not mean much to the average baseball fan. He watches a baseball player play the game and thinks that he ought to be happy just to be in the big leagues, and I guess there's something to be said for that. But to me, to be signed by the president of the club, in his office, before a special press conference meant something to me. It was a milestone in my career in more ways than simply salary alone.

People wanted to know if I didn't think I'd been underpaid, since Willie Mays and Mickey Mantle and other players had been making $100,000 several years before me. I'm not going to rattle any skeletons, but I'd pick up the papers and read about this guy and that guy signing for $100,000, and I'd be leading him in hits and runs batted in and home runs, but I wasn't leading him in salary. Yes, it had bothered me, but I hadn't said anything about it before.

"I think I deserved $100,000 a year several years ago," I told Bob Hertzel of the *Atlanta Journal*, and I meant it. It did startle me a little bit when I read the headline on the story the next day.

"I Deserved $100,000, Says Hank" is the way it read.

I guess I'd always been too easy to deal with. They'd offer me a contract and I'd nearly always signed without any argument. I realized the Braves had been having troubles in Milwaukee and weren't making any money. I felt that they had been paying me the best they could under the circumstances, but the circumstances were no fault of mine. I was still hitting the same and driving in the same amount of runs and hitting my home runs, and if the club wasn't drawing, they couldn't blame me for a bad situation. But I went along with it and made no kick.

When we moved to Atlanta, though, it was a different story. The club made $990,000 during the 1966 season, so the papers said. Here I had been in the big leagues fourteen years and I still wasn't making $100,000. I'd been living in the shadow of some pretty big salaries, too.

I know that Warren Spahn had made $75,000, and Ed Mathews was making $60,000, and Lew Burdette and Red Schoendienst had made $50,000, and a lot of others had made big money. It was a heavy pay roll, and that had held me back, though I had been the Most Valuable Player and led the league in batting twice and runs batted in three times and home runs twice. Still, I wasn't getting anything above "scale," I guess you'd say.

When it came to dealing for the $100,000 at last, I found out early I was going to get that. How I wanted it was what held us up, because this was the latest I'd ever signed.

I've never been thrifty—not exactly a spendthrift, but not thrifty. I'd reached the age of thirty-three, and was realizing that these checks weren't going to keep coming in forever. I'd never done any investing, never gone in on any of these schemes that people are always approaching ball players with. Oh, I did dabble with a couple of them, when I was much younger and not smart enough to consult somebody, and they had cost me money. But the only thing I owned outside of my home in Mequon was forty acres of land close to Mobile. Since then I've bought a house and moved my family to Atlanta.

Now I was interested in a deferred income. My lawyer, John Cleary of Milwaukee, had advised it, and I had talked it over with Barbara and we thought it was a good idea. We worked it out so that I'll draw a certain part of my salary each year and the rest over a period of ten or fifteen years on an annuity basis after I'm through playing. They tell me that Willie Mays is the only other player who has a contract like that.

Anyway, here I was a $100,000-a-year man at last. We caught the plane from Atlanta to Mobile that night, the three of us. When we got there, my mama had fried chicken, as only she can fry it, and chocolate cake, two of the things she knows I love best, on the table for me.

I keep repeating about the two dollars, two pairs of pants and two sandwiches. When you leave home that way, scared and homesick before the train pulls out of the station, and you come home this way, a $100,000-a-year man, it just naturally stands repeating a few times. I can't think well enough to explain just how I really felt that night back home at the family table in Mobile.

We sat down and had a mighty nice homecoming dinner; then I left the next day for West Palm Beach in the happiest mood for spring training I'd ever been in since I reported as a rookie in 1954.

2

SOME HIGH-SCHOOL baseball players sign contracts for more than I make in a season—even at my present salary—just as soon as they graduate. Eddie Mathews told me they came to sign him while he was at his senior prom and gave him something like $50,000, just like that. I remember a story about a kid named Pettit who signed for $110,000 with Pittsburgh and had an agent handle it for him. But he never made it in the big leagues, Pettit or his agent.

The way it happened to me would never make the storybooks, and I signed twice, first with the Indianapolis Clowns, and then with the Braves. When my "take" for both signings was added, it came to expenses and a cardboard suitcase.

If I had waited in Mobile for a white baseball scout to find me, I don't know if I'd ever have been discovered for the big leagues or not. In fact, I was discovered originally by the Mobile Bears as a softball player. Mobile always has had a rather active city recreational program. You've heard of the Senior Bowl football game? Well, a lot of the money from that game goes into a special fund to promote the recreational program around the city. We never had a baseball team at my high school, so I played softball in the playground leagues.

One day a man named Ed Scott was watching one of our games. I was playing third base, and I can't remember what I did that caught his eye, but when the game was over, he called out to me, "Aaron, how would you like to play base-ball and make some money?"

Mr. Scott lived in our neighborhood, so I knew the man. It wasn't like talking to some stranger.

"I'll have to ask Mama about that," I said. "She doesn't want me to be playing baseball. She wants me to get an education."

"Oh, this is just once a week, son. You just play on a Sunday afternoon and make a little money, that's all. It's not every kid that gets a chance to play for the Mobile Black Bears."

"I know I can't if it's on Sunday," I said. "Mama won't let me."

"I'll be seeing you, anyway. You ought to play for the Bears. I think you could make the team."

I guess it was the next Sunday I saw Mr. Scott coming down the sidewalk toward our house. I'd already said some-thing to Mama about playing, and she had told me I wasn't playing baseball on Sunday. So I ran and hid. Mr. Scott stayed around awhile waiting for me, then finally left.

He did this about three Sundays in a row. I was hiding because I didn't want to get in trouble with my mama, but I'll have to tell the truth, and the truth is that I wanted to get a chance to play with the Bears. So one Sunday I just sort of hung around where Mr. Scott could see me, and he finally convinced Mama that I ought to be allowed to go play with the Bears, that this was a big opportunity, even if it was Sunday.

The Bears played in Prichard, which is a suburb of Mobile. A man named Ed Tucker owned the team, and he put me at shortstop, and I liked it. I liked it even better when they started paying me in real money. Sometimes I'd get as much as $10 a game, and I'd never seen that much money in my life all put together.

I ought to set the record straight here. I said I wasn't a bonus boy. That's not just right accurate. One week I was a bonus boy. I was doing so well that they gave me two dollars extra.

The Tuckers lived right down the street from us there in Mobile. One Sunday I had a big day. I don't remember now just what I did, but they liked it. The next day I was walking by the Tuckers' house when Mrs. Tucker called me in.

"Henry, you did so well yesterday, I want to do something a little extra for you," she said.

She reached into this big black handbag she always carried and pulled out two dollars. "Here's a little bonus for you this week. The way you played yesterday, you surely deserve it."

Every so often, one of the famous black barnstorming teams would come through Mobile, like the Indianapolis Clowns or the Kansas City Monarchs, and play the Bears, because they were the strongest black team in town. When the Bears had these games with the barnstorming teams, though, they would bring in other players from teams around Mobile to play for them.

This is how I got my first break, when the Clowns came through Mobile to play the Bears in 1951, and I was playing shortstop for the Bears.

The Clowns had a traveling secretary named Bunny Downs who handled all their business affairs, and after the game was over that day, this fellow Bunny Downs wanted to talk to me.

"How old are you, kid?" he asked me. I was pretty scared. He was dressed like a dude and he was a stranger, not like Mr. Scott, because Mr. Scott lived in my section of town.

"Seventeen," I said.

"Are you still in high school?"

"Yessir."

"When do you get out?"

"I'll graduate next year."

"Do you always play shortstop?"

"I play anywhere they want me to play."

"That's a nice attitude. How would you like to play for the Indianapolis Clowns?"

"I don't see no reason why not," I said.

You'll notice I didn't get very enthusiastic. Somehow or

another, I figured I'd never see this guy again, so I really didn't think much of it. Then there was the problem of convincing my mama that I was old enough to leave home. So why not say why not?

I'll have you know that Mr. Bunny Downs was as good as his word. He said, "I'll send you a contract next year. You'll be hearing from me."

The next spring I got a contract in the mail offering me $200 a month to play for the Indianapolis Clowns. $200 A MONTH TO PLAY BASEBALL! You can't imagine how big that looked to a poor boy in Mobile, Alabama. It even looked big to my mother, who had not been inclined to be impressed by baseball before. In fact, neither was my daddy. My daddy, Herbert Aaron, was a hard-working man. He was brought up on a farm close to Camden, Alabama, a town that never would have been known outside of Alabama if it hadn't been for some racial trouble there a few years ago. When he moved to Mobile, he got a job with the Alabama Drydock and Shipbuilding Company, and became a boilermaker's helper.

I don't know what that means myself. I do know that it took him away from home a lot when I was a little boy, and Mama was left to run the house and look after all us kids. You hear and read about other big-league players and how they grew up playing catch in the backyard with their daddies. Not me. My daddy was working too hard to have time, and was bringing us home $75 or $80 a week—sometimes it got to $90, when he got overtime—to keep us fed and some clothes on our backs. The athletic strain in my blood comes from both sides of my family because my father played baseball and so did some of my uncles.

I've always heard that two of my mama's brothers would have been fine baseball players if they'd had the chance. One was sort of lazy, though, and the other was a "mama's boy," the way I get it. I'll have to say this for the "mama's boy"—he spent more playing time with me than any of my older relatives, but he had an odd way of "charging" me for it.

His name was Uncle Bubba, and when Uncle Bubba would come to our house, I'd always ask him to play catch with me. "Stroke my head a hundred times and I will," he'd say. That was always his price.

I'd get a comb and stroke Uncle Bubba's head a hundred times, then he'd get up and go out in the yard and play catch with me. That was really my very first experience with baseball.

I got my wires crossed with my daddy when I was (and I'm guessing again) about sixteen years old. I'd just started playing with the Mobile Bears and I was beginning to feel like a big shot. One day in the spring I was on my way to school and I stopped to peek through this poolroom door. I hadn't reached the age when I was bold enough to hang out in poolrooms, but my experience as a "big athlete" was giving me courage. I saw on a board in the poolroom that Brooklyn was playing somebody that afternoon. Jackie Robinson was playing for the Dodgers then, and I guess that, because he was the first black to play in the major leagues, he was sort of an official hero to every little black kid everywhere. So I decided to stick around and listen to the game on the big radio they had in the poolroom and watch the scores on the boards.

That just happened to be a day when work wasn't pushing at the Alabama Drydock and Shipbuilding Company, and who should come along on the way home early but Herbert Aaron, who had been laid off until things got better. My daddy caught a glimpse of me inside that poolroom, crooked his finger at me and invited me to come along home with him. He'd just happened by, just happened to see me and then just happened to spend the next two hours talking with me.

He didn't punish me or anything. He just wanted to know what I was doing out of school and in a poolroom.

"I was listening to the baseball game," I said. "Jackie Robinson plays for Brooklyn and I want to be a baseball player, and I'll learn more about how to play second base listening to him play than I will in a schoolroom."

My daddy wasn't an educated man. There didn't seem to be much point in a black getting an education in Alabama at that time, anyway. But he and my mama had made up their minds that their children were going to get educated.

"You don't think these fellows playing in the big leagues are dumb, do you?" my daddy asked me.

"No, but they didn't learn how to catch, or how to hit a baseball in a classroom," I said. "I've made up my mind. I want to be a baseball player."

"You can still be a baseball player and get you an education, too."

We had an old car, and it was parked in our yard, and we sat in that car and talked and talked. I told him I was going to drop out of school when I got a chance to play baseball.

"Son, I had to quit school because I had to go to work to help make a living. You don't have to. I put fifty cents on that dresser each morning for you to take to school to buy your lunch and what else you need. I don't take but twenty-five cents to work with me. It's worth more to me that you get yourself an education than it is for me to eat, and you aren't going to drop out of school until you're through."

That's a lesson that I learned from my daddy that stuck —until that contract arrived from Bunny Downs. I still had three weeks left before my senior year in high school was finished. I'd had some offers to play football in college. Florida A & M had talked to me about a scholarship. But my mind was made up. I wanted to play baseball. The money looked easy, and it was a game. Why try to lie about it? Some people are geared for some things, and some people are geared for others. I wasn't geared for college, and I knew it. I was barely geared for high school.

I promised my mother that I would come back and get my diploma (and I did later) if she would let me sign that contract and go play baseball with the Indianapolis Clowns. There was a lot of crying. She didn't want her little boy leaving home, and there was a lot of talking, but one morning in May, 1952, my mother, two of my sisters and a brother all went down to the railroad station in Mobile to see me catch a train for Winston-Salem, North Carolina, where the Clowns were having their spring training. And there was a lot more crying and hugging.

I had a seat on a day coach. I sat by myself and never said anything to anybody. The only thing I can remember doing is wondering if I shouldn't get off that train and turn around and go back home to Mobile as fast as I could get there. Every time that train would pull into a station, I'd really say, "The next station this thing stops at, I'm getting off and going back."

But I never did. I ate those two sandwiches, and so I had nothing but my two dollars and two pairs of pants left when the train finally pulled into Charlotte. I got off there and caught a bus the rest of the way to Winston-Salem.

Every time I see a kid come into spring training and start complaining about something that's not just right, I feel like going over to him and saying to him, "Hey, kid, if you think this is bad, you ought to have been with me when I was with the Indianapolis Clowns in Winston-Salem, North Carolina."

Man, you talk about primitive. We stayed in an old hotel upstairs over a poolroom. Everything in town smelled like tobacco, because Winston-Salem is a big tobacco town. And it was cold. It was May, but it was still cold there.

That wasn't the only way it was cold, either. The older players greeted me like I was a disease. Most of them had been with the Clowns for several years, and they weren't greeting any green kid with open arms. A new player coming in meant somebody had to go. They didn't say anything to me, and I didn't say anything to anybody, and that's the way it began.

It wasn't more than a month and a half until that was ended. I had my second signing and I was on my way again.

3

A MAN NAMED SYD POLLOCK owned the Indianapolis Clowns. He didn't live in Indianapolis. He lived in Tarrytown, New York. The Clowns didn't live in Indianapolis, either. They lived in that bus, and wherever they were playing that day. I never did see Indianapolis.

We worked out in Winston-Salem a few days. I'll never forget that first day. The only equipment I had was an old pair of spikes I'd been wearing three or four years and a beat-up glove. When we got out on the playing field one of the older players curled up his lip and said, "Where you get your equipment, kid, from the Salvation Army?"

They passed out warm-up jackets, and there was one for everybody but me, and, like I said, it was cold.

After we broke camp—if you can call it that—we got on that bus and started moving. Now, if I tried to tell you where we played and who we played, I'd be lying. I never paid any attention to geography. I just put on my uniform and played and dressed and got on that bus and rode all night and put on my uniform again and played again, and this was the way it went. The only time we slept in a hotel was on Saturday nights. We'd usually get to some town and stay for the weekend. After the Sunday game, it was back to that bus and the highway again.

I got off to a good start, hit real good and caught everything that was hit to me, and when we got to Buffalo, New York, which was sometime in June, I heard that some

17

scouts from the big leagues were interested in me. You are supposed to get excited about something like that, I guess, but I never was the excitable kind, so I acted like I wasn't paying any attention to it.

Inside, I was busting wide open I was so excited. I guess I'll die of a heart attack one of these days from keeping all this stuff inside me. That's what they say—the excitable kind lives a long time, and the quiet kind keeps it all inside until some day something has got to give and it's his heart.

The way I got the story later, the New York Giants had somebody on me first. Then this fellow Syd Pollock, the owner of the Clowns, wrote a letter to John Mullen, who was farm director of the Braves, who were still in Boston. Pollock was needing some money to meet his pay roll, and he'd always had a pretty good thing going with the Braves.

He put a P.S. at the bottom of the letter that said this: "We got an eighteen-year-old shortstop batting cleanup for us."

That was all. Just that little P.S. I don't know exactly what happened next, but I've read that Mullen checked the Clowns' schedule and saw that we were coming into Buffalo. The Braves had a scout named Dewey Griggs, who ran a semipro baseball club in a town close to Buffalo, so Mullen called Griggs and asked him to go take a look at me.

Well, he got me on the right day. We were playing the Kansas City Monarchs—and don't ask me what Kansas City was doing playing Indianapolis in Buffalo—and I went on a tear. I read what Dewey Griggs said about it later in a story in the *Saturday Evening Post*.

"They were playing a Sunday double-header in the International League park," he told this writer, "and this kid had seven-for-nine. He hit one home run over the left-field fence and one over the right-field fence. He made five double plays. He ran on his heels, but that didn't bother me. What did bother me was his arm. He didn't throw the ball. He flipped it."

Between games, Griggs came down to the dugout to talk

to me. "Can't you throw any better than that?" he said.

"Oh, sure, I can throw any way you want it thrown," I said. "I just been throwing enough to get them out."

Soon after the second game started, I had to go back "in the hole" back of third to backhand a ball. I came up with it and gave that throw everything I had and got the runner with plenty of feet to spare.

Next thing I knew, Griggs was in talking to Pollock, and Pollock was talking to John Quinn, general manager of the Braves. He told John Quinn that he'd give him an option on me for $2,500. That meant that they could look at me for one more week.

I was too young to know or care or have any idea about how deals like that were made then, but there are times now that I think about it when I want to kick myself. A Paul Pettit gets $110,000, and a kid pitcher named Billy Joe Davidson gets $100,000, and you know what I got out of the deal when it was all over? A cardboard suitcase.

You see, the Giants were after me and the Braves were after me, and I had the right to sign with either team I wanted to. If I had been one of these smart kids, I'd have said I'd go with the club that made *me* the biggest offer. I didn't have to go with the one that made Syd Pollock the biggest offer.

But that was the way it worked out. I did have a chance to go with the Giants. They wanted to send me to Sioux City, Iowa. I had the contract in my hand. But the Braves offered me $50 more a month to play at Eau Claire, Wisconsin, in the Northern League, Class C, than the Giants offered me to play at Sioux City in the Western League, which was Class A, and so I took the Braves. It seemed to me like they were willing to be fairer with me.

That's the only thing that kept Willie Mays and me from being teammates—$50 between Sioux City and Eau Claire.

The Clowns had reached Charlotte, North Carolina— seemed like I couldn't get away from that town—when Pollock and the Braves closed the deal, and this was where the big money was.

I'll have to go back to the *Saturday Evening Post* article again to fill you in on how that took place. That story said that Pollock wanted $10,000—$2,500 down and the rest of it as I moved up in the Braves organization. If I spent sixty days in the big leagues, Pollock got the last payment.

John Quinn called Griggs one day, so it said in the *Post*. "We've got to make our decision in a hurry," he told Griggs. "It's up to you. Is this fellow worth $2,500?"

"Mr. Quinn," Griggs told him, "I like this boy this much— I'm willing to put up the $2,500 myself."

So the Braves closed the deal. Pollock called me in and told me. Griggs had a contract with Evansville, a Braves farm club in the Three-Eye League, and I signed it. I was now a real professional. In keeping with my new and exalted status in life—that's another line I read in a magazine—I also moved up in travel accommodations. Me and my new cardboard suitcase boarded a plane in Charlotte and took off in the general direction of Eau Claire. I was to be on option from Evansville.

I keep mentioning that cardboard suitcase. That was my bonus. After I signed, Syd Pollock gave it to me for a going-away gift and in undying appreciation of the $10,000 I was putting in his pocket. But, as I said, I didn't know any better then, and it really didn't make any difference to me, and I don't know why I let it bother me now. Oh, I do know, too: I just hate to look back on something and realize that somebody took advantage of me because I was a kid who didn't know any better.

Unconsciously, though, and unintentionally, I almost took the $10,000 right out of Syd Pollock's pocket after I got to Eau Claire. I was unhappy, real unhappy in Eau Claire.

Let's go back to the very start of this little adventure, the plane ride. When I got on board that airplane in Charlotte, I was shaking all over. That's no exaggeration. I was scared stiff. I was darn sure that that big machine wouldn't be able to stay up there on nothing but air.

Another thing, by this time my teammates on the Clowns hated to see me go. I was hitting over .400 and helping the team in a big way, and they had come to love me after that frosty reception in Winston-Salem. In fact, they had a nickname of affection for me. They called me "Little Brother."

An old-time player named Ray Neal, sort of the kingpin of the club, put that name on me.

When I left the Clowns, then, it was sort of like ripping up more roots, because I was finally feeling at home. The only reason I was glad to get to Eau Claire was to get off that plane. I'd always said they'd never get me in an airplane. You say a lot of things you don't mean to do, but when the time comes you find out you'll do the very same things because you have to. And I rode this plane because I had to.

I shouldn't have been as unhappy as I was in Eau Claire. I had two other blacks for friends on the club—Wes Covington, who later played for the Braves, the Cubs, the Phillies, Kansas City and the Dodgers in the major leagues; and a catcher named Julie Bowers, who never made it to the big leagues. Wes got a bad name later in the big leagues, mostly for shooting off his mouth. He developed the nickname of "Kingfish" because of it.

The year after the Phillies released Wes, some sports writer was asking manager Gene Mauch of the Phillies why he was so gray-headed for such a young guy. (Gene was just over forty at the time.)

"You try managing Wes Covington for five years and see what it does to the color of your hair," he told the sports writer.

Well, in Eau Claire, Wes was good company. I had no complaints there. We could have had better living arrangements. We stayed in the Y.M.C.A., me and Wes and Julie rooming together, and we roomed together on the road. Our road trips were usually for three-game series, and we weren't away for long stretches.

We traveled pretty good, too. No bus smelling like gas

fumes and bologna sausage sandwiches and sardines and pork and beans. We traveled by automobile. The jumps were long—425 miles to Fargo-Moorhead, 385 miles to Aberdeen and 325 miles to Sioux Falls. These were the largest ones, but we were comfortable.

A guy couldn't have asked to break in under a better manager than Bill Adair. (Marion Adair in the record books. Bill is his nickname.) He was from Montgomery, Alabama, and I think that because he was a Southerner he was even a little more understanding of the little black kid he had playing beside him. You see, he was the second baseman as well as the manager.

But I was still unhappy. "Homesick," I guess, is a better word for it. Another thing, there was only one black resident of Eau Claire, and we didn't have anybody out cheering for us like I'd been used to. The one black who lived there was an old man, a sort of a character who would stand on a street corner downtown flipping a fifty-dollar gold piece. I'll never forget that, just standing there on the corner flipping that gold piece. I took up the habit myself, except that I broke in with a dime instead of a fifty-dollar gold piece.

So after I'd been there about two weeks, I was ready to pack and head for Mobile. Before I left, though, I decided to call home and tell them I was coming. With my mama, it was all right. She didn't give me much argument about it. But my older brother, Herbert Jr., was home at the time and I could hear him in the background.

"Here," I heard him say to my mama, "let me talk to him a minute."

Herbert had been a good athlete himself, but he never got a chance to play professional ball.

"Man, are you out of your mind?" he said. "Don't make a fool out of yourself. I just wish I'd had the chance you've got."

"Well, come on up here, if you think it's so great," I told him.

"Henry, don't make a mistake," he said. "If you come

home, you're making a big mistake. I know you're home-sick, but see if you can't stick it out."

To tell the truth, I had already packed my bag and it was on the bed ready to go. I hadn't talked to anybody on the club about it. I was just going to go. Talking to Herbert sort of knocked that in the head right at the time. Then something great happened, a real shot in the arm.

I had been in the league eighteen days when they picked the squad for the all-star game. I was the shortstop. That wasn't too much to brag about. There weren't any other shortstops burning up the league. None of them ever got close to the majors. There was a guy named Forrest, from Superior, who led the shortstops in fielding that year with something like .920. As a group, Northern League short-stops that season weren't known for their gloves.

Making the all-star team, though, was a big boost to me, especially after being in the league such a short time. It gave me something to be proud of, and to get my mind off things that were bothering me, like being homesick and a long way from Mobile and playing with white ball players. That was the first time, see, I'd ever played with or against white ball players, and there's no point in trying to cover it up. It did bother me. So when I made the all-star team it made me really feel like I "belonged" for the first time.

I went on from there and had a good season. I was voted Rookie of the Year in the Northern League, and I wound up second in hitting. My average was .336. A fellow named Joe Caffie who played at Duluth led the league with .342. I think he had a few trials in the major leagues a little later, but he never did stick.

Don't let anybody try to kid you about my fielding. According to the fielding averages, I was making an error about every ten plays. But they were told in advance in Eau Claire that they weren't getting any Marty Marion.

When John Mullen, the farm director for the Braves, had called Bill Adair from Milwaukee to tell him that I was on the way, he'd said, "We're sending you a shortstop. At least we think he's a shortstop. We don't know whether he can play or not. Don't know how good a shortstop he is, but we do know one thing—he can swing a bat."

Actually, so I found out later, I was on a thirty-day look. They hadn't told me. It was a private arrangement they had with Syd Pollock. I guess if I hadn't stuck he'd have made me give him back that cardboard suitcase.

I wish I could remember what happened to that suitcase. It's the kind you'd like to have stolen, just about what a thief deserved.

Pretty soon after I got there, Bill Adair called me over one day and said he wanted me to meet somebody.

"Henry, this is Billy Southworth," he said. I sort of stood up a little straighter and minded my manners. I hadn't met any big baseball people before, and Billy Southworth was big in my book. I remembered that he'd managed the Braves the last time they won a pennant.

"Mr. Southworth is scouting for the Braves now and he wants to talk to you a little about your throwing."

"Yes, Henry," Billy Southworth said, "have you ever tried to throw the ball any other way, maybe sidearm or overhand?" That was still bothering them.

"No sir, I never have," I said. In fact, I never even thought about the way I threw the ball. I just got it out of my glove and got rid of it as quick as I could. It was more of a flip than a throw, from down about my hip.

"Well, I was just wondering, that's all. I like the way you handle the bat. Keep it up." That was all Southworth said to me.

Adair told me later that they were thinking about trying to change me over, but that I was throwing everybody out so they decided to leave me alone.

They really weren't counting too heavily on me as a shortstop anyway. They had Felix Mantilla on their Class B farm club at Evansville, hitting a ton and a real glove man. He was the shortstop they figured would be coming up next in Milwaukee. They were sure my future wasn't at short, but they never told me. They just never bothered to fool with my throwing at Eau Claire.

If they had, it might have saved me one of the roughest experiences I ever had in baseball, and a near tragedy.

Cleveland had a fine prospect on their Northern League farm club at Fargo-Moorhead, and this is another one of those cases where I can't remember the name. All I know is that they thought he was major league material. Well, one night in Eau Claire this kid gets on first, and the next batter grounds to Adair. I come across the bag as the middle man on the double play, and this kid is out so far that he's not even going into a full slide. From where I was flipping that ball, then, his head was right in my line to first base. My throw hit him smack in the ear. You could hear it all over the ball park, like a shot. "Pow!"

He rolled over and flopped there real still. I thought he was dead. It scared me to death. He wasn't dead, but his baseball career was. The impact damaged his inner ear— something that had to do with keeping his balance—and he never was able to play again.

I felt bad enough about that, but when Eau Claire played at Fargo-Moorhead the next time, they really let me have it. Those fans booed me every time I came to bat. As far as they were concerned, I'd done it on purpose. Man, they ought to have known I wouldn't do anything like that. That thing shook me up for two or three weeks. I'd have had dreams some nights, and just about every time I had one, somewhere in it this guy would come sliding into second base, and every time he slid I'd wake up shivering and sweating.

The season of 1952 looks like a good one on paper. I'd made the all-star team, "Rookie of the Year" and second in hitting in the league, but Eau Claire was tough for me. That Class C league was a lot more rugged than that .336 average of mine made it look. I thought it was the toughest ball I'd ever played. I had a fantastic season at Jacksonville, Florida, the next year, but that Sally League pitching looked a lot easier to me than that Northern League pitching.

A lot of things were changing, though, and I was a year older and somewhat wiser and gaining confidence. Besides, when the Northern League season ended, I really got a bolt of happiness. Bill Adair stopped me one day, and said, "Henry, I've got some good news for you."

"What's-at?" I said. I still wasn't going around wasting any words.

"You're going to spring training with the Milwaukee team next year."

Milwaukee was still in the American Association then. They called the team the Brewers, and they were the Braves' triple A farm club.

"That's good, is it?" I said. I didn't know then. I never read the papers. I knew I was in Wisconsin and that Milwaukee was, too, but you could have told me Eau Claire was bigger than Milwaukee and I wouldn't have argued about it.

"That's triple A. That's a big break," he said.

One big thing I hated about not coming back to Eau Claire: I was going to miss Bill Adair. He had been a lot more than a manager to me. But I was about to get the best break I ever got in managers. I wasn't going to make it with the Brewers. (For that matter, the Brewers weren't going to make it to Milwaukee, either, that next spring. In the middle of March, 1953, the Braves announced that they were moving from Boston to Milwaukee, and the Brewers were transferred to Toledo.) They optioned me to Jacksonville, and an Irishman with a long face and a chin sharp enough to slice a loaf of bread came into my life. His name was Ben Geraghty. He was the kind of manager a player never forgets.

4

I'M NO CRUSADER, not in the way they use the word now. Never wanted to be. Let's get that straight before we go any further.

I'm not running away from any responsibility or any fight, understand. I believe in a man being able to live like a human being and enjoying the privileges that any other man enjoys in his country. I haven't always been able to enjoy these privileges, either.

The winter after the Braves won the World Series in Milwaukee in 1957 I went back to Mobile for "Henry Aaron Day." I was honored and flattered, of course. It was a mighty special day in my life, but something happened while I was there that took some of the edge off.

Since I was working for Miller Brewing Company at the time, I was carrying this movie of the World Series around with me and showing it at meetings and dinners on a public relations basis. While I was in Mobile this group invited me to be their guest at dinner, show the World Series film and make a little talk. I told them I'd be glad to, and asked if it would be all right to bring my wife.

"No, it's a stag affair," the man told me.

"Fine, then I'd like to bring my daddy," I said. He'd never had a chance to go to anything like that.

Well, the man squirmed and hemmed and hawed and finally told me I couldn't bring him.

"Then you don't want to see the film then," I said.

That ended that conversation.

Several years before that, when I was younger and frightened by such things as this, my brother Herbert Jr. was on his way to work early one morning when the police picked him up in Mobile. He had to be up awfully early to get to his job and it so happened that the police were looking for a "peeping Tom" some lady had reported.

Just because he happened to be on the street and because the police were looking for "some black," he was picked up. They took him to the place where the woman had reported the peeper and made him stand on a brick wall so she could look out of a window at him.

All she had to do was say, "That's him," and Herbert would have been in prison. She said it wasn't Herbert, but this was the kind of fear we lived in when I was growing up.

I've had to drive long hours with my family just looking for a place where I could feed them, or even let them go to the rest room. I know that feeling of having a man look through your car window and say, "I'm sorry, but we don't have a rest room for colored people." Not being ugly, understand, but in a nice way just telling you he didn't want your business.

Thank the Lord, that has changed. That part of the fight is over. When I say I'm no crusader, I'm saying I'm not going out and stir up trouble or do things that aren't within the law to draw attention to myself for any cause. I have my beliefs and I'll stand up for them. That doesn't mean I'm standing shoulder-to-shoulder with Tommie Smith, or Muhammed Ali, or Bill Russell. Their way of doing is their own business. But this is a baseball book. I'm a baseball player. And I want to keep it that way, although I must report on my 1953 season as a player, which was a season spent "crusading," but not in the way we think of it now.

Remember, now, in 1953 I was just nineteen. My birthday is February 5, so I had turned nineteen just a few days before I reported to where the Milwaukee Brewers were training in Kissimmee, Florida.

Not only was I nineteen, I was a young nineteen. What is that word they use for it? "Naive," which I guess is a nice way of saying "dumb."

Naturally, when I reported to the Milwaukee club I expected to play the season with it. I never had had any trouble making any team before. All I'd had any experience at was going up.

I thought I was getting off to a pretty good start, too. One day I hit two home runs over the right-field fence. I was really getting their attention, I said to myself. I sure was, I found out.

Tommy Holmes, who had been a great hitter for the Braves and had later managed the team, was managing the Brewers. In 1945 he had the hottest streak any hitter ever had in the National League. He got at least one hit in thirty-seven straight games, and that's still the league record.

I didn't know any of those statistics then, and didn't care. All I can remember of Tommy Holmes from that spring of 1953 is what he said after I hit the two home runs over the right-field fence.

"He'll never be a big league player," he said to John Mullen, the farm director. "He can't pull the ball."

"You really don't think he can make it?" Mullen said.

"Not a chance, the way he pushes the ball," Holmes said.

Now, that's a strange thing to me. Later I heard that Holmes was one of these fellows who tried to teach his hitters to push the inside pitch to the opposite field and pull the trigger—in other words, lay into it—on the outside pitch. I don't know what he expected of me. When I heard what he'd said, though, I told John Mullen, "Send me to Waycross, then. Send me anywhere. I'm not going to get a chance to make this club."

Waycross is a little town in south Georgia where the Braves trained their farm clubs then. The base was an old Army airfield that had been used for training pilots during World War II. It wasn't anybody's Fontainebleau or Grossinger's. It was pretty rugged and rustic, an old barracks sitting out in a forest of pine trees and equipped with a personal squadron of mosquitoes for each man. It wasn't too much of an improvement over life with the Indianapolis Clowns, except that it wasn't on wheels and you didn't have to sleep sitting up.

That was where I first met Ben Geraghty, and I'm going to tell you more about him later. Mullen assigned me to the Jacksonville club in Waycross. Geraghty was the manager. He did more for me than any manager I ever played for, and I guess he was one reason I didn't realize I was "crusading" because he crowded out a lot of the stuff and never let it get close to me.

Jacksonville was in the Sally League then. That's about as Southern as you can get, next to cornpone and camp meetings. The other teams in the league were Columbia and Charleston in South Carolina, Macon, Columbus, Augusta and Savannah in Georgia, and Montgomery, Alabama. There never had been any black players in the league before, or in any professional league in the South before. The bigger cities, like Atlanta, Birmingham, Nashville and Memphis, never did have any black players because there must have been some kind of unwritten agreement in the Southern Association not to have any.

Now here I was at Waycross, trying to make a job for myself in a Southern city where no black had ever played professional baseball before. I was still under an Evansville contract. That's the way they do things on major league farm rosters: assign you to some club in the organization, which doesn't mean a thing except as the draft goes. I was on Evansville's roster, I had trained with Milwaukee, but I was trying to make Jacksonville. They could leave me on the Class B roster and I couldn't be touched in the big league draft.

Out there in that old air-base camp at Waycross, the idea of playing for Jacksonville didn't register with me. There were a lot of other black players around wearing all kinds of names on their shirts, like Cedar Rapids, Eau Claire, Evansville and Jacksonville. Wanting to stick with the Jacksonville club made sense because it was the highest of the classifications there, Class A.

One day I was leaving the clubhouse for practice. Ben Geraghty caught up with me soon after I walked out the door.

"How'd you think you'd like to play with me in Jacksonville, Henry?" he said.

"That's what I'm trying to do, Skip. Hadn't you noticed?"

"Of course I've noticed. That's the reason I'd like to have you. But I did want to mention to you that you'd be the first black player that ever played in the Sally League. Does that bother you?"

"I don't guess so," I said. That shows you how dumb I was. It sounded pretty important to me to be first at something. "Of course not." I was getting more confident every step I took.

Ben was a little serious now. "It won't be easy, son. You ought to know that. But I sure want you on my team."

He got me. He got me, Horace Garner, a long, string-bean center-fielder, and Felix Mantilla, who was a Puerto Rican kid they were training to be the Braves' next shortstop. I was the second baseman.

This was the second of three positions I was to play in three years—shortstop at Eau Claire, second base at Jacksonville, and my first year in the majors I moved to the outfield.

Here I was now, a new kid, in a new town, in a new position, in a new league, bucking an old tradition. You know, what they call the "Southern way of life." I've got nothing against the "Southern way of life." The South has always been good to me. But here I was in the middle of a situation.

There's only one way to break the color line. Be good. I mean, play good. Play so good that they can't remember what color you were before the season started.

I had a great spring. I hit a ton of home runs. The first time we played in Jacksonville, we lost an exhibition game to the Boston Red Sox. The score was 20–1. I got the "1," a home run. That didn't hurt in getting me introduced to the people.

The season was a big one for me. I batted .362, drove in 125 runs, made 208 hits, 36 doubles, and scored 115 runs—and led the league in all that. Then they elected me the "Most Valuable Player in the League." As one sports writer put it, "Aaron led the league in everything but hotel accommodations."

It must have been bad, the way the black players were handled, but I'd never been anywhere before; I'd been raised in the South, and this was the way I was accustomed to seeing blacks treated. So I knew what to expect, and I think Garner did, too. Mantilla was just two years away from Puerto Rico, though, and it was puzzling to him.

Besides, I was having such a good year and I was so loose that I must have been a barrel of fun. At least, that's what I read in the newspapers from time to time.

I was having a batting slump sometime during the summer. It was a rare one and it didn't last long, or I wouldn't have been a .362 hitter. One day I picked up the paper, which I didn't do very often—I was sort of like the kid who wanted to hear bedtime stories, tell it to me, but don't make me read it—and I see this story about how I'm busted out of my slump because Stan Musial has helped me.

Wow! You can imagine how Stan Musial would help a nineteen-year-old kid in another organization he never heard of before—particularly since I didn't even know and had never even seen Stan Musial. Later on, after I got to the big leagues and got to watch him close up, I'll have to admit that Musial became an idol of mine. Always was, but you can idolize a guy better close up than you can miles away. After I got to watch him play, I saw what a really great hitter this man was, how he met the pitch, hit it to any field, just made the pitcher almost afraid to throw him anything. He could have helped me out of any kind of batting slump I had, I know, but that wasn't the way it happened in that summer in Jacksonville.

The way the story got out was this:

We had this guy on the Jacksonville team named Joe Andrews. He was a big kidder. Everybody liked Joe and was always joshing with him.

Well, one night Joe said to me, "Henry, whatchu doing to break out of that slump? Man, you been up two nights without a base hit? That must be driving a hitter like you crazy."

"Oh, I called Stan Musial about it," I said to Joe. Never cracked a smile, just sat there pulling on my stockings and saying that.

"What did Stan tell you to do?" Joe said. The grin was off his face now. I guess he was serious, but I didn't know it.

"Oh, he told me to keep swinging," I said.

"How about that!" Joe said. "How about that!"

That night I got back on the track again and got two doubles and drove in some runs, and they tell me later that Joe was telling the story all around the clubhouse and this newspaper man picked it up. Next day this writer came up to me and wanted *me* to tell *him* about it.

"Man," I said, "I never called Stan Musial. In the first place I haven't got the money for long distance, and in the second place Stan Musial doesn't know me."

"But you told Joe Andrews you did," he said.

"I'm liable to tell Joe Andrews anything," I said.

I was beginning to get a little bit of a reputation as a "character" out of innocent stuff like that. I unconsciously contributed to it with the way I used bats.

One day pretty late in the season the business manager of the Jacksonville club, Spec Richardson, said to me, "Henry, are you sure you still don't need any bats? I'm taking orders again today."

"No, it looks like we got plenty over there," I said.

"I know *we've* got plenty, but what about you? You haven't ordered a bat all year."

"Oh, I just use a lot of different ones. I didn't know I was supposed to put in a special order."

Then he told me. He told me that ball players actually ordered their own special kind of bats with their names burned in the meat end. I could have my own special bat with "Henry Aaron" on it. The kind of teams I'd been playing for—the Bears, the Clowns and even the club in Eau Claire—hadn't told me that. I'd just been going to bat with any kind of bat that felt good. Most of the time I'd been using a pitcher's bat, a fellow named DiLorenzo.

Oh, that brings up another "character" story.

We all printed our names on our duffle bags that we used on the road. DiLorenzo, though, just put "DiLo" on his. All year long I thought that was his name, "DiLo." He even had it on the bat he used, and I knew his bat a lot better than I knew him. In fact, his bat and I got along real good.

All of this didn't bother me. It was good, clean fun, and made me feel like I really "belonged" as a regular guy. A mighty lot of good things happened to me that year in Jacksonville, and a lot of it has had a lasting effect on me. We won a pennant. I had a great year. It gave me confidence, and really was the most important season I ever spent in baseball in many ways, none of it having to do with "crusading."

When I use that word "crusading," I probably oughtn't to. It really has nothing to do with that 1953 season in Jacksonville. And when I say I spent that season "crusading" and didn't know it, what I mean is that it was several years later before I realized that people were looking back on that turn of events—of Garner, Mantilla, and me and the other black players being in the Sally League—as a great breakthrough for the black in sports. Blacks had finally been accepted in the major leagues. Now they were being accepted in the South, and there were people who had said that it never would happen in "slavery country."

It wasn't more than a year or so before blacks were playing even in those little towns in the deepest part of Georgia. Willie McCovey broke in in a little town named Sandersville, and was voted the most popular player on the team. Julio Navarro, who was a pitcher with the Los Angeles Angels and Detroit later, broke in in the same town.

Several other little towns, like Dublin and Vidalia in the Georgia State League, had black players. Their popularity depended on how well they played, not on their color, and I know that because I've talked to some of them about what it was like in those towns.

Montgomery, the capital of my own home state, was the worst town in the Sally League. It was about the only town in the league where we got "nigger" thrown at us. Those fans started on us on the first trip into Montgomery and never let up. They threw every word in the book at us —some that couldn't pass in "Who's Afraid of Virginia Woolf?" I thought they'd get used to us after a while, that they'd settle down and get off our backs, but it lasted the whole season.

Strangely enough, Montgomery was the only town where the black players were put up in a hotel. Don't get the wrong impression. It wouldn't rival the Waldorf, or the Chase. It didn't have any crystal chandeliers or fancy cocktail lounges. As I recall, it did have one potted plant in the lobby, which would barely pass for a storage closet in most hotels. No air conditioning and, in summer, three of us to a room, it got mighty hot in Montgomery; a "private" bath —down the hall—and all the other luxuries you would expect in a situation like that.

It was called the Ben Moore, just like a man's name. It wasn't too bad at the time. I was still comparing hotels to that seat on the Clowns' bus, and anything slept better than sitting up with Jenkins snoring beside you. It just looks bad as I look back on it now.

In all the other towns, we stayed in private homes. We traveled by bus, and the bus would take the white players by the hotel where they were staying. Horace and Felix and I would sit there watching them unload. It was a silent kind of thing. The white players might have been joking and laughing when we drove into town, but when the unloading started they would get quiet. Hardly ever said anything. They didn't like this any more than we did, but we all knew we couldn't do anything about it.

After they unloaded, then the bus would take Garner, Mantilla and me to the house where we were staying. Actually, I think we had it better than the white players. Those people in private homes couldn't do enough for us, and on top of it all, we were getting home cooking.

There were only two "incidents" that disturbed the scene on a racial basis that season, and I'm not even sure one was based on race. It took place in Macon.

The Macon team had an old pitcher, a tough-looking guy who always looked like he needed a shave. Felix was mighty young-looking then, had almost a baby face. When he would come to bat, this pitcher would growl at him.

"Pickaninny, ain't you too young to be away from yo' mammy?" Stuff like that. Not loud. Not long. Just a thing or two to try and scare him so he wouldn't play his best. Felix was having a great year.

One night in Macon this old pitcher was pitching Felix pretty "tight." One of the pitches hit him, and by this time Felix was boiling. Felix charged the mound, and the Macon players charged Felix, and the Jacksonville players charged the Macon players. About this time, a couple of hot-headed fans jumped out of the stands and ran out on the field. Police moved in and more police came out on an emergency call, it said in the paper the next day, but it was all broken up before anybody got hurt.

If you wonder where I was when the turmoil was taking place, I was watching just as close as I could. I've never been much for fighting and even less for brawling. I did move in and help keep Felix out of it after somebody had pulled him away from being the center of attraction.

I'd call that more a baseball brawl than a racial brawl. If Felix had been white as a sheet, pitchers would have been throwing at him, the way he was hitting. Pitchers didn't throw much at me that season. As wild a swinger as I was, they were afraid I might hit it, and so they tried to keep the ball away from me rather than close to me.

The other so-called "incident" was more political than anything else. The all-star game was played in the city that was leading the league on July 4. Savannah was the leader at the deadline time, and so the all-star game was played there that year.

I was elected the second baseman. The way I was going at the time—and I hope I'm not letting my pride get out of hand right here—I was about the hottest news in the league. Savannah papers wrote it up big that I would be there, and how sensational I was going.

The Savannah papers also wrote that Governor Herman Talmadge of Georgia would be there to throw out the first ball. That created an interesting situation, because Mr. Talmadge was a pretty strong segregationist and here he was scheduled to appear at the first Sally League all-star game in which blacks were playing. Then coincidence began to go to work.

The night before the all-star game I was trapped in a run-down between third and home in a game in Jacksonville—against the Savannah team, in fact. During the chase, the Savannah catcher—a big guy named Moose Williams—stepped on my foot, and his spike ripped the nail off one of my toes. That toe was really a mess the next day. I couldn't have run ten feet.

Some of the newspapers said that it wasn't that serious, and that I was using the toe as an excuse not to be at the all-star game because Mr. Talmadge was going to be there. Now, I don't want to sound like an ignoramus and I don't want to say anything that even sounds like I wasn't respectful of our political leaders, but if somebody had given me a test on Southern governors, I'd have flunked it. I couldn't even have told you what the Governor's first name was, but I could tell you that that toe hurt.

As it turned out, Mr. Talmadge didn't show up and I didn't show up either, and neither one of us was absent because of racial affairs. Some kind of pressing business kept Mr. Talmadge away, and you already know why I wasn't there. I think some of those silly people thought I didn't show up because I was afraid, or something.

What made it really look worse was this: the toe that

couldn't have been played on the night of the all-star game was all right two days later when we began playing the schedule again. The swelling went down, the hurt went away, and it didn't bother me any to run on it again, and I was back in the line-up. It was just one of those things, but people looked sort of suspicious at me because it happened that way.

I ought to point out here that just getting to the major leagues didn't eliminate segregation. You know, I don't like that word. Every time I use it, it makes me feel like I'm complaining. I feel like I'm charging somebody with a crime. I don't feel that way at all. This country has been good to me and I've had a great life.

Moving from Jacksonville to the Braves didn't change a lot of conditions. It didn't make me not a black any more. The white players stayed in one hotel and the blacks stayed another place in Bradenton, Florida, where we were in spring training. They stayed in the Manatee River Hotel, and the way they growled about it, I gathered that it was no palace. They didn't like the food. They didn't like the rooms. They didn't like the elevators. It was an old hotel, but they'd have grumbled if it had been new, because a baseball player gets pretty restless during that long spring training grind.

The Braves put up the black players in a private home, with a Mrs. Gibson, who had a big place on Ninth Street. She was an elderly lady—around seventy, I'd guess—and she was mighty good to us. Bill Bruton, who was sort of the straw boss among us, stayed in the "big" house, as we called it. The rest of us stayed in a little house back of the "big" house—the "penthouse," we called it. It was nice and comfortable, and the food was good. Mrs. Gibson always had a sister come down from the Carolinas to help her with the cooking in the spring.

That first year, my rookie year of 1954, the black players on the Braves were Bruton, myself, Jim Pendleton, Charlie White and George Crowe. I was the kid of the bunch and

I didn't have much to say. I just ate and slept and watched television.

When we traveled around the state for exhibition games it was the same way. We stayed one place, the white players stayed in the hotel. We could usually find some place where we could eat together, but there was one little town in Florida I'll never forget: Clewiston, where they manufacture sugar.

Every time we'd make that long jump from Bradenton to Miami for an exhibition series, we'd get up at six o'clock and make Clewiston our lunch stop. Well, the white players all ate in one restaurant, but the black players had to go down the street across the railroad tracks to eat. It wasn't the kind of place Duncan Hines would recommend. In fact, it wasn't much at all for food. It was a "black café," and not a good one.

When we barnstormed through the South on the way from spring training to Milwaukee, it wasn't good. The white ball players stayed in the hotel, we stayed in private homes or run-down hotels. Same old thing.

The team bus would be waiting at the ball park to take the white players directly to the airport, escorted by the police and their screaming sirens. The black players had to scramble for a cab, or take leave the best way they could, go to where they were staying, shower and get to the airport the best way they could.

Once, in Mobile, Bruton, White and Pendleton all three got left behind. They ran into a traffic jam and got to the airport late. Our plane was already gone, and you think that didn't rip it a little bit.

"What I ought to have done," Bruton said later, "was rent a car and charge it to the ball club."

"What you ought to have done," Charlie White said, "was be born white. You didn't plan ahead."

"You're White," Bill said, "and that ain't doing you a lot of good."

Nothing changed very much along the living lines until

Birdie Tebbetts came to the Braves as general manager. John Quinn had made an honest effort to get all the team together, but elements stronger than any of us busted that up.

He announced one winter that the Braves had reserved living quarters at a motel across the Manatee River from Bradenton in the little town of Palmetto—the Twilight Motel. It was a nice place. It would have been an improvement over the Manatee River Hotel, except that buses would have had to have been called out to take the players back and forth to the ball park—that is, if it ever had come off.

During the winter a tornado hit the place and just about tore it down, and so it was back to the Manatee River Hotel for the white players and back to Mrs. Gibson for us.

When Birdie took over, he called me to his office one day in Milwaukee.

"Henry, you can level with me and help us both out," he said.

"About what?" I said. I couldn't figure out what he was driving at.

"Well, there have been some complaints about the living conditions of black players in the league. Bill White"—he was with the Cardinals then—"has been talking to the club owners about correcting them. Are you satisfied with conditions as they are in spring training?"

"No, I'm not," I said. He'd asked me to level with him, so I leveled. "I think we ought to live together as a team. We play together as a team. I think we ought to eat together, or at least have the opportunity of eating at the same places."

"If you've felt this way, why haven't you said something about it before?" Birdie said.

"I've resented it, but I didn't say anything about it because I didn't think it would do any good. When I first got to the majors, I was just happy to be here. Mrs. Gibson's place is a nice place to stay, and all the other players seemed happy enough."

"Does Mrs. Gibson still treat you fellows well?"

"Sure, she treats us real nice, but I think we ought to stay together as a team and live as a team."

Well, Mrs. Gibson heard about it later and took it wrong. She thought I'd gone to Birdie to complain about having to stay there. I hadn't, but that still didn't make any difference to her. She was losing a good income.

Anyway, the next spring we were all together at last in a new motel in downtown Bradenton, and everybody was just one big, happy family, I guess you'd say.

You can see, then, that the problems of being a black didn't cease just because I was promoted from Jacksonville to the big leagues. I lived with it well in Jacksonville, really hardly ever gave it any thought. The black fans piled into the parks around the league to see us play, and made us feel like we were among friendly people. The people in Jacksonville were just great to us, and it was while I was there that something pretty special happened in the way of a family life.

The ball park in Jacksonville was located in the black section of town, on Myrtle Avenue. It isn't there any more. They built a new one later after International League baseball came to town.

I was on my way out of the park after practice one day in the spring, and crossed the street to mail a letter in a drop box. I saw this cute little girl coming down the street. I know you're supposed to remember exactly what happened when you met the girl you love, but I'm a little cloudy on just what took place next after I saw this cute little girl.

Anyway, we met. I found out she lived right down the street across from the ball park. Her name was Barbara Lucas. She was living at home and going to business college. She had been going to Florida A & M, but it came time for one of her brothers to go to college, so she had dropped out to give him a chance. The cost was a lot less for her, living at home and going to school there in Jacksonville.

I learned all this while walking down the street with her.

She said she was on her way to class at the business college. I lived down the street a few blocks with Mantilla and Garner in a rooming house. She lived in a section known as "Durkeeville." I told her I wanted to see her again, and she said all right, but I'd have to come by the house to get her, as her mother wouldn't let her go off downtown to meet some boy. I said I'd be by.

That was the team's first day in Jacksonville after breaking camp in Waycross. The rest of that baseball season I reckon I spent as much time at the Lucases' as I did at the ball park. I'd go by their house every day. Barbara and I would go to the movies. She'd come to the ball games, and we'd go out to eat after it was over. I got to eat some of Mrs. Lucas's home cooking. I got to talk to older folks who sort of filled in for my own family while I was away from home. So it was just natural that on October 6 that year Barbara and I were married.

Getting married developed some sense of responsibility for me. In about a year we had our first child, a daughter named Gail. I've never had any trouble settling down since. You don't see me in any of the night spots, kicking my heels, doing the watusi, looking some "camp-following" woman in the eye and buying her booze, or wandering around after curfew. If I wanted to, I would, I guess. I'm just built the other way.

Two days after we were married, Barbara and I were off and running. The Braves had made some arrangements with the Caguas ball club in Puerto Rico for me to spend the winter there learning how to play the outfield. They had tried me at shortstop in Eau Claire, and at second base in Jacksonville. They had watched me at bat for two years, and they had decided that I was ready for the major leagues as a hitter, but not as a second baseman.

"The way we look at it," John Mullen, the farm director, told me over the telephone, "you've got too much to learn at second base, but you can make it in a much bigger hurry as an outfielder. Would you be willing to go to Puerto Rico and play for the winter?"

"Sounds all right to me," I said, "if I don't have to learn to speak Spanish."

"All right, then, you're going to report to Caguas. Mickey Owen is the manager. He's an old major-league catcher. He used to be with Brooklyn and the Cardinals. We think he's a good baseball man. That's why we're sending you to him.

"Caguas—that's the name of the team. Think you can remember that?" Mullen said.

"If you'll write it down for me, I can," I said. "I told you I don't want to bother learning Spanish."

5

My ARRIVAL IN the major leagues was pretty dull—no drama and no excitement, absolutely none. I just arrived, that was all. My bags and I got to Bradenton, Florida, and we were sent to Mrs. Gibson's to stay and there I was, Henry Louis Aaron in the big leagues.

After all, I was just a kid up from a Class A league. Sure, I'd had a big season, but that was against Columbia, Macon, Augusta, Savannah and those towns, not the triple A's.

I wasn't even on the Milwaukee roster. I didn't have to be protected from the baseball draft, so the Braves had signed me to a contract with Toledo, which was their top farm club in the triple A American Association. That's where I expected to play—in Toledo or maybe Atlanta. Tommy Holmes was gone as manager by that time, and I didn't have him to worry about.

You'll recall that Holmes was the manager who'd seen me hit home runs over the right-field fence in spring training the season before and had said, "He'll never play in the big leagues. He can't pull the ball."

If he'd have been nice, I might have been able to save his job for him. All he'd have had to do was tell the Braves he wanted me, and he could have had me. I couldn't promise that I'd have had the same season I had at Jacksonville, but I think I'd have hit a few for him, even if I did hit them over the wrong fence, and I think I'd have driven in

44

some runs for him. Instead, he was fired in May, and George Selkirk took his place and won a pennant with the team.

Although there was no drama involved in my arrival with the Braves, there was some involved in my staying with them—in fact, a whole heap of it.

During the winter, the Braves had made it pretty clear that they planned to strengthen. They had moved from Boston to Milwaukee, and from seventh place to second place all in one year.

"Braves Shop for Left-fielder." "Braves Dicker for Second Baseman." These were the headlines of the winter in the newspapers.

Sid Gordon had played left field the season before, and he had hit pretty good—.274 and 19 home runs, the book says. But Sid had to hit home runs not to clog up the bases. He was getting old and slowing down. (I'm quoting, you understand. I wasn't there and don't know a thing about it other than what I read in *The Sporting News*.)

The Braves had brought up a kid named Jack Dittmer and put him at second base, but they decided that he couldn't do the job on defense. So they made two big trades during the off-season.

They got Bobby Thomson from the Giants to play left field, and they got Danny O'Connell from the Pirates to play second base. The Thomson deal got most of the attention because it involved Johnny Antonelli, a pitcher to whom the Braves had given a $100,000 bonus to sign. They gave him up; and they gave up Don Liddle, a good left-handed pitching prospect; and they gave up Ebba St. Claire, who could have been a real good big-league catcher if he hadn't got too fat; and they gave up Bill Klaus, an infielder, and $50,000. I don't have to tell you, then, that they had a lot riding on Thomson.

Any way you wanted to look at it when spring training started, I was out. They'd already decided I wasn't a second baseman. That's why they sent me to Puerto Rico to take lessons in the outfield. They weren't expecting me to be able to play the outfield yet, and that's why they traded for Thomson. They had finished so high the season before that they thought they might be able to trade themselves into first place, I guess.

The first few days of spring training, hardly anybody knew I was around—or if they did, I didn't know it. You know how these sports writers are about a new kid in spring training, if he's got any kind of chance at all. They're all over him, checking the color of his eyes, the size of his waist, his ma and pa and his love life. Some of them would see me and say, "Who's that kid?"

Somebody would answer, "That's Henry Aaron."

"Henry who?" And pass on.

Of course, I don't guess I was any well of information that spring. If I said three words in a row, it was an upset. I just wasn't any kind of talker at all.

I remember one day some writer from New York came up to me, and said, "Say, Henry, tell me what it was like, being the first black in the Sally League."

"I wasn't," I said.

"That's what all the stories say, that you, uh, broke the color line in the South."

"Two other guys were on the team, too."

"Two other blacks, you mean?"

"Yeah."

"Who were they?"

"Felix and Horace."

"Felix and Horace who?"

"Garner and Mantilla."

"Felix Garner and Horace Mantilla, right?"

"No, just the other way around."

"You mean Horace, uh . . . oh, there's Bobby Thomson, and I've got to see him."

That ended that interview, and I was relieved.

When exhibition games started, I'd go in for somebody around the seventh or eighth inning, or pinch-hit, but nothing more. Then we went to St. Petersburg to play the

New York Yankees on a Saturday, March 13. Those were the "frontier" days of travel in Florida. The Sunshine Skyway, connecting the St. Petersburg side with the Bradenton side of Tampa Bay, hadn't been built, and when we traveled from one side to the other we rode an old ferryboat. I learned to try to dodge those trips later on, until the bridge was built, but I was happy to be among the traveling squad that day.

It was getting late in the game. I had already been in as a pinch-hitter, and was showered and dressed and standing in a little alleyway between the third base stands and the bleachers at Al Lang Field. It was still there, last time I looked, and it's the passage the players use going to and from the field.

I was standing there drinking a Coke when Thomson got hold of a pitch and hit a line drive to left field. He tore around first and went into second with a big slide. Then he didn't get up. I could see his leg doubled up underneath his body and he was just lying there on the ground like he'd been shot.

Our equipment man, Joe Taylor, ran out on the field, and players started gathering around. Then they sent for a stretcher. I knew something big had gone wrong. I just stood there drinking that Coke, really not thinking anything, except that I was glad it wasn't me.

"What happened?" somebody asked me.

"I dunno," I said. "Looks like Thomson hurt his leg."

I didn't say anything else, just stood there drinking that Coke. They brought him right by me on that stretcher, brought him so close I had to stand out of the way to let the stretcher-bearers by. He had one arm over his forehead, but I could see the pain in his face.

"He broke his leg, I think," somebody said.

I didn't realize it then. Heck, I wasn't mature enough to realize anything but sunup, sundown and mealtime. Anyway, that was my ticket to the big leagues going by me on the way to the hospital. Bobby Thomson, the man they traded for to play left field, wasn't going to get to bat again until July 14. In the meantime, the Braves had to have somebody in left field.

By all rights it should have been Jim Pendleton. He had had a big season the year before. He had come on big in a few tight situations, and had done so well he was playing like a regular at the last. But prosperity got to him: he'd shown up for spring training big as a blimp and out of shape.

The other candidates were Dick Sinovic, who had a lot of power, batted .342 on the Atlanta farm club, had a good arm but couldn't run; Billy Queen, who could play several positions, hit 18 home runs, batted .281 on the Toledo farm; Pete Whisenant, a real "character" of a ball player up from Atlanta, batted .266 and had some power and could run and throw; Bob Thorpe, who had been with the club three years, but was trying to get over the effects of a broken ankle himself; and George Metkovich, known as "Catfish," who had been with the Pirates and Cubs the year before, but was on his way out of the big leagues.

I wasn't even on the roster, which I repeat here for the reason that you can look through the National League "Green Book" for 1954, under the heading of "Braves Introduce," and you won't find my name. You find some kids named Bill Casey, a catcher; Bill Denney, a pitcher; Ben Johnson, another pitcher; Collins Morgan, an outfielder; Ted Laguna, a catcher and a funny, funny guy; Glenn Thompson, another pitcher, and Sinovic and Queen, but no Aaron.

At the hospital the news was bad. Thomson's ankle was broken, sure enough. That made a pretty gloomy mess out of all of us. He'd been going good and it looked like the Braves had made the right deal. The sports sections were full of it the next morning. We went back by the old, slow ferryboat to Bradenton for the night, then came back to Tampa the next day to play the Cincinnati Reds. We are now about to get to the moment I'll never forget. I was about to become a major baseball player, Henry Louis

Aaron, from two sandwiches, two dollars and two pairs of pants, to the Indianapolis Clowns, to Eau Claire on the first airplane ride of my life, to Jacksonville to Left field, Milwaukee, Wisconsin, U.S.A.

We were getting our bags ready to leave the clubhouse at Bradenton that Sunday morning, a bright, pretty day. I remember that. Charlie Grimm picked up my glove, threw it to me, and said, "Kid, you're my left-fielder. It's yours until somebody takes it away from you."

I really never thought too much about it at that time. I'd read stories about other ball players being told they were with a team to stay and winding up that season playing left bar-stool in Saginaw, Michigan, or coming to a new club after a trade and being told, "We traded for you to play you, son," and winding up in the dugout.

In fact, I really never have thought about it a lot until this very second. But that was when I became a regular in the big leagues. I never have been out of the line-up since, except when I was sick, hurt or resting, and there hasn't been a lot of that in my big-league life.

Nevertheless, before that first season was over, I was going to know that awful feeling that Bobby Thomson felt on that Saturday afternoon in St. Petersburg.

6

I'VE NEVER BEEN much for clowning around. I'm not the serious kind, moody, "vanting to be alone," like that old actress from Sweden. If I got something to say, I'll say it. If there's a gag going, I'll laugh as big as anybody and sometimes throw in my two-cents' worth. But when it comes to gathering the gang around and layin' 'em in the aisles with some of my hot comedy, that's not me.

When I got to the big leagues, though, you'd have thought one of baseball's biggest jokers had hit the scene. Some of the stuff I've read about myself in those early times after I got to Milwaukee have left me wondering if I should laugh or sue.

Of course, Charlie Grimm was responsible for a lot of it, all in good nature, understand. Charlie was a fun lover and a real great guy. He wasn't beyond stretching the truth a long way, especially if it got a bigger laugh. Sometimes some of the things he'd tell on me made me sound like a real kid from Hicksville, and then sometimes he'd make me sound about twice as smart as I really was.

I didn't read a lot in those days, after I got past the box scores. I didn't read them a lot. I knew what I had done the night before, and if it was good I was happy, and if it was bad, I didn't need to make myself any sadder by seeing it in print. So most of these funny little yarns that came up about me in my first couple of years in the big leagues I never read until I was older, and wiser, and a little more tolerant than I would have been, I guess.

Another thing I was able to realize later that I wouldn't have realized then was that the Braves were doing their best to get all the mileage they could out of me. I was just a kid, twenty years old, up from the bush leagues, taking a regular job on a team with a chance at winning a pennant. I was "good copy," except that I wasn't "good copy" at all. I was just a kid who spoke when spoken to, usually.

It's a funny thing, I really wasn't scared or nervous. I guess I should have been, but I wasn't. We opened the season in Cincinnati in 1954, and I was the left-fielder. I hadn't even been on the roster until the day before we opened. I'd really come to think I was going to play for Atlanta that season. Little did I know, until later, that the Southern Association was not yet ready to accept Negro players.

One black actually did stick with the Atlanta farm club for about two weeks. He was a kid named Nat Peeples, an outfielder. An odd thing was that the only game Peeples played in was in Mobile, my hometown. He played that one game, didn't get a hit and was farmed out to Jacksonville a few days later. And so the old Southern Association managed to finish its life a few seasons later untainted by a black base hit—which, I suppose, those old club operators would claim sort of maintained the league in the "Southern way of life."

Anyway, I had come to expect, in my ignorance of things, to play the season in Atlanta. The day before the season opened in Cincinnati we worked out in County Stadium. We had gone into Milwaukee for an exhibition game with Cleveland, then had a day off. After the workout that morning, Charlie Grimm met me in the clubhouse.

"Henry, Mr. Quinn wants to see you," he said.

In fact, Mr. Quinn had left a notice in my box at the stadium, but I hadn't thought there was any big hurry about it.

"He wants to see you now, Henry, so you'd better go on up."

John Quinn was sitting at his desk in the upstairs part of the stadium. I'd never been up there before. I didn't have any historic feelings as I went into his office. I just went in to deliver the body, like a kid called in by his high-school principal.

"You've had a great spring, Henry, and we're proud of you," Mr. Quinn said. "I don't guess this'll come as any great surprise to you, but we've bought your contract from Toledo and I want you to sign a Braves contract."

I don't remember saying anything. He had this piece of paper on his desk, a regular baseball contract. I can't even tell you what the salary was. I didn't look. I didn't care. I figured that anything John Quinn did was going to be fair, anyway.

I signed my first major league contract. I was a Milwaukee Brave. It reads a lot more exciting now than it seemed at the time it happened.

The next day in Cincinnati, I was the left-fielder. Bud Podbielan pitched for the Reds, and I was o for 4 in my first game. But I wasn't o for 4 because I was scared or nervous. I just didn't get any hits. I may have been a little overanxious. Podbielan wasn't a power pitcher. He threw a lot of slow stuff, and I was overswinging trying to get the bat on the ball.

Anyway, whatever funny things I did in the first stage of my life with the Braves I didn't do because I was scared or nervous. Willie Mays says he was a scared kid. I wasn't. Maybe I wasn't smart enough. And if I was being funny, it wasn't on purpose. You've got to remember here, too, that Donald Davidson, a funny little man himself, was publicity director for the Braves then—he's the traveling secretary now—and Donald was doing everything he could to make me the kind of colorful fellow that fans wanted to come out to watch.

Donald was the first fellow who began calling me "Hank." No big thing, understand. But I'd been "Henry" to everybody else until then. Hank made me sound a little more like a colorful athlete, I guess—a little more like an athlete and a little less like somebody's handyman around the house. I liked it.

Donald was the fellow who put out the story about why I'm number 44. And it's a true story.

My first season with the Braves, I wore the number 5 on my uniform. It was assigned to me. I didn't get any choice. Numbers really never made any difference to me, in high school, or with the Clowns, or at Eau Claire, or at Jacksonville or in Puerto Rico. I took whatever they put on my back and let it go at that. When I got to the big leagues it was different. Don't ask me why. I just became number-conscious. I wanted to be a double figure.

I saw Donald one day, and I said, "Hey, Donald, how about me trading number 5 for two numbers?"

"Like what? You're so skinny, I don't know how a little b____d like you could carry two numbers around."

You've got to understand Donald Davidson. I think he was born cussing. It's just his nature. He's a little guy, and when I say little, I mean little bitty. About three-and-a-half feet tall. Really, the smallest traveling secretary any big-league baseball club ever had. And a good one. Donald was always good to me, so the language is standard procedure.

"I don't mean just any kind of double number," I said. "I mean like 22, or 33, or 44, something like that."

"Henry, dammit, don't you know that all the great ones were single numbers?" Donald said. "Babe Ruth was No. 3. Lou Gehrig was No. 5. Joe DiMaggio was No. 9. Stan Musial is No. 6 Ted Williams is No. 9. Mickey Mantle is No. 7. And you want to carry two numbers around?"

"That's right."

"What's wrong, don't you want to be great?"

"I can be great and two numbers, too."

"Awright, I'll see what I can do."

It didn't make any difference to Donald. If it wasn't worth arguing about to him, it wasn't worth anything at all. Besides, Donald liked to needle everybody in sight.

The next year when I got to spring training, number 44 was hanging on my locker. I've been number 44 ever since. Makes no real difference, but I like the sound of it for some reason or another. Like you like the sound of a new car or some instrument. Besides, there have been some great double numbers in sports, and I think that really had something to do with my wanting one. Red Grange was 77, Tom Harmon was 99, Charlie Justice was 22, Honus Wagner was 33, after baseball teams finally started wearing numbers, and Bobo Newsom, the pitcher, was 00. (For a fellow who's not so good with statistics and history, I'm surprising myself. Actually, somebody looked these up for me.)

The guys who collected Henry Aaron stories in those early times made a lot over my nonchalance. I remember reading a story in one of the Milwaukee papers, and this was what Charlie Grimm said:

"You can't make a Willie Mays out of him. He's not the spectacular type. Everything he does, he makes it look easy. He'll be around a long time after Willie's gone."

That was pretty safe to say, since Willie is three years older than I am.

You read about my first airplane ride, from Charlotte, North Carolina, to Eau Claire, Wisconsin, so you know I was no experienced eagle of the airlines. Flying didn't exactly appeal to me right at the start, and I didn't mind mentioning it, but I didn't go around "soapboxing" about it.

Duffy Lewis, the old Braves' outfielder, was our traveling secretary in those days. Somebody asked Duffy one day, "How does that Aaron kid like flying now?"

"Dunno," Duffy said. "He won't give us a chance to find out. He's fast asleep before the plane leaves the ground and he doesn't wake up until it lands."

That got old Duffy a laugh or two, but I didn't recognize the kid he was talking about. I did sleep a lot on trips, but not until I was sure that pilot was going to be able to get us off the ground, and then I slept with one eye open and one foot dragging.

Charlie Grimm liked to tell the one about the day I got a telegram from Ford Frick.

It happened in the spring of 1955. Several of us checked in early at Bradenton and got a few days' jump on spring training. Frick notified the club and each player that they were being fined for doing it. Charlie walks into the clubhouse, hands me this wire and I stuff the thing in my locker.

"Better look at that thing, Henry," he said. "It's from Ford Frick."

"Who's he?" I said.

You think that one didn't travel fast. Of course I knew who the Commissioner of Baseball was. I didn't understand "Ford Frick" the way Charlie said it. But, the more I think about it, the more I like the story. It made me sound like a pretty cool kid. Bo Belinsky had to plan his "cool." All I had to do was open my mouth and there was somebody standing around waiting to put my foot in it.

One of the rich ones came from John Quinn. We'd had a little trouble getting together on salary after the '55 season. I had finished the season having put in my only time at second base in the major leagues. The club was having trouble there. Danny O'Connell quit hitting, and so they shoved me in there for the better part of the last month.

The next winter, my contract came in the mail and I called John Quinn to talk to him about it. Some man wrote in a magazine later that I said, "Hey, Mr. Quinn, did you send me Danny O'Connell's contract by mistake?"

I won't say that I did and I won't say that I didn't. It makes such a good story that I'm not going to deny it, even if it does make me sound a little like a smart-off.

Another thing came up, just because I happened to come from Mobile, that didn't make me sound or read like an authority on local history. Worse than that, it made me sound like an upstart.

A lot of writers would ask me if Satchel Paige had been any inspiration to me in baseball. I didn't play it smart. I didn't say, "Of course, Satchel Paige was a big inspiration to me. As a small boy, I used to watch him pitch and wanted to be a big-name player like him."

I didn't say that because I not only didn't know Satchel Paige came from Mobile, I'd never heard of Satchel Paige. Oh, I may have heard the name around Mobile, but I never thought that *that* Mobile Satchel Paige was *the* Satchel Paige, if I thought anything at all about it. But when I was asked the question, I'd answer the truth. I'd say, "I don't know Satchel Paige." The way it came out in print made me sound just like it read—an uppity black kid just striking it rich.

I still haven't met Satchel Paige, but you can bet that I have read up on his history. I've read up on it enough not to say that I used to watch him pitch when I was a little boy. That would make me the oldest player in the major leagues, because I don't think Satchel has pitched in Mobile since World War I.

There were a lot of rough edges to be buffed off this boy when he got to the Braves. Since I wasn't aware of them, it didn't bother me, didn't warp my personality or make me self-conscious about being a non-sophisticate, which seems like a good word for it. Whatever I may have been, though, I wasn't a funny man. I didn't go around making myself the life of the clubhouse. If what I said had any humor in it, it was the natural, undistilled stuff. It came off the top of my head. I wasn't creating "lines."

I came to the Braves on business, and I intended to see that that business was good as long as I could.

7

Ike Delock was a right-handed pitcher. Not exactly the kind of guy you'd remember a long time for his pitching, and I'm the guy, you know, who said he wasn't much for remembering names and dates and statistics. Well, Ike Delock is a guy I won't be soon forgetting.

He was an average-sized pitcher, and an average pitcher. He pitched for the Boston Red Sox a few years, had a good season or two, then his arm went bad.

You remember I wrote about the first exhibition game we played in Jacksonville when I was a rookie in the Sally League—when Boston beat us, 20–1, and the only run Jacksonville got was a home run I hit, which had only the effect of cutting the margin from 20 to 19 runs at the time?

Ike Delock was my pigeon. He was the pitcher off whom I hit the home run in Jacksonville.

The Red Sox trained in those days at Sarasota, which is about ten miles from Bradenton. From ball park to ball park, it may be even less. The name of the Red Sox's park was Payne Park, and it was a big one, pretty rightly named for a hitter, but a pitcher's friend.

I hadn't played much before Bobby Thomson broke his ankle, but the one significant game I had played took place in Payne Park. Delock was pitching for the Red Sox again, and if I must say so myself—usually a batter won't slander any pitcher who's still pitching, afraid of a jinx, or something—that Delock did throw some nice, fat, fast balls.

He threw me one that day we played the Red Sox in March, 1954, and I hit it over that long left-field fence (I'm thinking it's 390 feet out there), and it landed among a bunch of trailers in a trailer park.

It was the first home run hit there that spring, they said, and they also said it was bound to be the longest that would be hit.

I mention that particular home run, because I've always felt it had a lot to do with my staying with the Braves. In other words, when Thomson got hurt, Charlie Grimm might have thought of two or three other guys for left field. He might have pushed Jim Pendleton into shape. He might have wanted to make another trade. But when he threw that glove to me and said, "Left field is yours, kid, until somebody takes it away from you," I think he still had the picture in his mind of that home run sailing over the fence in Sarasota. I'm going to think that way, anyway.

I hit two more home runs that spring, one of them off Jack Harshman, that cleared the center-field fence in the Bradenton park. It was no Payne Park, but to center field it was over 400 feet. I batted over .300 in exhibition games, and so the job was mine. To me, though, the regular season was a disappointment. I got a slow start and never did really develop a full head of steam. Besides that, I kept reading in the Milwaukee papers during the season that the Braves had lost their chance at the pennant when Thomson broke his ankle. That didn't do a lot for my confidence, either. But I didn't say anything. I was still the silent kid. I didn't want to say anything that was going to open a trap door and find myself on the way to Toledo.

One day in Bradenton during spring training, Bob Wolf, the baseball writer for the *Milwaukee Journal,* and a pretty straight shooter in my book, was sitting in the dugout listening to me talk to some visiting sports writer about my first season as a Brave.

"It was a great year for me, because I got a break that put me in the big leagues, but I disappointed myself as a player," I was telling the other guy. After the other guy left, Bob moved in.

"Hank, I just heard you say that your first season was a disappointment to you," he said. "You can't really be serious, can you?"

Then he pulled out the record. "Twenty-seven doubles, 13 home runs, 69 runs batted in and .280 average—I'd say that's pretty good for a rookie."

"Not if you been used to hitting .340 all your life," I said. "I was hitting over .400 with the Indianapolis Clowns."

"What do you think Willie Mays hit his first season in the big leagues? Or Ty Cobb, or Rogers Hornsby, or even your pal Ed Mathews? Neither one hit as much as you did Cobb didn't hit but .240. Mays hit .274. And Hornsby, the great Hornsby, he didn't hit but .246."

"Still don't make me feel any better that I didn't hit but .280," I said.

"What did you expect to hit, .400?"

"Not my first season," I said. "Some day I'd like to hit .400. I guess that's really what I'd rather do than anything else in the big leagues, be the next player that hit .400. A lot of guys are hitting 40 home runs these days, and a lot of guys are driving in a lot of runs. But nobody has hit .400 since Ted Williams. I'd like to be the next one. I'd like to win a batting title and I'd like to be the most valuable player, but most of all I'd like to hit .400."

"You hit .400, Hank," Bob Wolf said, "and you'll be all those things and have your own television show."

That's really how I felt then. I can't remember the year, but it had to be before 1956, because it was before I'd led the league in hitting, and the first time I did that was 1956. But I really believed I was going to hit .400 in the big leagues before I was through. There were a lot of things I hadn't learned about major league pitching yet, and major league travel, and the fast pace of living in the major leagues.

I'm thoroughly satisfied now that I'll never hit .400 in

the big leagues. In fact, I don't think any player will ever hit .400 in the big leagues again, unless the rules are changed giving the hitter more of a break than he's getting now.

You take the spitball, for an example. Of course there are pitchers in the big leagues throwing the spitball. I've played on teams with them and I've batted against them. I don't say that the spitball is an unhittable pitch. A lot of these guys throwing it don't know how to use it, but a lot of them do and do it well.

I'll bet you Lew Burdette would have been out of the major leagues two or three years before he was if it wasn't for his spitter. He threw one of the best ones. Don Drysdale of the Dodgers threw it, and Gaylord Perry, and Frank Linzy, the one-time relief pitcher for the Giants, and Phil Regan, who didn't become an outstanding pitcher until he started using it for the Dodgers, and a lot more.

When the Braves were playing the Giants once several years ago, Billy Loes, the sort of eccentric pitcher who had broken in with the Dodgers, was pitching. There had been one of those spitball furors going on about that time. Well, Loes spits a big glob on his fingers, winds up and throws me a big fat lob that was supposed to be his joke of the spitball. I swung and knocked the thing out of the park.

I guess what Loes was saying—if he ever had a serious thought in his life—was, "If you're going to have the spitball, legalize it. If not, rule it out and enforce it."

That's about the way I feel. My own view is, legalize the spitball, then at least the batter will know it's coming.

That's just one of the hitting hazards we have today. Another is the twilight games. You hear a lot of talk about night baseball, but that's not too bad. At least everything is consistent then. It's twilight baseball, twi-night double-headers, early-starting games in daylight time zones, those in-between times when there isn't enough daylight left and when the best lighting system in the world can't make anything out of twilight but twilight. That's the toughest time in the world to hit. You start off hitting in broad daylight, then twilight, then night, all in the same game. You can't tell me that those old .400 hitters would have been .400 hitters under those conditions.

I've got to admit that when I look at some of the records of the old-timers, I darn near choke to death. Those cats really knew something about this game we don't know today. Some baseball men have called me "the greatest right-handed hitter since Rogers Hornsby." Since I've looked at Rogers Hornsby's record, I've been willing to give up hitting .400 as my ambition and settle for that reputation, if somebody will only make it official—the "greatest right-handed hitter since Rogers Hornsby," I mean.

I'd never really looked at Hornsby's record until we started working on this book. One afternoon in West Palm Beach, Florida, during spring training of 1967, Furman Bisher spread the *Baseball Register* open to Hornsby's lifetime record in the major leagues, and I've got to confess that I developed some kind of new respect for myself. What I mean is, I decided I must be some helluva kind of a hitter if anybody is crazy enough to compare me with this man.

In the first place, I took a look at the bottom of Hornsby's record, where it says, "BRTR, Games 2259, .358," and I said, "Man, you can't be serious. You mean that .358 is his lifetime average? Whoo-o-o-o-o-o-eeeee!"

Then I looked down a string of his averages, from 1920 to 1925—.370, .397, .401, .384, .424, .403—and I said, "If that happened today, Congress would investigate this guy. You know no man ever had batting averages like that. This is got to be a misprint."

Well, I've got a new respect for the man they have compared me with. I guess of all the things that have been said about me since I've been a major leaguer, nothing has really meant as much to me as that thing about being the best right-handed hitter since Hornsby. And then, that didn't take hold until I really took a good, close look at his record. I'm sorry I never got to meet that man now.

I don't think the public really appreciates what some

little thing can mean to a baseball player. There's nothing like a pat on the head or a kind word to turn a ball player into a terror. You play a schedule of 162 games a year, you can't go into every one inspired, with all your juices turned on. There are not that many kinds of different inspirations.

But something a man says to a player or about a player can really get him playing on a level he never played on before, just because at a certain time when it's critical the player will let that little thought run through his mind and he feels something inside him that tells him he's really capable of doing something he never thought he was capable of doing before. I don't know if I'm saying it right or not, but that's about as well as I can put it.

I won't try to convince you that what Charlie Grimm said in the spring of 1956 caused me to lead the National League in hitting that season, but it didn't hurt. I always liked Charlie, and I've said that, and I think he liked me. Leastways, I can't think of any time when he was unfair to me, or when he went out of his way to "chew me out." So whatever Charlie said about me would mean a little something extra to me.

This happened on the day we played our first exhibition game that spring—played the Philadelphia Phillies in the Bradenton park. They started a kid pitcher named Jack Meyer. He's dead now. He had a heart attack in the spring of 1967. Wasn't but about thirty-four years old, but was pretty wild, they tell me. That sort of described his pitching, too: threw hard, but wild.

The first time I faced Meyer that day, he threw me a knee-high fast ball, really too low for a strike, but I golfed it over the center-field fence, which was about a 425-foot drive.

Meyer was a right-hander. Then the Phillies switched to Ron Mrozinski, who was a left-hander. The second time up, Mrozinski threw me an inside fast ball, and I hit it over the center-field fence, another 425-foot shot.

Of course my performance was rather prominent in the

conversation after the game. Some of the writers asked Charlie Grimm about me, and Charlie said, "There is the guy who's liable to be leading the league in hitting this season, and several seasons after that."

I led the league in hitting that season. I batted .328. I'm sorry to say Charlie wasn't around long enough to enjoy it. I woke up one morning and read in the newspaper that he had been fired and that Fred Haney, one of the coaches, had been hired to take his place. I never really have been too bothered about who's managing the team. I figure I've got to play the same, no matter who's the boss. I hated to see Charlie go, but I got used to Haney and we won pennants with him, so you can't knock that

What Charlie said about me, though, stayed with me, and I tuned it on inside me from time to time and it did mean something to me on the way to the batting championship. At last I felt like I was a big leaguer. I'm not cocky. Some guys used to say I had the "big-head." I didn't say a lot. They didn't say much to me. I just went my own way and tried to stay clear of some people because I didn't have anything to say.

I'm not cocky, but I believe in myself. I believe I'm a good hitter. I had been a disappointment to myself in Milwaukee because I hadn't been hitting in the high figures. Leading the league that year at last convinced me that I was finally becoming big league as a hitter.

That first season became an even worse disappointment to me—really left me pretty low when I finished it off the way Bobby Thomson started it. I guess you've got to say that this was fate at work. His broken ankle gave me the chance to play, and I paid a pretty price for it. I broke a leg, the right one (same one Bobby broke), sliding into a base (same way Bobby broke his).

It happened on the Sunday before Labor Day in Cincinnati. We were playing the Reds a double-header. Bobby had started the first game, but I came in to run for him after he got a hit in the seventh inning. I came to bat later in the game and got a double. We won that game, 11–8.

I started the second game, and we really turned it on the Reds again. I got 4 hits and was 5 for 5 for the day. Our dugout was alive, and you had that feeling that something great was about to happen to this ball club. We were still in the pennant race. We were just five games back of the Giants, who were leading, and right on the Dodgers' tails. And we had one big series left with the Dodgers.

We were winning the second game—and we won it—going into the eighth inning. Then I got the hit that did me in, my fifth hit of the day. I hit a screamer to center field and went tearing into third for a triple, but I had to slide for it. My left foot got caught in something. I never knew what it was. But it got caught so that I couldn't hook with my right leg, and my right one crumpled up under me.

Snap! I'm not going to say that you could hear it all over that part of town. I didn't even hear it myself. I didn't feel it too much until they started moving me around, and I knew then I was hurt bad.

You'll never guess who came in to run for me—Bobby Thomson himself. They took me to Christ Hospital and I was there for three weeks. Bobby begins the season in the hospital and I take his job, and I end the season in the hospital and he gets his job back. By this time, though, I knew something I didn't know when Bobby went to the hospital.

I knew I could play in the big leagues. I had to have 5 for 5 that last day to hit .280, but I knew then that I could hit in the big leagues.

I was a pretty despondent boy when they wheeled me into that operating room at Christ Hospital. You know how hospitals are, anyway. They sound like everybody is waiting for somebody to die. No noise. Everybody moving around like they're walking on tiptoes. They acted like if they spoke out loud they'd break my other leg. Then something funny happened, if you can call anything funny about a broken leg.

Actually, the break was down around the ankle, and the doctors wanted to go in and place a pin in it. But something developed they hadn't thought of before. I still wasn't twenty-one years old, and they had to call my parents to get permission. I was old enough to have a wife and a baby, but not old enough to give the doctor permission to operate on me.

They put in a call for Mobile. Well, my mother panicked. "Don't you go cutting on my child!" she said.

"But, Mrs. Aaron, the boy has a broken ankle," the doctor said. "All we want to do is put a pin in it. It won't change anything. It will only make the ankle heal and grow stronger as it heals," the doctor told my mother.

Finally, my dad got on the phone. He told the doctor, "If it's got to be done, it's got to be done." And so they operated and set it.

What I really didn't realize was that I was getting a double break—one bad and one good. The Korean War was on then. I'd registered for the draft in Mobile, and my papers had been transferred to Milwaukee. Donald Davidson came into the clubhouse one day and told me I was due at the draft board the next morning at seven o'clock.

I remember when we walked into that place, there must have been two hundred guys standing around there. Donald had picked me up and drove me down. I said, "Look, Donald, they already got about two hundred guys. They don't need me. Let's go."

I can't tell you what Donald said. This is supposed to be a clean book.

Anyway, my number had come up. I was due to report in October. Naturally, when I broke my ankle, that put me on the deferred list. My country calls me, I'm ready to go. But I'm not looking for any wars to fight. I don't hate anybody bad enough to shoot 'em. I didn't want to go to war. I wouldn't break my ankle to keep from going, but since it happened that way, and my draft board had to reclassify me, and it kept me from losing some good baseball years, I'm not going to turn liar and say that I'm mighty sorry I didn't get a chance to be a soldier.

So, anyway you want to look at it, even my own ankle

break was a break for me. By the time the draft board got around to me the next time, I had three children, and that took care of my soldier's career. I was ready to play the next season. I had had what the people I worked for thought was a good rookie season. We didn't win the pennant. The Dodgers kicked our teeth out in that big series. The Giants won it and took Cleveland four games in a row. But the Braves' time was coming. We were all going to grow a little bit each season. A pennant wasn't far off.

8

There was this little story in *The Sporting News* of September 12, 1956:

> The Milwaukee Civic Progress Commission took its first steps on August 30 toward providing for a suitable celebration if and when the Braves win the National League pennant.
>
> The plans call for decorations on the city's main thoroughfare, Wisconsin Avenue, and a welcome home celebration if the Braves should clinch the pennant on the road.
>
> The commission also instructed its planning committee to draw up a suitable symbol for decorative purposes, probably an Indian swinging a bat, and the parks and recreation committee of the County Board of Supervisors voted to authorize the addition of as many seats as possible to County Stadium if the Braves cop the flag. At the present time, the stadium capacity is 43,117.

On the same page there was another story just chock full of happiness for the Braves. The headline said:

> "Braves' flag boom given louder roar
> by club's big guns."

The story, written by Bob Wolf of the *Milwaukee Journal*, began:

> Milwaukee's pennant stock, already booming, went even higher over the Labor Day weekend. The Braves'

1–2–3 punch of Henry Aaron, Eddie Mathews and Joe Adcock finally started clicking on all three cylinders.

Until Aaron finally got going and joined Mathews and Adcock, Manager Fred Haney never could get his three power men hitting together. First one and then another would slump, but the fact that the Braves kept winning was in itself a happy commentary on their chances. . . .

You can see, then, that Milwaukee was ready to award the pennant to the Braves. But the best thing about our finish was all the planning. The Dodgers beat us out on the very last day of the season.

We led the league 126 days. The Dodgers led the league only seventeen days, but they led the last day and that was the right day.

For us, it was a strange season, any way you want to look at it. We started off hot. We were in first place the whole month of May. Then, whatever we had going for us we lost. When we came to our senses, we were in fifth place. That was about the middle of June.

Back in the spring, before the National League season opened, a writer from New York, Milton Richman, had printed a story that said, "Charlie Grimm will have the Milwaukee Braves in first place by June 15, or he'll be out of work."

I can't say for myself that this thing had any effect on Charlie. I don't think I was capable of seeing that deep beneath his skin. But some of the older players kept talking about it.

"That story is eating on Charlie sure as hell," I heard Johnny Logan saying one day. "Don't try to tell me it's anything else, because I can tell something is bothering him."

"No guy who has been around as long as Charlie has is going to let one newspaper story get to him," Ed Mathews said.

"Don't take much to bother some people," Joe Adcock said.

"Take more than that to bother me," Logan said.

He was right. Nothing bothered Logan much. I've been

out in the country and watched cattle standing in a rainstorm chewing on their cud. Just standing there. Lightning and thunder and the rain coming down and running off their hide, and them just chewing their cud. Sort of reminded me of Logan. He had a temper. I don't mean he didn't get riled up. But when it came to the way he played, I think Johnny Logan thought he was going to be playing shortstop for Milwaukee forever.

"Whatta you think, Henry?"

Logan was talking to me. "I don't think," I said. "I just come here to hit." I didn't want to get messed up in any clubhouse politics.

A few days later we were in the clubhouse, most of us dressing or reading mail, or getting ready to dress. The door opened and John Quinn, the general manager, walked in. You could tell by the set of his mouth that he hadn't come there to pin any ribbons on anybody. Just the night before we had blown a game to the Giants, and I mean we blew it. We'd kicked it away.

Joe Taylor, the clubhouse man, cleared the place of everybody but players, coaches and Charlie Grimm. John Quinn started talking.

"I make it a practice of staying out of the clubhouse," he said, "but there are times when even I can't make a principle like that stand. I've asked Charlie's permission to talk to you and I'm going to talk straight from the shoulder."

Man, by the time he was finished there wasn't a player in the room who wouldn't have liked to crawl under the door and out.

"You haven't been hustling. You've read the stuff in the papers about how great you're supposed to be this season, and you're taking it for law. Well, I can tell you this: you're letting the fans down, you're letting the club down, you're letting Charlie Grimm down, but worst of all, you're letting yourselves down. When you start acting like you want to play baseball again, you'll start winning again."

He wheeled around and walked out without another word.

Now it was Charlie's turn. I'd have thought this was

playing it Charlie's way. In other words, it looked like the front office was blaming the players, not Charlie. But when he stood up his face was red. There was an angry curl in his lips.

"I don't know how much longer I may be here," he said, "but as long as I am, nobody is going to talk to my players like that. You're hustling so much you're pressing. I can see that. Maybe it's necessary to live with you every day to see that, but I can see it. I know you want to win as bad as I want to win, and I'll defend the way you've been trying as long as I'm here."

I can't say to this day that it wasn't a "team" job, a strategy that John Quinn and Charlie had planned to get us on our toes. One thing that would make me believe that it wasn't, though, was this. I heard a few days later— after we had lost ten out of thirteen games, and we were still falling flat on our faces, and rumors were flying everywhere that Charlie was going to be fired—that he had gone into Quinn's office one day and demanded to know where he stood. And the way I heard it, what Quinn told him didn't clear the atmosphere very much. Charlie was left hanging just as he had been, no promises, no vote of confidence.

Maybe it was a sincere act—Quinn sincerely blasting us, and Charlie sincerely defending us. But I still wonder.

None of us had to wonder long about the rumors, though. The club was in New York after that bad home stand— we won five and lost ten—when it happened. We'd left Milwaukee just the day before. I don't know why Quinn waited until we were in New York to make the move, unless he wanted the situation to simmer down some before we walked out on the field again at County Stadium. Charlie had managed in Milwaukee when it was minor league, and he and those people had a running romance going.

It was June 16. We were staying at the Commodore Hotel. We were opening a series with Brooklyn, but the club always stayed at the Commodore when we were in New York City. We had an off day. I walked into the lobby of

the Commodore and ran into Warren Spahn. He had a
funny look on his face.

"Charlie just got it," he said.

"Fired?" I said.

"Fired," Spahn said.

We'd heard that Quinn was flying in. First, there was
some talk and some newspaper writing that he was coming
in to make a big deal. The players knew better. Still, I can't
say that it wasn't a shock. It's sort of like somebody in
the family with cancer dying. You know the person can't
get well, but you're never ready for death.

Charlie was popular with the players. All of them liked
him because he wasn't the kind to "chew you out." I liked
him especially because he gave me my chance. He tolerated
my mistakes when I was a green kid. I don't make any
bones about it: I couldn't have taken the criticism then,
green as I was, the way these young players have to take it
today. (But I'll get around to some managers I have known
and some I have liked and some I could have lived without
a little later in the book.)

"Haney's the new manager," Spahn said.

"What's Charlie going to do?" I said.

"I don't know," Spahn said. "Quinn's here now and I
guess they'll get that worked out. I hate to see Charlie go."

I said previously that I had read about it in the paper.
Well, I really didn't know it for sure until I picked up a
paper that night. I *knew* it, but that confirmed something
that I'd sort of hoped inside wouldn't come off.

There is something magic about a change, though. I
can't deny that. We got cranked up again. We won eleven
games in a row, like all we needed was a new leader. All
we needed was a kick in the britches. Anyway, winning
eleven in a row put us back in first place. Then we lost our
momentum, or whatever it was, again. At the All-Star break
in July, Cincinnati was in first place.

That was the way it went. Up and down. Twenty-five
guys on a seesaw. I was going to win the batting championship. I was going to hit .328, but the next highest guy—

Bill Virdon of Pittsburgh, who wasn't that kind of hitter—had an average of only .319.

On the way, though, I had my slumps, like that story said. At one stretch I hit in twenty-five straight games. Herm Wehmeier, then with St. Louis, stopped me. (Remember that name, Wehmeier. I'll get back to it again, and we'll all hate him together.) Then I went into a slump. No, not a slump—that word's not bad enough for it: I fell flat on my face. For the rest of that month, which was August, I couldn't order a base hit from Sears, Roebuck.

I wasn't a streak hitter. I still don't consider myself a streak hitter. The only other real bad slump I can think of was during the early part of our first season after the Braves moved to Atlanta. I was about 2 for 24 there at one stretch.

The Sporting News was as puzzled by it as I was. In fact, it said, "Aaron is not what could be called a streak hitter. In his two previous seasons in the majors, his average did not vary more than 10 or 15 points once the campaign was well under way."

During the month of September we were in and out of first place again, but we went into the last three games of the season a full game ahead of the Brooklyn Dodgers. We had it. It was right there in our laps.

The Dodgers did have one break on us. They were finishing up at home against Pittsburgh. We were finishing up in St. Louis. We each had three games to play.

On the first day of the series, Brooklyn was rained out. We should have been. We lost to St. Louis, 5–4, but we still had a half-game lead. We win the next two, it makes no difference what the Dodgers do.

, Now remember that guy Wehmeier. He was a right-handed pitcher with freckles and reddish hair. Never really had a big season in the majors. He'd pitched for Cincinnati and Philadelphia before. The Phillies had traded him to the Cardinals that season, and that was one deal you could have bet would never have had any effect on the pennant race. And you'd have lost.

Herm Wehmeier beat us out of it. Warren Spahn pitched his guts out in St. Louis in the second game. The Cards got only three hits in eleven innings. We might as well have left our bats in the clubhouse, for we weren't making a dent in Wehmeier. The only run we scored came on Bill Bruton's home run in the first inning. We got eight more hits off Wehmeier. I got three, but we couldn't get a rally going. It came to a sudden end in the twelfth inning. Stan Musial hit a double, and Rip Repulski hit a double behind him, and Wehmeier beat Spahn, 2–1.

I was just getting used to silent clubhouses. I've heard some pretty quiet ones since then, but up to that time that was the quietest one I'd ever heard. I wanted to hide from Spahnie. You don't know what to say to a guy who has pitched a game like that and you've done nothing to help him and he should have won and he's lost. Best thing to do is take a shower, get your clothes on, and get out of there before somebody says the wrong word. And leave by the back door. Mrs. Spahn may be waiting at the front door for you with a shotgun.

That was the key game. You see, we went into it knowing that the Dodgers had taken a double-header from Pittsburgh that afternoon. The heat was on us. I guess you'd have to say that we buckled, the guys who carried the big bats. We came back and won on the last day of the season, but the Dodgers won, too, and it was over. That World Series check we'd been taking to the bank in advance was wiped out. The Big Winter became the Longest Winter. I never knew a longer one.

I'd had a fine season. As a ball club we'd had a fine season. I'd led the league in batting. Lew Burdette had led the league in pitching overall. Spahn had won twenty games. We had drawn over two million people in Milwaukee again. But the Dodgers had won the pennant. Man, you talk about something hurting. For the first time in my life in the big leagues, I really knew what hurt was.

Something took place in the clubhouse after that last game that made it smart a little more. On the inside, I think, the players were kind of pleased with themselves for beating the Cardinals that day. We hadn't completely folded. We'd played with one eye on the scoreboard, because no matter what we did in St. Louis, it didn't mean a thing if the Pirates didn't beat the Dodgers.

We took hope when we saw that the Pirates had knocked Don Newcombe out of the box in the eighth inning, but Don Bessent saved the game in relief and there went our chance at a tie. But we still had something left to preserve, now that the pennant was out. We *had* to beat the Cardinals, or Cincinnati would tie us for second place.

So we won. Burdette beat Vinegar Bend Mizell 4–2. We had saved second place, so we were sort of pleased with the consolation prize. The clubhouse wasn't quite the morgue it had been the night before. The club was breaking up for the season, and a lot of guys were saying good-by. Then Haney called us to attention. Most of us thought he was going to thank us for coming through on the last day and saving second place and making him look like the kind of manager that Charlie Grimm hadn't been. We were in for a surprise.

"Boys," he said, and you could feel the ice in his voice, "Go home and have yourselves a nice winter. Relax. Have fun. Get good and rested, because when you get to Bradenton next year, you're going to have one helluva spring."

Then he left. Fred never was one to hang around the clubhouse long after a game.

9

I WANT YOU to know that Fred Haney is a man of his word. What he said in October he remembered in March. I think that he had managed the rest of the year—after Charlie Grimm was fired—on a sort of a trial basis, but by the end of the schedule he was strong in the saddle. He knew that he was going to be seeing us again, and he must have spent the winter planning his "mean" spells.

The batterymen reported early, pitchers and catchers and a few coaches. The rest of us checked in on February 27. I flew in and went to Mrs. Gibson's. I was still in the "penthouse." I might have been the "batting king" of the National League, but I was still one of the penthouse boys. Bill Bruton, as the senior member of the colored players, kept his position in the "big house."

Wes Covington was back, Humberto Robinson—he was a pitcher—was back, and Jim Pendleton was back, but we had two other new guys, Felix Mantilla and Juan Pizarro. Mantilla wasn't new to me, but he was to the penthouse. Pizarro was just a kid then. He'd had a big season in Jacksonville. He'd been going so great in Jacksonville that several sports writers had written that the Braves should have brought him up to help us sew up the pennant.

That first morning at the park Haney called a team meeting. We'd suited up, and he closed the door and let us know why we were there.

"Gentlemen, the first thing I want you to realize is that

75

we're here for one purpose—to get in shape," he said. "By the time the season opens, you're going to be ready to play. Anybody got any questions?"

Nobody had any questions.

He never mentioned the 1956 season. With him, that was spilt milk, water over the dam, a $7,000 check you couldn't get cashed. He just told us what was ahead. We already knew what was behind.

I won't say that spring training, 1957, was like training for the Boston Marathon. I never ran in the Boston Marathon. But I got a pretty good idea of how I'd train if I was planning to run in the Boston Marathon. I'd get Fred Haney to get me in shape like he got the Braves in shape in 1957.

The third day we were in camp we played an intrasquad game. That day and every day when we had infield practice, batting practice, or any kind of formal practice or intrasquad game and somebody made an error, everybody dropped what he was doing and took a lap around the park.

A home run was considered a "mistake." The pitcher shouldn't have thrown it. You booted a ball, that was a "mistake." The fielder shouldn't have made an error. We were there to practice being perfect, and the less perfect we were the better shape we got into.

That Bradenton park isn't the biggest park in the world. With a good wind, home runs pop out of the place. But it sure got bigger and bigger and bigger the more I ran around it. By the time we broke camp, I swear that I knew every blade of grass around that fence by its first name.

I was still rooming with Pendleton when we were on the road, and I couldn't help but think that if we'd had Haney's kind of spring training in 1954, the year I reported to the Braves as a rookie, I'd never have got my job. When Bobby Thomson broke his leg, Pendleton would have been in such good shape that he'd have been Charlie Grimm's man for left field.

This time, though, Pendleton didn't survive it. We were in Jacksonville for an exhibition game, on the way north, and the telephone rang one night for Pendleton. It was Haney calling. I hadn't seen Jim.

That telephone rang, and it kept ringing until morning. Haney, Donald Davidson and Duffy Lewis all called wanting Pendleton. Jim never did show up. Half the time you never knew where Jim was, anyway.

The next morning I found out why he had been so much in demand the night before. The Braves had traded Pendleton to Pittsburgh for Dick Cole, who could play all around the infield. Haney had had Cole when he managed the Pirates, and he wanted him for the bench.

Now my roomie became Felix Mantilla, and I liked this. We had been teammates in Jacksonville, and we had spent that winter together in Puerto Rico, and our wives were good friends. You don't think too much about roommates until you get one that isn't a good "housekeeper"—what I mean is, one who not only is the careless, sloppy kind, but also seems to be headed to the bathroom every time you start and never seems to sleep the same time you sleep.

Sometimes there is a purpose in roommate assignments. A lot of times the club will put men together because they figure one fellow has some kind of quality that will rub off on the other fellow. Sometimes it works, and sometimes it's bad.

Take the spring of 1966. When I got to West Palm Beach, I went straight to the clubhouse at Municipal Stadium, where the Braves trained. I wanted to know about schedule, locker, transportation and the general details, and I just wanted to get out to see some of the guys before I put on my uniform the next day.

Somebody asked me, "Who you rooming with, Henry?"

"I don't know," I said.

Donald Davidson walked by, and he is the man who handles those things for the Braves, being the traveling secretary, director of games and public relations director on the road.

"You're rooming with Clarence Gaston," Donald said.

"And don't show him any of your bad habits." He cussed and laughed. This meant he was kidding.

"Who's Clarence Gaston?" I said. I didn't know who Clarence Gaston was.

"He's the man who's going to be the next right-fielder after Henry Aaron," Donald said.

He wasn't kidding this time, I found out later. Gaston was a good-looking kid who had had a great season in the minor leagues. The Braves had big plans for him, and since he was about twenty-one years old and I was thirty-three, it was possible that he might be the next right-fielder. That didn't bother me. You know that some day you're going to open the door and the guy who's going to take your job is going to be standing there. That doesn't bother you. You know the time is coming. You just want to put it off as long as you can.

Clarence Gastons don't bother me. But I think I bothered Clarence Gaston. He was a tall, thin, shy kind of kid from Texas. Texans aren't usually shy, but this kid didn't say ten words. In fact, he stayed away as much as he could. He had friends his own age and kids he had played with, and he could talk to them. We didn't have anything in common— except right field, and he wasn't going to get right field for a long time yet.

Opening that 1957 season with Mantilla for a roommate was a break for me. We were about the same age. We got along. We had things in common. Felix was good for my frame of mind, just a little something extra to open the season with.

We were picked to win the pennant. Sports writers had voted, and they elected us. That did something for my frame of mind, too. Of course, some of the reasons why they picked us didn't pan out at all, but they figured that since we had come so close the year before we wouldn't let it get away again. That much of the reasoning was right. I don't think I ever saw a team open a season as determined to win as we did in 1957.

The writers were picking us, when you boiled it down to

the reasons in uniform, because of our "Big Five" pitchers, Warren Spahn, Lew Burdette, Bob Buhl, Gene Conley and Ray Crone, and because Red Murff, a relief pitcher, had been great in the spring. We needed help in the bull pen.

Well, Conley had just an average year, 9 and 9. Crone wound up the season with the New York Giants. Murff wound it up in Wichita. Red was no kid; it was just his second season in the big leagues, but he was thirty-five years old, had a bad back and couldn't work as often as a good, reliable major-league relief pitcher should be able to work.

Our season began in Chicago, and it began in shape. Hancy had said it: "This team is going to open the season in shape to play." And we did. We were slim, trim, hungry and ready to play. I know I felt that we had something to make up for.

We rode down to Chicago from Milwaukee by bus the day before the opening game. We worked out at Wrigley Field. We stayed at the Edgewater Beach Hotel. I went to sleep that night with Lake Michigan under my window and the lights of the city dancing in the water.

I was ready to play.

10

ON APRIL 16, 1957, there was a big explosion in Nitro, West Virginia, that killed four people.

You could buy a Mercury Monterey automobile for $2,575, new.

A little boy got too close to a leopard with a bad disposition and was nearly clawed to death in a New Orleans zoo.

I read all this in the newspaper. I noticed the Nitro dateline because that was Lew Burdette's hometown, and that name always made me wonder what kind of a town a town named Nitro would be.

You could turn on your television set and watch Jimmy Dean doing a morning show on CBS. He wasn't a big name yet. He was just working on it.

If you liked the nighttime kind of shows, you could see Paulette Goddard on Ford Theater in "Singapore." If you liked your movies "live" instead of on the Late Show, you could see Henry Fonda in "Twelve Angry Men," or E. G. Marshall and a bunch of other actors I didn't know in "Bachelor Party." I didn't go.

Or, if you liked your entertainment outdoors in the fresh air and daylight, you go to Wrigley Field in Chicago and see the "Cubbies" play the powerful Milwaukee Braves. "Cubbies" is a name that one of the Chicago sports writers, Jim Enright, uses for the team.

Two Cubs of the day before were Cubs no longer. Overnight Chicago had traded two veterans—catcher Ray Katt and third baseman Ray Jablonski—to the New York Giants for outfielder Bob Lennon and pitcher Dick Littlefield. That was in the morning paper, and the Chicago writers were pretty excited about Lennon. He sounded like something special. He had hit 66 home runs one season in the Southern Association.

Lennon didn't get to Chicago in time to see the Braves win the first of the ninety-five games they were going to win that season, or the Cubs lose the first of ninety-two they were going to lose. (He didn't stay around long enough to help them lose many, either. He was soon on his way back to the minor leagues.)

A crowd of 23,674, small even for Chicago, especially with Milwaukee playing, came out for the opener. It was what you would call routine. Spahn pitched a four-hitter. The Braves won, 4–1, and we got all four runs in the sixth inning.

> Henry Aaron, the 1956 batting champ, whistled a single to left. Mathews drilled a triple down the rightfield line for the tying tally and Adcock's hit registered Mathews with the tying marker. After Bobby Thomson fanned, Logan rammed a Rush pitch into the centerfield bleachers.

That was how Red Thisted told the story of our four runs in the *Milwaukee Sentinel*. Ah, "the 1956 batting champ" was a line I'll have to admit that I sort of rolled around in my mind a little. I liked the sound of it. It represented one ambition achieved, but I had something more in mind. At least we got a start like we didn't want to have to look back to see if anybody was gaining on us.

We won nine of our first ten games. I was hitting about .400, and we looked like a team. Even little things that had gone against us in the stretch in 1956 turned our way now, and I cite you the name of Bobby del Greco as Prime Example Number 1.

I'll remind you that Del Greco had played center field for St. Louis in our last series of the '56 season. Well, on that black Saturday night, when Herman Wehmeier beat Spahn 2–1, this Del Greco had made two inhuman catches against us. He climbed walls, he flew through the air, he did somersaults, and he caught the baseball twice when it broke up rallies.

Baseball is a game of no heart when it comes to the flesh market, and the Cardinals had shown their appreciation to Del Greco by trading him to the Cubs during spring training. He was playing center field for the Cubs when they came to Milwaukee for a series the Monday following opening day. One of the Braves hit a soft pop fly to him early in the game, I mean the easiest kind of thing to catch. And the Del Greco who had made those fantastic catches in St. Louis dropped it. You wouldn't believe it. He dropped that simple fly, Bob Rush—the Cubs' pitcher—began coming apart, and we beat Chicago 9–4.

The next day, though, we got the news. It wasn't going to be a cake walk. A young catcher named Cal Neeman, who had never hit a home run in the major leagues, hit one that beat Burdette 3–2 in the tenth inning. It was the first game we lost, but to show you how tight the race was and was going to be, it dropped us into a tie for the lead with the Dodgers.

By May, Fred Haney was having closed meetings, and I tell you he wasn't wasting any kindness on us.

"You're playing like you played last September," he told us one day. This was about the middle of May. Cincinnati had won nine in a row and passed us.

Oh, man, you think that didn't bite. "You're playing like you played last September," and I don't think I have to explain that statement.

In other words, "You're blowing it early this year."

This was a team thing, make no mistake about that. I think I've always been a team man. I'll have to admit here, though, that in one of the stories on Haney's meetings something else that Red Thisted wrote in the *Milwaukee Sentinel* made me feel my responsibility. Here's what he said:

It is a little unfair to fault Henry Aaron individually for the recent string of defeats but it may as well be admitted now that when Henry isn't swishing that bat with authority, the Braves are in trouble. He has made two hits in the last 14 appearances and driven in one run in that time.

When Mantilla saw that in the paper, he said, "It looks like Thisted taking a rap at you. You're hitting .385. What does he expect, .500?"

"I don't think that's a rap," I said. "He's just saying if I'd hit more, we'd win more. I gotta agree with him."

"That not 'swishing the bat with authority,' that no rap?" Felix said.

"Not the way I look at it, if I ain't got but two hits in fourteen times up," I said. "I don't call that authority."

Yeah, you can read "rap" into that, but you know why that story pleased me? It told me that people were expecting me to be the leader. If you're going to be the big man on your ball club, you've got to be able to carry your load. This was really one of the first times I could remember reading any story that said, in effect, "As Aaron goes, so go the Braves." So I've got to say that I liked it. It indicated that I was reaching my maturity as a leader of the team, and with Spahn, Mathews, Adcock, Burdette and Del Crandall on the same roster, this was a situation that I coveted.

There was another sign of it showing, too. Pitchers were beginning to throw at me pretty regularly. I guess this was another form of recognition. I wasn't going to sit down and write them letters of appreciation. But it told me that there was a new kind of respect around the league for the guy with "44" on his back.

Don Drysdale was new in the league and already at work on that reputation of his. You know what they said about Drysdale: if it's his wife and she's crowding the plate, he'll brush her back. He was just a kid then, but you know that most of these brush-backs don't take place in a pitcher's mind. They come from some genius on the bench who never has to face the consequences.

One night in Brooklyn, Drysdale threw two straight pitches right at my chin. The first time might have been an accident, but when he threw the second one, that made it pretty obvious what he was about. After the game I was quoted as saying, "It didn't bother me. That punk doesn't throw hard enough to hurt me."

Man, if there has ever been a misquote, that was one. Drysdale threw hard, and he could hurt, and it bothered me. But I hope he didn't notice it. Maybe he was trying to avoid the accident that had happened to Don Newcombe in an exhibition game in the spring.

We were playing Brooklyn in Nashville, Tennessee, on a barnstorming trip north. Big Newk wound up and let me have one around the head my first time up. I got up, brushed off the dirt and hit the next pitch for a single. Later, in the same game, he knocked me back again. The next pitch was a strike and I knocked it out of the park.

The only time I ever really spoke out about bean balls was in St. Louis in the '57 season. Sam Jones and Larry Jackson used to throw at me like I was the target in one of those carnival booths. Finally, I had had enough.

"I'm going out there and get me one of those gentlemen the next time they throw at me," I told a reporter.

One of the older players, Adcock, told me that was the worst thing I could do, start jawing about bean balls in the papers. "All you're doing is inviting more bean balls," he said. "Do whatever you feel like doing, but don't talk about it in the newspapers."

I thought it over, ran it through my mind, and began to realize that getting mad about it wasn't going to make it any easier on me. I stopped showing any concern about it and started getting more hits, and sure enough, Jones and Jackson stopped throwing at me.

I can't blame a pitcher for "brushing back" a batter, I mean if the guy is on a hot streak and he's beginning to intimidate you. But there's a big difference in the "brush-back" and the bean ball. One is a legitimate weapon, as I see it, and the other is a murderous weapon.

There was something else bothering the writers of Milwaukee about this time, and they were beginning to bother me with it. Haney was batting me second in the line-up. Mathews was batting third, Adcock was batting fourth and Thomson was batting fifth. The Milwaukee writers, who never were especially in love with Haney, wanted to know why the Braves' best hitter was not batting third or fourth? I would have liked to be batting third or fourth, but I wasn't letting it prey on my mind. Mathews, Adcock and Thomson represented power, and you want your power in the meat of your batting order.

Thomson *had* represented power, but he was having his troubles. In fact, it wasn't long before he was gone. But at the time he was supposed to be delivering, he was hitting about .150.

I'd lie if I said I didn't think more and more about moving out of second place in the batting order the longer we played that season, Thomson going like he was. I tried to cover it up, though.

One of the Milwaukee writers I didn't know too well, Cleon Walfoort, asked me one day, "Are you happy batting second?"

"I don't think about it too much. Besides, I get to hit more often up there."

"Don't you think the league's leading hitter ought to be batting third or fourth, though?" he said. He was pushing me a little now.

"Maybe I'll score a lot more runs up there, and scoring runs is important." There's no hitter in baseball willing to swap a good, clean, crisp base hit for a run. Or any kind of base hit, for that matter.

"Henry," Walfoort said, "did I read in the spring that you would like to bat .345, hit 35 home runs and bat in, say, at least 100 runs? And then, didn't you say, 'But I don't see how I can knock in 100 runs batting second because there just aren't that many men on base when I come up?' "

He was right. I'd said it. I mumbled something. I don't

remember what. It must not have been worth printing. I never saw it in the paper, anyway.

An event was about to take place, though, that was going to change some things.

After that hot start, the club settled back into some uncertain ways. We'd win a few and lose a few. Cincinnati, Brooklyn and Philadelphia got in the fight with us, and I guess it was pretty obvious that we were suffering at second base. At least I read regular reports in the newspapers that second base was giving us trouble, and I could look across the clubhouse at Danny O'Connell and tell that he was carrying a cross. Usually, he was the life of the party, a good-humor man in the clubhouse who kept us loose.

I don't know how to describe Danny as a second baseman and be fair to him. I thought that he was a good third baseman, shortstop or second baseman, but that he wasn't nearly the second baseman he thought he was. He and Johnny Logan, the shortstop, didn't team too well. The baseball experts said he didn't make the double play like a pennant-winning second baseman should. He wasn't any dandy at it, but he wasn't the worst I ever saw, and after having some experiences as an "experimental" second baseman, who am I to judge other people who try to play the position?

Another thing, Danny was always trying something different. He'd purposely drop pop flies with men on base trying to trap a runner who was not paying attention. He'd pull other little tricks that you didn't ever see other second basemen try, and they'd have been great—if they'd have worked. They hardly ever did, and that was bad.

So we go into Philadelphia for a series. It's over the weekend of June 15, which is the deadline for trading between big-league clubs. We're in first place, but we're hanging on. Cincinnati and Philadelphia are both barking at our heels.

We win the first game, Bob Buhl beats Robin Roberts. Then that night the big event happens. The word gets around when we see O'Connell and Thomson come down from their rooms at the Warwick Hotel with their bags packed.

Some of the guys sitting around the lobby asked them where they were going.

"Back to the Giants," Thomson said. "We've been traded."

This was late at night. The trade was made right at midnight. Thomson, O'Connell and Ray Crone, one of our right-handed pitchers, were swapped to the Giants for Red Schoendienst. Three for one, no money involved. I guess that should convince you of how desperately the people in our front office thought we needed a second baseman. That, in the long run, you see, amounted to a mighty expensive deal.

Look at it this way. To get O'Connell from Pittsburgh, the Braves had given up Sam Jethroe, Sid Gordon, Max Surkont, and three kid pitchers named Larry Lassalle, Curt Raydon and Fred Waters out of the farm system. Plus $75,000 cash.

To get Thomson from the Giants, they had given up Johnny Antonelli, Don Liddle, Ebba St. Claire and Bill Klaus, plus $50,000.

Crone was developed in the farm system.

Now you can say that the Braves got three years of service out of Thomson and O'Connell, but they didn't win the pennant with them. That was the object of the deals. On the other hand, the Giants *had* won a pennant with Antonelli and Liddle.

Jethroe and Gordon were just about through, and neither of the three kid pitchers ever cut a wide swath in the majors. Raydon was the only one who ever spent any length of time with Pittsburgh, but you can ask yourself the question: what might they have done if they had come up under Milwaukee training?

Now the Braves had their second baseman, Schoendienst. When he arrived, it was a signal for a change in the order of things for me. No. 44 became the cleanup man, meaning me. Actually, Haney already had me batting fourth the day before, when we opened the series with the Phillies, but he didn't say anything to me about it until the next day, Sunday, when we got to Connie Mack Stadium. There wasn't anything special about the way he handled it. He simply walked by me in the clubhouse and he said, "Henry, now that we've got the 'Redhead,' I'm going to leave you in fourth spot. He'll be getting on base a lot and you'll have somebody there to bat in."

"Okay by me, Skip," I said.

So we played the Phillies that day with a batting order like this:

> Bruton, cf
> Shoendienst, 2b
> Mathews, 3b
> Aaron, rf
> Torre, 1b
> Logan, ss
> Pafko, lf
> Crandall, c
> And the pitcher.

That Torre was Frank Torre, not Joe. They're brothers, but at that time Joe was still a fat kid in high school in Brooklyn. Joe Adcock was the regular first baseman, but something was hurting him that day and he was sitting it out for some reason. It was just as well that we were getting used to Torre at first base. Exactly one week later, Adcock slid into second base in a game against the Giants, broke his ankle, and he was out most of the rest of the season. I'm surprised that Joe hadn't broken something before when he slid. He was a lot of man, and when he hit the dirt it was like a horse sliding. You could almost feel the ground shake.

We played the Phillies a double-header that day and won the first game 7–5. Schoendienst got two hits and made all the right plays.

The second game we lost, 1–0. Lew Burdette pitched a one-hitter, but we got beaten by Curt Simmons. Even the one hit they got off Lew was disputed. Joe Lonnett, a second-string catcher, hit a ball that Bruton got to just as he hit the outfield fence, and the scorekeeper, being a Philadelphia scorekeeper, gave him a double on it. Bruton said later that it should have been an error and that Burdette should have had a no-hitter, but that would only have made him the first pitcher who ever pitched a no-hit game and lost it in the National League.

Don't let me convince you that the Redhead's arrival cleared up all the Braves' troubles. It didn't. On the day of the trade, this is how the standings looked, as far as the first- and second-place teams were concerned:

	W	L	Pct.
Braves	32	21	.604
Cincinnati	32	24	.571

One week later we were down in third place. Honest injun! Third place, one game and a half behind! St. Louis was leading now.

And you think those newspapers weren't yowling loud and long? Just a few days after the deal this headline came out in one sports section: "Schoendienst Helps Braves at 2nd, But Who's in Left?"

When Thomson left the club, he was batting .236. He'd picked up some in the last few days, but .236 in left field, I'd have to say, won't win a pennant for you. Schoendienst came in from the Giants with an average of .307. You think I wouldn't trade a .236 average for a .307 average any day?

Oh, just to keep honest about it, consider all the angles. O'Connell left with an average of .235. I'm not going to try to convince you that the Braves would not have won the pennant anyway. I think we would have won it even with O'Connell at second base. I think we were that good a ball club in 1957, and that we were that dedicated to winning in 1957. But there were things that Red Schoendienst did for that ball club that couldn't be reproduced in plain, cold statistics.

I'd seen Red play before, of course, when he was with the Cardinals and the Giants both. But you don't notice a fellow as much when he's trying to beat you as when he's trying to help you win. I saw him make double plays I never saw a second baseman make before. I saw him make moves around that infield that I never saw ball players make before. He sometimes seemed to know where the next batter was going to hit the ball and he was there or he was moving somebody else around so the other guy was there. Red glued that infield together.

Just to make sure that they pleased all those critics as much as they could with the situation in left field, the Braves recalled Wes Covington from the farm club in the American Association, which had been moved from Toledo to Wichita by this time. Haney gave out a story that he would alternate Pafko, a right-handed batter, and Covington, a left-handed batter, in left field, and that was the way we went.

I'm happy to report that it worked—especially after "Hurricane" Hazle blew in.

I can't remember exactly when we went on top to stay. That race was jumbled on into August, first one team leading, then another. It finally boiled down to a battle between the Braves and the St. Louis Cardinals, and this is the way it went from about the middle of August until the night we salted it away. That is a night, I want you to know, that I shall never forget. It was the first real, big explosive one moment in my career.

But there was some ground to cover before we got there, and this fellow Hazle had a lot to do with covering much of it. If it hadn't been for an emergency, Hazle would have never made it to Milwaukee, and that goes back to a night game at Forbes Field on July 11.

The Pirates weren't very long on the long ball in those years, and one of their batters lifted a pop fly into short center field. Billy Bruton started in for it. Felix Mantilla started out for it. All I could do was stand there in right field with my mouth open and watch them run together. It was

like two sports-model cars running together, because both
those fellows could really move.

They wound up in a heap and just stayed that way for a
moment. Some of us got around them and helped them up.
Both of them were able to get around with a little help, and
they were taken to a hospital. Mantilla was out for about
a month.

With Bruton, though, it was another thing. He'd torn
some ligaments in his right knee, and he never played again
that season. He wasn't even around to watch the World
Series. He was at Mayo Clinic having some tests made.

When this happened, that brought about another change
in my life and brought "Hurricane" Hazle into the life of the
Braves, for which we all became duly thankful.

Somebody had to play center field, namely me. Now, I had
covered it all in the outfield. I had played left field my first
season in the league, after Bobby Thomson broke his ankle.
Then I had gone to right field when Thomson came back
the next season. Now I was going to be the center-fielder.

I didn't like the switch and there is no point in trying
to hide it. It was a feeling that had nothing to do with my
confidence in my fielding ability.

I was never like Willie Mays. We're two different types
altogether. He was Willie the Spectacular and I was always
Henry the Easy-Does-It, I guess you'd say.

At the risk of being called an immodest fellow, I'll take
the position right here that I did my job in right field all
the years I played there as well as Willie did his in center.
Some people have criticized my style. They've said I was too
nonchalant. Well, we didn't all come out of the same mold.
A lot of famous athletes do things a different way. I could
no more be a Willie Mays than Willie Mays could be a
Henry Aaron.

Willie was always geared to go at top speed, and he paid
the price for it. As he got older he was forced to take himself out of the lineup more and more because he would
almost play himself into exhaustion. Willie Mays was as
natural in the way he plays baseball as he was about brushing his teeth or combing his hair.

In other words, I didn't think he "showboated." He used the basket catch because it came natural to him. It was easier to him. The basket catch isn't easier for me, so I make the catch with my hands about chest high. I've always been taught that you should catch the ball in a position to make a throw if there should be a play on the bases. I can't make the basket catch and get in a position to throw. It's not natural to me.

I'm inclined to pace myself. I guess that's the best way to put it. Sometimes you're going to look bad playing this way, and I take that calculated risk. You hit an easy hopper to third base, you make a routine run to first, because fielding averages will show you that 98.7 per cent of the time that infielder is going to make the right play.

But let him boot the ball then get a glove on it again—and you, the base runner, get thrown out because you weren't running like you were competing in the National A.A.U. 100-yard dash, and you're accused of loafing. (I've got another story on the "loafing" line, but I'm saving it until I reach the chapter on managers.)

I can field. I've got three "Golden Gloves" in my den at home to prove that. The "Golden Glove" is what the two major leagues award to the man who has the best fielding average at his position. But I don't care to play center field. From my experience as a center-fielder, it seems to me to be the easiest position to play in the outfield. You've got one fielder on the right of you and another fielder on the left of you, and what you can't get to, they take. That simplifies the job a good deal.

If I had broken in with the Braves as a center-fielder, I don't think I'd ever have wanted to play any other position. By the time I got to center field in 1957, though, I already had a complex about it. I tell you, you watch Billy Bruton play center field for three years—especially from as close up as I was watching him—and it would give anybody an inferiority complex. I considered Billy one of the greatest center-fielders in the business. He played the position with his brain as well as with his physical ability. I came to depend upon him almost like a high-school player depends upon his coach. You get an idea of how intelligent Billy Bruton is when I tell you that he retired from baseball, after he had been traded to Detroit and played a few seasons, to take an executive job with Chrysler Motors.

So I felt a little like Raggedy Ann trying to play center field after Bruton.

There was no great formal ceremony about the switch. Haney wrote out the line-up card the day after Billy was hurt, and taped it on the wall of the dugout. After my name were the letters *cf*, and so I became the center-fielder.

I don't think there's any doubt that moving to center field took some of the edge off my performance as a hitter. As long as I played beside Bruton, I was confident. He and I worked together well as a unit. He knew my moves and I knew his moves, and it was comforting to know that the fellow playing beside you was going to be in the right place nearly all the time.

I have been close to the "triple crown"—that is, leading the league in batting average, runs batted in and home runs—three or four times. I've led the league in hitting and home runs, or home runs and runs batted in, or runs batted in and home runs, but never all three at the same time. I want this. I don't mind letting anybody know that I want this.

Well, I guess I had my best chance in 1957. I was leading the league in all three departments at the time Bruton was hurt and I had to make the switch. I was hitting about .340, had about 30 home runs and 75 RBI's. I was on such a hitting bash that the papers were beginning to look up Babe Ruth's home-run record. Bruton himself started that. We'd just beaten the tar out of Cincinnati on the Fourth of July. I'd hit my twenty-sixth home run. We were a happy group.

In the clubhouse Bruton hollered out, "Hey, isn't it about time somebody started comparing Henry's home-run record with Babe Ruth's the year he hit 60?"

Lou Chapman of the *Milwaukee Sentinel* looked it up, and found that I was just two games behind the Babe.

I don't say that I would have hit 60 home runs, not by any stretch of the imagination. In fact, I was pretty pleased with 44, which has become my magic number. It was the first of three times that I've had that total for a season.

I'm not saying that I would have led the league in hitting. With Stan Musial going along at a .351 clip, I'd have had a tough assignment to beat him. But after I got to center field, my home-run production fell off and my batting average fell off, too. I'm not going to blame it on anybody other than myself, but I'll tell you that playing with Wes Covington on one side of me and "Hurricane" Hazle on the other didn't give me a lot of confidence. Neither one of them ever won any prizes playing defense, and with me in strange territory, our outfield was not feared for its glove. There were times when we were like three calves trying to get to the feed trough at the same time. It's a wonder one of us didn't get killed before the season ended.

"Hurricane" Hazle was brought up from Wichita to fill the gap after Bruton got hurt. The first time I ever saw him, as far as I know—I'd never heard of him before, for sure— he was standing in front of a mirror in the clubhouse combing his hair. I was going to view that scene several times, because this kid spent a lot of time looking after his appearance. He had wavy brown hair and sort of cool, watery eyes that seemed to be looking somewhere else while he talked to you. He was a flashy dresser, and he wasn't about to go out on the street not looking his best.

I call him a kid. I thought he was. When I really got around to getting the details, I found out he was three years older than I was. Cincinnati had signed him for a pretty good bonus—about $50,000—and he'd been touring the minor leagues since 1950.

Ed Mathews told me that they'd been planning to bring up another outfielder named Earl Hersh. Hersh had been with the Braves before and had some power. I remembered him. But Ben Geraghty, my old Jacksonville manager, entered the picture again. He was managing Wichita then. When John Quinn called about Hersh, Geraghty told them that Hazle was the man they wanted.

"This guy is hitting .279 right now," Ben said, according to the newspapers, "but he can hit big-league pitching. He's a best bet right now."

I told you what a great manager Ben was. Well, he hit it again. Hazle—Bob was his real name—hit town with a bigger bang than any bench warmer you ever heard of. That's all he was supposed to be, a bench warmer, insurance for us. He was a left-handed batter, and he began to get a few calls in right field, platooning with Andy Pafko, and he got to hitting so Haney couldn't take him out.

It was just about that time that the hurricane season hit its peak in the Atlantic, and one came up that the United States Weather Bureau's people in charge of naming hurricanes called "Hazel." So, we had "Hurricane" Hazle, and it was a fit.

Down the stretch this guy almost carried us. He played forty-one games. He batted .403. (You remember that I said there'd never be another .400 hitter.) He hit 7 home runs, and he drove in 27 runs. He was unbelievable. I was hitting about .330, and he made me feel like I was in a slump. I thought I was having a pretty good season, and he made me feel downright embarrassed.

When it got down to the big pay-off, though—that real, big explosive moment I mentioned earlier—that was mine, all mine. I'm not the least bit ashamed to sound proud and possessive about it because it was the greatest thrill I've ever had in baseball. I've had some big thrills since, like hitting my four hundredth home run and making my twenty-five hundredth hit, winning the MVP, starting in All-Star games and winning a World Series. But this still is my *big* one. If it hadn't happened, we might not have been in the World Series.

Right after Labor Day, the Braves had gone into a slump. We lost eight out of eleven games. Look over our shoulders and there were the Cardinals right behind us, two and a half games. I guess that scared us.

We were walking up the ramp after losing one night, and we were a grim bunch. Logan was walking beside me, and Johnny was always talking, it seemed.

"Henry, have you noticed Haney lately?" he said.

"Of course I noticed him," I said. "I notice him every day. What do you mean?"

"I mean, have you noticed how pale he's getting?"

"I hadn't noticed him that much. You think he's sick?"

"I think we're all sick. How bad do you want to win this pennant?"

"That's a crazy question," I said. "All of us want to win it bad."

"Well, then, you can figure how it is with Haney," Logan said. "See, we blew it on the last day last year. If we don't win it this time, we'll still be back next year—I mean me and you, the players—but I'll bet you Haney won't be. We lose and he's gone this time."

I've never said Haney was one of my favorite people, and I've never said he wasn't. He was a different kind of manager. He didn't spend a lot of time kidding with the players, as Grimm did. He was the manager and we were the players, and he never let you forget it.

I began to notice him that night, the minute I walked through the door into the clubhouse, and I did feel something for Haney. Don't get me wrong. I wasn't feeling any more for Haney than I was for myself, but suddenly I wanted to win that pennant worse than anything. I don't know how many others began to feel the same way, or if Logan even talked to any of the rest about it, but the next day we began to win again. We went on a streak of winning. We won eight in a row. The eighth one did it, and that fell on the night of September 23, in County Stadium.

It was the first game of the big series with the Cardinals, their last chance. All we had to do was win one from St. Louis and that would lock it up.

I remember one of the little things that had nothing to do with the game. Everybody was shouting and throwing something, and County Stadium was losing its mind. But I remember looking up about halfway down the first base line and noticing the time on the big clock hanging above the fence.

It was 11:34.

Precisely at 11:34, twenty-six minutes before midnight, I had hit a pitch over the center-field fence with a runner on base and beat St. Louis 4–2. The score was tied, and we were in the eleventh inning. A relief pitcher the Cardinals had brought up from the minor leagues a little earlier was my pigeon. His name was Billy Muffett, a pudgy right-hander. That probably would have been the way they remembered him in St. Louis if he hadn't come back to the Cardinals in 1967 as pitching coach. So you can't say I picked a dummy for a victim. This guy obviously knew how to pitch.

Milwaukee went crazy, of course. I don't think anybody went home to bed that night. I did. I was tired. We celebrated some, but I guess we were so excited we couldn't really appreciate what had happened to us.

The next morning the papers had a picture of some of the other Braves carrying me off the field, and me grinning a grin like I'd been named the King of Wisconsin. I can't tell you who was carrying me, because you know something? —I don't remember that at all. If somebody had asked me the next morning how it felt to be carried off the field, I couldn't have answered. I didn't remember it.

But I remember looking up at that clock and seeing 11:34.

That was my shiningest hour.

11

I WISH I COULD WRITE about what it's like to play in a World Series and make you understand the feeling. You put on your uniform the same way, the personal equipment, the undershirt, the sanitary stockings and the outer stockings with the rubber bands that hold them up, the spikes and the shirt with "Braves" across the front. You do that for 162 games a year (in 1957 the season was 154 games), but there's nothing special about it then. That's your day's work. You're merely on the job like any other salaried employee.

But the World Series! Man, that's something different in every way. You do everything the same way, I said, and yet it's not the same way. You give every little act an extra touch, like a ritual. After all, you're going out on the field to play for the world's championship of baseball. Every eye that can see will see you a little better in a World Series. People who never go to a baseball game during the season will be watching the World Series. Celebrities who never read a box score and couldn't tell you what Cooperstown is famous for show up for the World Series. If you're playing in a World Series and your spine doesn't tingle some that first day you walk out of the clubhouse onto the field, you're dead and don't know it.

Our World Series with the New York Yankees in 1957 opened in Yankee Stadium and closed there. It was a long one and a busy one, running seven games from October 2 to October 10, and in between some real hell broke loose.

98

The Yankees took us in the first game with Whitey Ford pitching, and it looked like we were goners. He'd beaten Warren Spahn, our best pitcher, and I'd read somewhere that teams that lose the first game of a World Series don't usually win it.

Lew Burdette beat Bobby Shantz in the second game, then we flew to Milwaukee for the third. It was like a state fair when we got back there. Downtown Milwaukee was dressed up like the Fourth of July. Store windows were decorated, and businesses had banners hanging out saying, "Welcome Home Braves," "Home of the Next World's Champions," and all kinds of hoopla.

The Yankees flew into Chicago and came by train from Chicago to Milwaukee. A few miles out of Milwaukee some newspapermen got aboard, buttonholed Manager Casey Stengel and squeezed some quotes out of him. He made the mistake of saying something about Milwaukee being a "bush town," and they never let the old man forget it.

We played like a bush-town team in the third game. The Yankees bombed our pitchers, and our pitchers threw nothing but base hits or balls. Bob Buhl never finished the first inning. The score was 12–3, and it may have been for the best. It sobered the Milwaukee fans some. If we had come in from New York and swept the three games there, those wild people might have burned the town to the ground.

Everything you read about in sports seems to have a turning point, and I don't think there's any doubt about what was the turning point in the 1957 World Series. If it wasn't, it will have to do for a turning point in this book, because that's the way I saw it.

Back in June when we lost Joe Adcock—he'd fractured an ankle sliding into a base, you'll recall—our bench had been left short. We had Frank Torre to take Adcock's place at first base. There was no sweat there. Torre had always been a clever fielder. One year in Atlanta, when he played on the Braves' old farm club there, he had a string of more than one thousand chances without making an error, and everybody knows the first baseman gets more traffic than anybody on the field. By this time, his second season in the big leagues, he was becoming a pretty good hitter, too.

Just for insurance and pinch-hitting, the Braves bought an old-timer named Nippy Jones from the Sacramento club in the Pacific Coast League. Jones had been in the major leagues before. One year he batted .300 for the Cardinals, and he had played for them in the 1946 World Series, but he had had some kind of back trouble, and since the 1952 season with the Phillies he had been back in the minors.

I never did get to know him, except to say "hello" and ride elevators with him. He didn't say much, and I didn't know enough about him at that time to ask him any questions about his exciting career. He had a sort of a bony face and dark, sad eyes that were set deep under his brows.

He hadn't had much of a hand in our pennant-winning. He didn't get much of a chance, because as I said, Torre was taking care of first base in a great way. Jones played a few games and hit a couple of home runs, but he went to bat only about seventy-five times. He was the kind of a guy that a sports writer would identify as a "most forget-table" member of the Braves.

So we go into this fourth game of the World Series. We are now down to the Yankees, one game to two. Worst thing about it is, we're in our own ball park, but the Yankees have taken us apart, humiliated us before our own people in the only game we've played there.

We get to the ninth inning with a 4–1 lead, Spahn pitching. You've got to feel as safe as if you're in a bomb shelter, Spahn pitching with a 4–1 lead. We got the four runs in the fourth inning, all on home runs. Logan had walked. Mathews had followed him with a double, and I hit a home run over the left-field fence off Tom Sturdivant. Torre followed me with a home run over the right-field fence.

There wasn't any more scoring until the ninth inning, and it came like a bomb. I could see people filing out of the ball park as the Yankees came to bat. They were heading for their cars, pretty sure that the Braves had won and tied the series at two games apiece. But the Yankees got two men on base, and with two men out, Elston Howard hit a home run over the left-field fence and the score was tied 4–4.

We could have folded then. I really believe that. You never saw a quieter dugout in your life when we came in from the field. We all looked as if we'd been watching a murder. I don't remember anybody saying anything, unless it was the usual routine, meaningless stuff about going out there and gettin' 'em.

The Yankees shut us out in the bottom of the ninth inning, then they took the lead in their half of the tenth. Hank Bauer hit a triple that scored Tony Kubek, and so we went into our half of the tenth on the short side, 4–5, and it began to look as if we were dead for the whole series, as well as the fourth game.

Spahn was due to be the lead-off batter in the tenth inning. He was always a good hitter, and I think any of us on the Braves would just about as soon see him at bat in a clutch as a lot of our regulars. Surely, we'd as soon have seen him up as Nippy Jones. But Haney called for Jones to bat for him. In any other situation—what I mean is, if Spahn hadn't been tired—it wouldn't have been that way. Haney was taking him out as a pitcher now, not as a batter. Besides, Spahnie was a left-handed batter and the Yankees had Tommy Byrne, a left-handed pitcher, in the game. Jones batted right-handed.

He stepped in and Byrne pitched. It was low and looked like it was in the dirt, and the ball got through Howard. The next thing I know, Jones is jawing with the plate umpire, Augie Donatelli, and as I said before, Jones wasn't a very talkative sort. But he was talking now, and he was having it out with Donatelli chin to chin. I didn't know what it was all about until I heard Red Schoendienst holler from the on-deck circle.

"Hey, Augie, it hit his foot! It hit his foot!"

While Donatelli and Jones were arguing, the ball came rolling between their feet and just died there. It had hit the retaining wall and bounced back. Jones suddenly reached down and picked up the ball and showed it to Donatelli. Nobody in the crowd knew what was going on, but there was some flutter of anticipation going around, and when the fans saw Donatelli wave Jones to first base, a roar went up.

What happened was this. When Jones looked down and saw the ball at his feet, he also saw a black spot on it left by the polish on his spikes. He picked up the ball, showed it to Donatelli, and, as I heard him telling sports writers in the clubhouse later, he said, "Here, see the shoe polish! Doesn't that prove it?"

He was on his way to first base before Haney could even get out of the dugout. The Yankees argued back. Stengel came out and grumbled some, but Jones had his base. He held it about ten seconds. Haney sent Mantilla in to run for him, and Jones faded away into the obscurity of the dugout. He'd left us something to go on, though, and we took it and ran, though I didn't have a hand in it. My turn at bat never came up.

After Stengel finished arguing—and I guess he dragged it out some to get a relief pitcher heated up—he sent to the bull pen for Bob Grim, who was a right-hander. Grim pitched to Schoendienst, and Red sacrificed Mantilla to second. Logan was up next, and he really clothes-lined a drive to the left-field corner. Mantilla scored, and we were tied now 5–5.

That bought up Mathews, and this was the reason I never got to bat. I was kneeling in the on-deck circle with a box-seat view watching it all. Grim tried to slip a fast ball by Mathews, but Ed caught it on the nose and hit a home run over the right-field fence. Ball game, 7–5, from death to life again. The series was tied 2–2. We knew we could win then, but not if it hadn't been for Nippy Jones. I believe that.

There's a strange little point of interest in the case of Nippy Jones. The day that pitch hit his toe and he argued his way to first base was his last appearance in the major leagues. He never came to bat again for the Braves.

The next season he was back playing first base in Sacramento. I looked it up. He could still swing a bat. He had an average of .302 in 1958. His record shows 2–0–0 for the World Series of 1957, but as far as I'm concerned, he was the man with the turning point.

Burdette beat the Yankees in the fifth game. Lew was nothing but great. The Yankees got seven hits off him, but he shut them out 1–0, and we got revenge against Ford. Whitey was the loser.

We flew back to New York that night leading the series 3–2. All we needed was one game, but Bob Turley beat Buhl in the sixth game. Buhl was a fast ball pitcher, and what he threw the Yankees seemed to love. He wasn't the loser, though. He was knocked out in the third inning, when the Yankees scored twice, and Ernie Johnson, who's now one of the Braves broadcasters in Atlanta, relieved him. We tied the score in the seventh, 2–2, but Hank Bauer hit a home run off Ernie in the Yankee seventh, and that was the game. Ernie was the loser.

In the last game, Haney had a choice: Spahn or Burdette. He could start Spahn with three days' rest or Burdette with two days' rest. I wish I could make some tremendous revelation here on why he decided on Burdette instead of Spahn. After all, Spahnie was our ace, our big winner, our bread-and-butter pitcher. He had won twenty-one games. Burdette had won only seventeen. Burdette never even qualified among the league's fifteen leading pitchers in *The Baseball Guide*. The average fan would have said, "If there's a critical game to be pitched, my pitcher would be Warren Spahn."

Haney's pitcher wasn't Warren Spahn, and I guess the reason built up in the World Series itself, not in the course of the season. The Yankees had beaten Spahn in the opening game and roughed him up pretty good in the fourth game— the key game that we won in the tenth inning. Spahn was the winner, but he was already out of it when Mathews won it with a home run.

Burdette had whipped the Yankees twice. Maybe he had his "wet one"—the spitball—going for him. Out in center field you can't tell much about a pitcher's spitball if an umpire standing behind the plate facing him can't detect it. So I back off from any discussion of that. And I want to tell you another thing: players don't run around the clubhouse talking about the spitball like it's a fast ball or a curve ball, unless it's a spitball some pitcher on some other team is throwing.

In other words, to put it in plain, simple baseball jargon, Burdette seemed to have the Yankees' number, and Spahn didn't. He was stronger, too. With two days' rest, he went at them again and took them again, and he was just as great as he was in the fifth game.

Burdette shut them out again 5–0, and you ought to be reminded that the Yankees had been shut out only one time during the regular American League season.

You can imagine the rest: wild celebration in the clubhouse; jubilation and much champagne on the charter flight back to Milwaukee; insanity at the airport and on the streets in Milwaukee. I suppose that if you've seen one World Series celebration you've seen them all, but I kind of doubt that, when I stop to think again of Milwaukee on the night of October 10, 1957. Those people were out of their minds. We got involved in the damnedest parade you ever saw, from the airport into town, and around town, and it seemed like it would never end. I can't remember when I got to bed that night. I was asking Ernie Johnson not long ago if he could remember what he did that night.

He said, "You know something, it's all a blur to me now. I remember the flight back to Milwaukee. I remember the mob scene at the airport. I remember the parade, but I don't remember any of the little fine details. I don't remember when I went to bed. I don't remember even getting home. I'd have to ask my wife. She'd remember, because she was seeing it all from a different angle."

In other words, anything that I might say about the victory celebration after we got back to Milwaukee would be strictly hearsay. Some say I had a great time. I hope I did. I know I had a great time winning the World Series.

It was a good series for me. Something happened in it that made it just about as sweet to me as the $8,924.36 I got for my share.

One of the newspapers was trying to pick a World Series hero before it was played—and I bring this up now because I've heard people whisper little things about me and pressure, and how we don't get along too good. (A lot of this is based on my record in the Major League All-Star game, but we'll take that up later.) Well, this paper predicted that the stars of the 1957 World Series would be Mickey Mantle for the Yankees and Henry Aaron for the Braves. But when it came down to picking the star of the whole thing, the outstanding player on both teams, Mantle got every vote but one.

I didn't see it at first. Mantilla said something to me about it one morning when he came into the clubhouse. We were having a workout before the series started.

"You are already the hero, I see by the paper," Felix said.

"What hero?" I said.

"The World Series hero. This vote the paper took. They vote on you and Mantle. Here, see?"

Felix showed me the paper, and I was looking at it.

"But they don't give you a chance with Mantle," he said.

He didn't have to tell me that. I could see it for myself. I didn't say anything. I don't think I showed any kind of emotion, but I was having some emotions inside me. I'm that kind of guy, and I don't guess I have to tell anybody who has watched me play baseball.

Emotions? Yes, I've got emotions, but they don't come through. Some people have to explode when they get moved one way or another. Henry Aaron, he keeps all his emotions inside him. I get the jitters before the first exhibition game in the spring. I get the jitters before the All-Star game. I told you how I felt tingling, and all that, before the World Series. But outside I guess I look the same. I take this game seriously and I take life seriously, but it just doesn't come through this hide of mine. So I went into that World Series fully conscious that these experts expected Mickey Mantle to run me off the lot.

I said to myself, "Okay, Henry, let's see who's the best man, you or Mickey Mantle."

When it was over, I felt that I had justified myself. I got one of our 5 hits in the first game. Mantle got 2. In the second game, I started the Braves on their way to the first run, and I was sort of pleased that Mantle was the victim. I hit a ball to deep center field, and Mickey apparently misjudged it. Anyway, the ball went over his head to the wall and I got a triple. Mantle was hitless that day.

In the third game, I hit a home run and drove in 2 runs. Mantle had 2 for 3 and a home run. In the fourth game, I hit the home run that gave us a 3–0 lead. Mantle missed the fifth and sixth games, except to pinch-hit. He and Schoendienst had gotten tangled in a spill on a pick-off play in the third game, and his shoulder was injured.

In the fifth game, I hit a single that moved Mathews into position to score the only run on Adcock's single. In the sixth game I hit another home run, and this would have brought out the tape measure if it had been hit by Mantle. Turley was pitching. He had handcuffed me up until then. He struck me out in the second inning and got me on a grounder in the fourth. Leading off the seventh, though, I got a fast ball I liked and hit it all the way into the Yankee bull pen, in the deep part of left field. In the seventh game, I singled twice and drove in a run. Mantle was back for this game, but he only had a single.

Now, I take you to *The Baseball Guide* for Fred Lieb's final summary of the 1957 World Series, and this is what he had to say about the action when it came to who outdid whom:

Following Burdette among the Braves heroes was outfielder Hank Aaron, 1956 National League batting champion and 1957 leader in home runs and runs batted in. Hitting safely in every game, Hammering Hank was the only .300 hitter among the Milwaukee regulars. He led both teams with a .393 average, smashed three homers, drove in seven runs and was an agile workman in center-field.

I accumulated 11 hits and 22 total bases. I talk like I'm on the defensive, and in a way I am. I am defending myself against those people who like to interpret my nonchalance, or my loosey-goosey ways on the baseball field, as meaning that I'm not a bear-down player, and that when the pressure's on, Aaron's off. One thing I especially didn't like about myself, and that was futility at bat when I could have put us back in that third game. It's true, I hit a home run and a single and drove in two of the Braves' three runs, but look at another hidden statistic: I also left eight other runners on base in three more times at bat. That's a statistic I wish I hadn't reminded myself of.

Since Mr. Lieb mentioned my work in center field, I might as well take this opportunity to talk about "that catch," which I mentioned earlier. It was the first real major controversial situation that I was ever connected with, and it's still in the air. People even now ask me about "that catch."

It happened in the first game in Milwaukee. It wasn't any great money play. The only real difference it made was that the Yankees might have scored a half-dozen runs or more in that inning instead of three. Right at that red-hot moment it was a big play. As it turned out, us losing 12–3, it wasn't but nobody seems willing to forget it. And I don't mind. My answer is the same for everybody. I made the catch. I swear to you that I did.

Bauer led off the first inning and grounded out. Kubek hit Buhl's next pitch over the right-field fence. Bob was shook up a little by that. Kubek was a Milwaukee boy, you see, and there were enough Kubek fans in the house to make a lot of noise for the hometown kid. Buhl would have been shook anyway, but this seemed to shake him a little more.

He walked Mantle and Berra in a row. When he tried to pick Mantle off second base, he threw the ball all the way to me in center field. Now he had men on second and third and McDougald at bat. McDougald hit a sinking liner at me and I started after the ball, and the more I ran for it the more I realized I'd never be able to make a normal catch. Just as I got to it, then, I fell to my knees and skidded into the ball and just barely got my glove under it. The Yankees screamed I didn't catch it, but the umpire in left field signaled that I did, and he was closest. He could see it.

Pictures in the newspapers the next day showed the white of the ball in the grass. They ran the pictures in a series, showing the ball in my glove, then out of my glove, then back in my glove again. I'm not certain that they got the pictures in the right order myself. The man who made them might have made the mistake. Anyway, this series of pictures was used, especially in the New York papers, to make it seem that I really hadn't caught the ball.

All I've got to say is to repeat myself. I made the catch. There would be no point in lying about it at this late date if I hadn't.

I'm not trying to say that I'm any great fielder. I have my faults as a fielder. Sometimes I lose a ball in the lights, or I get a bad jump or I make a false move in the wrong direction. I did that in the All-Star game in St. Louis in 1966. I made a bad move, tried to correct it and couldn't, and Brooks Robinson got a triple on it and almost beat the Nationals for the Americans on that one play.

I've had some great plays, too. I haven't got a collection of them like Willie Mays. There was one I made in St. Louis, in old Busch Memorial Stadium, that some of the Braves still insist was the greatest they ever saw. It was a pure accident, but I made it.

Some Cardinal hit a line drive to my right, and I was going full speed after it. It had rained, and the field was slippery. When I started to slow down, I slipped and began a skidding fall, and as I did, I threw up my meat hand. Just as I did, the ball struck it and through some means that I can't explain, I held the ball in my bare hand, skidding and falling at the same time.

Now if I could say that I then got up, wheeled and made

a mighty throw that cut down a base runner, I'd be willing to allow you to call me a great fielder. But I didn't.

I don't think this catch on McDougald in the World Series was any great play. But I bring it up again after all these years because I don't want the Yankees still thinking I put one over on them. I made the catch.

12

I couldn't recognize it as it was happening. You can't blame this on my youth. There were a lot of people older, wiser and more experienced in baseball and the rise and fall of empires than Henry Aaron, who were living right in the midst of it and couldn't see it either. But after the World Series of 1957, when we beat the Yankees in seven games, everything else for the Braves in Milwaukee was downhill—a degree or so at first, then more and more as the years flew by.

I don't mean we did everything like we were coasting. I mean everything was in a decline. We were losing a little bit of something we had had, but we didn't get to the point that we knew it until it was too late. Then there was nothing we could do about it.

I don't blame it on any particular group—the managers we had, the players or the front office. It was a team disaster. We all had our part in it.

This sounds strange to you, I suppose, considering the fact that we won another pennant in 1958, and that we carried the 1959 race to a play-off with the Los Angeles Dodgers. Do you realize, though, that if we could have changed the results of just two games between 1956 and 1959, we could have won two more pennants?

In other words, what I'm saying is this. *The Braves should have won four pennants in a row, not just two!* The kind of ball club we were, the kind of talent we had in reserve in our organization and the kind of backing we had from fans and executives, we should have won four pennants in a row.

Instead, we blow one in 1956 on the last weekend of the season. We blow another, 1959, in two straight play-off games. We win one, and take the World Series like the champions we were. We win another pennant, and get a lead of three games to one against the Yankees in the World Series—and blow that.

Do you realize that we, the Braves of 1958, were one of only three teams that ever led a World Series 3 to 1 in games and lost it?

Maybe that's really when we got on the roller coaster, in the World Series of 1958. Maybe there's a little more logic in establishing that as the beginning of the collapse rather than lumping in the whole 1958 season. After all, we did win the pennant that season, and we won it big. We didn't have the record we had in 1957. We were 95–59 —.617 in 1957. We dipped to 92–62—.597 in 1958, but we beat out the Pirates by eight games. We had it sewed up by September 21, when Spahn beat Cincinnati.

"Had it not been for injuries, the Braves might well have made a shambles of the race just as the Yankees did in the American League," *The Sporting News* said.

At one time or another we had Bob Buhl, Wes Covington or Red Schoendienst either hobbled or out of the game altogether. Buhl started the season as if the National League wasn't going to be good enough for him. He won four in a row, then came down with some sort of trouble in his shoulder. From the middle of May to September we didn't have him. He won only one more game that season, yet we won the pennant without this guy who had won eighteen games for us the year before. Two of the young pitchers picked up the slack—Carlton Willey, who was called up from Wichita after it became obvious Buhl wasn't going to help us; and Joey Jay, who looked like he was about to grow out of the baby stage and become a real pitcher.

Schoendienst broke a finger in July, but another kid

picked us up here. Mel Roach had been signed to a big bonus contract and had spent two useless seasons on the bench right after the Braves moved to Milwaukee. Now, when he was really needed, he came through. He was recalled from Wichita and hit over .300 while he filled in for Red, but Roach came a cropper, too. He tore some ligaments in a knee on August 3 and he was through for the year. In fact, you might as well say he was through for life, for he never was the same again and he retired just a few seasons later.

Covington developed a bad press later. In Milwaukee, he was a contributor. He never was a great fielder. He used to show us a picture on the wall there in County Stadium of him making a real circus catch in the World Series of 1957, and he'd give us that big "Kingfish" laugh of his and say, "That's genius, guys, that's real genius!" But he wasn't only not great, he wasn't even a consistently good fielder.

That year, though, in just ninety games, Wes drove in 74 runs and hit 24 home runs, playing on two bad knees. You can see he contributed, but those knees kept him out of the game so much. He'd hurt them both trying to make a catch against a wall in spring training.

Another blow to us was that Billy Bruton didn't get back in the line-up until sometime in May. He'd gone into surgery after the collision with Mantilla in the middle of the '57 season, and he took that long to mend.

Yet, we win the whole kit and caboodle by eight games with a patched-up line-up at times and only one full-time .300 hitter named Aaron—and him not having the kind of season he'd had when he was the Most Valuable Player of the year before. I didn't have a disgusting year. My batting average, in fact, was four points better, and I'd be willing to settle for a lifetime average of .326. But I hit 14 fewer home runs (30), and drove in 37 fewer runs (95). That's not the half of it. At the middle of the season, I wasn't hitting .300, but they still voted me into the All-Star game. It would have looked bad if the Most Valuable Player of the year before hadn't made the All-Star game, I guess. I made the seasonal All-Star team as right-fielder, and the Gold Glove team for defense, and wound up third behind Ernie Banks of the Cubs and Willie Mays of the Giants in the MVP balloting.

The one thing that really held us up during the 1958 season was the pitching. Our guys led the league in earned-run average with 3.21. Spahn and Burdette were twenty-game winners. Jay had an ERA of 2.13. Willey had an ERA of 2.70. Don McMahon was great in the bull pen. It was good that all this worked out the way it did, because Buhl and Conley were of no use at all and the rest of the bull pen wasn't anything you'd pin a rose on.

Oh, I should mention that we were able to win it in '58 without any heroics from "Hurricane" Hazle. You may have noticed the absence of his name in this account of the season. After May 24 there was a definite lack of Hazle: that was the date when the Braves sold Hazle to Detroit in the American League for the waiver price, which was about $20,000. He had played in twenty games and was batting .179 when he left us. I don't know what happened to the guy. He still combed his hair as much as ever and was the same flashy dresser, but not the same ball player who batted .403 the year before.

I'm going to be just as brief about the 1958 World Series as I was lengthy about the 1957 World Series. It's not one of my dearest memories, beginning with the personal point of view. I hit well enough—.333. But I didn't hit a home run and I didn't drive in but two runs, both of those in the same game, which we lost—the sixth.

What happened in that series was sort of a tip-off on what was about to happen to the Braves over a period of seasons, and to some extent was an indication of why it had taken us so long to get off our bottoms and play like champions when we were the best team in the National League that season.

We opened this World Series against the Yankees in Milwaukee, and Spahn beat Ford in the first game 4–3. Burdette beat Turley in the second game 13–5. Pitching really had little to do with that game. We scored 7 runs in the first inning, during which Turley was able to get only one man out. When we caught the plane to New York that night, most of us were thinking that the World Series was over and that we were the greatest baseball team known to man. Even Burdette hit a home run that day, and our dugout was busting out all over with cheer and confidence when he jogged in from his blast.

We lost the first game in New York. Larsen shut us out. One game we get 15 hits and 13 runs, and the next game we can't get a run off Larsen. But Spahnie was next, and he shut out the Yankees 3–0.

Now there was no question about it. It was just a matter of time. We were the greatest and we all knew it, but we didn't go around talking about it. It might have been better if somebody had popped off a little about how great we were, then somebody could have shut him up, and we would have all been reminded that humility is something that even great teams have—even teams as great as the Milwaukee Braves of 1958.

Next game, darned if Turley didn't shut us out 7–0. The same guy we'd tortured in Milwaukee gave us 5 hits and beat Burdette. It wouldn't have made any difference who was pitching for the Braves the way we were hitting that day.

Now we had a day off to fly back to Milwaukee. You could tell on the plane that we weren't quite sure we were as great as we had thought we were the day before. There was a lot of talk now about who should pitch. Haney had the three young pitchers—Willey, Jay and Pizarro— all fresh and ready; alternatively, he might have planned to come back with Spahn. But Spahn had had only two days of rest, and he had pitched his guts out both times he'd started.

I don't like to make decisions like this even ten years later, and I surely wouldn't have wanted to make it then. My feeling was, though, that we should have gone with Willey. He was a curve ball pitcher with good control and a mild sort of kid with tough insides. The situation wouldn't have got to him, in other words. Another point in his favor: he'd have been pitching against Ford, who had had only two days of rest. In case we did lose, then we could have come back in the seventh game with Spahn with an extra day of rest, and Burdette to back him up in the bull pen.

We had dinner out with the Brutons the night before the sixth game, Barbara and I. It wasn't anything special, just a little treat for the wives. We took them to one of the finest places in Milwaukee named Eugene's. It really wasn't much of a pleasant night out, because everywhere we went everybody wanted to talk about the World Series. They weren't feeling too good in Milwaukee by that time—the fans, I mean. They were already talking losing talk, and I guess they could sense what was taking place.

Bruton didn't have much to say about the pitching choice —not that Billy and I ever sat around and spent a lot of time making like baseball brains.

"You've got to go with your best," Billy Bruton said. That was his way of saying he'd pitch Spahn.

When I got to County Stadium the next day, I found out it was going to be Spahn while I was putting on my uniform. Willey sat across the clubhouse looking low and unhappy.

For nine innings, Spahn was great. In the tenth, the Yankees scored 2 runs off him and tore him apart. We scored one in our half of the tenth. I singled Logan home, and was on third base when Frank Torre hit a soft liner to McDougald, which ended the game.

Now it had to be Burdette in the seventh game. No choice. If you didn't go with Willey in the sixth game, you couldn't take such a gamble now. It wouldn't have been a gamble in the sixth game. It was definitely a gamble now.

The Yankees beat Burdette, 6-2. It was over.

Changes began to take place during the winter. By the next spring, the Braves were not the same Braves. They never were again as long as we were in Milwaukee.

13

WE HAD ALL grown complacent. We could never perform at our best as a team until we were being criticized or unless we had our backs to the wall. The better things were going, the worse we went—if you know what I mean. I can back that up with figures.

From May through August of 1959, we lost more games than we won. When September came, we suddenly realized what we were playing for. It was win or no pennant. We won fifteen of our twenty last games, and tied the Dodgers. When people talk about that season, you'll hear them say, "The Braves blew the pennant."

Not so. We had to make a comeback even to tie the Dodgers for first place. What we blew was the last game of the play-off in Los Angeles. So old baseball fans remember us as "blowing." *The Baseball Guide* pronounces our play that season as "indifferent," "up and down" and "weird."

We should have seen it coming in spring training, I guess. I got to the clubhouse one morning in Bradenton just in time to hear that Haney had called a team meeting. Closed doors. Nothing but players, coaches and Haney.

"What's up?" I asked Bruton.

"Haney's teed off," Billy said.

"About what?" I said.

"Because Tebbetts is teed off, I guess," Billy said.

The name of Tebbetts comes to you as sort of a strange sound when you talk of the Braves, doesn't it? Well, that

116

was one of the winter changes. Birdie Tebbetts had left Cincinnati in August of 1958—either quit or was fired as manager—and showed up in Milwaukee as executive vice-president in October.

What a change for the players! Tebbetts was a big man with the needle when he managed the Reds. He jawed as much as any bench jockey, and he wasn't anybody's kind man with the rough language.

Now we were supposed to look upon him as an executive, Our Leader. He wore double-breasted suits, sat in a swivel chair and tried to look like the guy who hadn't given us every knife in the book.

And where did this leave our old friend John Quinn?

Well, now I'm getting ahead of myself. Let's go back to Bradenton, where Haney is having a called meeting.

"Somebody close that door," he said. Somebody closed the door, and everything got quiet.

"I don't know if you guys came to Florida this spring to be playboys or ball players," Haney began. "You've won two pennants in a row. You've been in two World Series in a row. You've carried home some pretty fat pay checks. You've also started carrying home some pretty fat asses. What's wrong, don't you like the big leagues? Don't you like the Braves? Don't you like yourselves? Well, if you don't, keep it up the way you're going and about half of you are going to wind up in Wichita. . . ."

And he took it from there.

We did have a sloppy spring. We were just going through the motions. We were all moving around like a bunch of King Farouks. We played like we were fat, rich and spoiled. Back home in Milwaukee, the fans were spoiled, too. They read the stories out of Florida, first Haney blasting us, then Tebbetts, and then even mild-mannered John McHale blasting us.

Oh, yes, that was another name—John McHale.

All of these are my opinions, you understand. I may be wrong and I may be right, but they amount to what I think of what was happening at the time.

I never could figure why John Quinn got bounced out of his job. That's what it amounted to, as far as I'm concerned, when Tebbetts was moved in. The stories said that Tebbetts was replacing Joe Cairnes, who was not a baseball man but who had been president of the Braves in title. Lou Perini, the owner, needed Cairnes for some construction assignment.

In came Tebbetts, a baseball man to replace a man who was not a baseball man. John Quinn began looking around. I think he got a raw deal. I know he was thinking he got a raw deal.

Sometime in January, the Phillies hired him as general manager. I was shocked. I got the morning paper one Sunday and read the news. That's how I found out about it. This was one of the saddest parts of my career, because John Quinn was one of the best friends I had in baseball. He dealt with me like a man, and he gave me advice and he was nice to me and my family.

About two weeks later we got the next news blast. John McHale, who had been with the Detroit Tigers, had been hired to replace Quinn as general manager. Now, we had an executive vice-president, a general manager, no John Quinn and no club president, except in name only. And Haney was the manager, and people told me that Haney and Tebbetts didn't like each other at all.

You can imagine, I guess, what spring training was like, the players not knowing what to expect from Tebbetts or McHale, and wondering what was going on between Haney and Tebbetts.

It was, as the book says, a weird season, though for me, nothing less than my greatest as far as averages went. I hit .355 and led the league again, and batted in 123 runs and hit 39 home runs. Mathews led the league in home runs. He hit 36. His batting average was .306, his best in the majors. We had Spahn and Burdette winning 21 apiece. So none of the internal club politics seemed to bother us.

We did have our troubles at second base. Schoendienst

119

developed tuberculosis and spent most of the season trying
to get well. In the meantime, we had everybody but Tebbetts in his swivel chair trying to play second base. Our
list of second basemen that season read like a roll call—
Mantilla, O'Brien, Wise, Cottier, Avila, Roach, Morgan and
finally Schoendienst.

I was afraid they might even think about ol' Henry for
second base again. I was sitting in the dugout one day
while Haney was making up the line-up, and I heard one
of the coaches say something about me.

"What about Henry?" the coach said. "He played it in
the minors."

"He even played it for a month in the majors," Haney
said. "I was at Pittsburgh then. Hm m m m-m-m."

I didn't bust right in, but a minute or so later I got up
and started walking by, and I said, "I'm willing to bat like
Hornsby and I'd like to have his averages, but I want to
leave second base for him. I think the man deserves something to himself."

I never heard any more about second base. I don't think
they were ever serious, anyway.

Schoendienst came back to join the club about the first
of September. He hardly played any at all, but I think that
just having him on the bench helped the team get its pride
back. You can't say that it hurt any, for he was in there
with us all through that September stretch drive. We played
the Dodgers head-to-head down through the last week of the
season, and we both won on the last day of the regular
season, bringing about the play-off. And, oh-h-h-h-h, that
play-off!

There were no grounds for a tie in the first place. You
compare the Braves and the Dodgers that year position by
position, and they just weren't as good as we were, except
as a team. We were mostly a bunch of individuals, not a
team. We had two twenty-one-game winners, the home-run
king, the batting champion and all that, and all they had
was Memorial Coliseum in Los Angeles and the shortest

left-field fence in baseball. What it boiled down to was that the Dodgers wanted to win more than we did. I know they wanted to win more than the Milwaukee fans did.

The first play-off game was scheduled in County Stadium, and you'll find this hard to believe, but in that town of fanatics, of the people who had painted banners and held parades until three o'clock in the morning in honor of the Braves who had won pennants and a World Series in 1957, only 18,297 showed up to see us play.

That had some effect on us. There was a lot of dugout talk about it that day. Maybe the fans were thinking like we were thinking. Our attitude was, "Okay, we'll take it now and get on with the World Series business."

Maybe the fans were saving up for the World Series. Maybe.

I don't buy that, though. I think the fans had become just as spoiled as we had. I think they were sitting at home —it was an overcast day with some rain—and were saying, "Ho hum, so the Braves are going to win another pennant. What else is new today?"

Willey had to pitch the first game. Spahn, Burdette and Buhl pitched themselves out in the series with the Phillies that ended the season. I always thought that kid was going to be a terrific pitcher. He sort of got frozen out by the Spahn-Burdette-Buhl combine, and never got the chance he should have got. I always compared him with Carl Erskine, the old Dodger pitcher. Good curve, good control, good habits.

Yet, as much as I liked Carlton Willey, there was something about starting him in a game this important that didn't add up, if you wanted to measure the situation by the World Series of the previous year, when Haney had started Spahn with just two days of rest instead of taking a chance on Willey then. In the World Series, we had three chances to win one game. In the play-off against the Dodgers, we had to win two out of three, and if we lost the first game in Milwaukee, then we had to win two in Los Angeles, on the Dodgers' own crazy grounds, the Coliseum. In other words, lose one game and you were half dead already.

Willey had not been the pitcher in '59 that he was in '58, either. Something had happened to his change-up. He hadn't had a chance at starting a game since the first of August, and in between those two starts, Haney had used him for only three innings of pitching.

It was pretty hard to make sense out of it, except for one thing—Willey was a good pitcher that day. The only trouble was, we lost. The powerful line-up that included the home-run king and the batting champion couldn't get but six hits off Danny McDevitt and Larry Sherry. John Roseboro, the Dodger catcher, hit a home run in the sixth inning and beat us 3-2.

On the plane to Los Angeles that night, we were still sure we were going to win it. You know, we were simply the superior ball club. I could tell that by looking around me on the plane. Mathews sat in front of me reading a magazine. He was the world's best third baseman. Crandall sat across the aisle: All-Star catcher. Spahn and Burdette, as usual, sat together. They were like twin brothers in those days, always together. They were twenty-one-game winners. Bobby Avila sat up front with Mantilla. Avila had led the American League in batting one time. The Braves had traded with the Boston Red Sox for him when Schoendienst got sick. Bruton sat next to me, and as far as I'm concerned, there was no better defensive center-fielder in the game.

We even sat and talked about how we were going to use our World Series tickets, and who was coming in for the games. We all needed extra tickets because we'd be playing the White Sox—they were already winners in the American League and waiting for the National League to come up with a champion—and with the games so close together, everybody would want to see the whole series.

"Maybe 'Good Kid' will let you have some of his," I said to Billy. "He won't be needing them. His family's not around."

"Good Kid" was George Susce, one of the coaches and

our bull pen catcher. He got the name "Good Kid" because he was always calling everybody else "Good Kid."

Billy walked back to where "Good Kid" was sitting and was back in the seat in just a minute or two.

" 'Good Kid' says we got to win it first," Billy said as he sat down.

We started off in Los Angeles like we were going to run the Dodgers out of their play pen in the very first inning. Mathews walked. I hit a double that sent Mathews to third. Frank Torre was batting fourth that day, and he singled. We had a 2–0 lead right off the bat. Burdette was fresh and ready now, and it looked like we finally had things going our way.

We looked truly superior, like the superior team that we were, all the way into the ninth inning. At this point, our lead was 5–2. Since the fourth inning, Burdette hadn't allowed a Dodger to reach base. I was already working out my World Series ticket allotment again. Out there in the bull pen, "Good Kid" was waiting to be shown. In a few minutes, "Good Kid" was so busy he needed two sets of hands.

With Burdette going and a three-run lead in the ninth, you've got to figure you're safe. But Wally Moon, Duke Snider and Gil Hodges opened the ninth with singles. "Good Kid" warmed up McMahon, and Haney called for him with Moon, Snider and Hodges on base and nobody out. You still had to like our chances with McMahon going. He was big and strong and at the peak of his relief pitching career then.

I took a look over my shoulder at the bull pen. Spahn was warming up now, throwing as fast as he could. Haney was going to throw everything at them. I think this was the very moment when I first became really worried about winning it. The sight of Spahn, our ace, warming up in the bull pen was enough to tell me that somebody higher than me was also pretty worried.

Spahnie didn't get warmed quick enough. He should have been pitching to Norm Larker, who was a left-handed batter. Larker greeted McMahon with a single that scored Moon and Snider. Now it was 5–4. Hodges was on third, and still nobody was out.

End of McMahon.

Spahn came in. He got Roseboro, also a left-handed hitter, but Carl Furillo tied the score with a long fly. Hodges tagged and scored after the catch.

I think we sort of wilted then. We'd had it won. Now the Dodgers had got tougher than we were, and they had tied it. We had nothing left. Stan Williams, a big right-hander, mowed us down like he was Walter Johnson and we were the local Junior Legion team. We never got a hit off him in three innings.

Bob Rush was pitching for us with two men out in the twelfth when the hammer dropped on us. Hodges walked. This didn't look fatal. But Joe Pignatano—he was catching for the Dodgers now—singled him to second.

This is the way it ended, a crazy, cruel way for a great team (and the Braves were a great team until then) to come to its end. Furillo hit a ball through the middle. It took a high, twisting hop. Mantilla, my friend, was playing shortstop now. (Logan had been hurt on a play at second base in the seventh inning.) Felix went hard to his right and gloved the ball, but he had to make a quick turn to get the throw off to first. The ball hit in the dirt, and Torre, our best defensive first baseman, couldn't get it without leaving the bag. Hodges, of course, was on the go when Furillo swung, with two men out, and he scored the winning run.

If you're keeping score, the play was ruled an error on Mantilla, but what difference did that make? We'd had plenty of chances to lock it up before. No point in putting the blame on Felix. By that time, there was no winning for us anyway. If it hadn't been him, it would have been somebody else.

By that time, I'd become used to such clubhouse scenes. Like a death in the family. Nobody spoke. I can't recall a sound, except those of men undressing and packing and spikes on concrete and the showers running. I've never heard such loud water in my life. It seems that water runs twice as hard and sounds twice as loud in a quiet clubhouse as it does in a happy clubhouse.

Then we had another ordeal to face. We had left our bags in the Ambassador Hotel—a show of confidence. We had to go back to pick them up before we went to the airport. One man cried. We all felt like crying, but only one man let the tears come through. I'll never forget him.

It was "Good Kid" Susce. He was an old-timer. He had been around in this game for thirty years. He had a face full of lines and lumps. There was a lot of geography in that face. It was a deeper blow to him because it was probably his last chance at a World Series check. "Good Kid" sat on the bus and cried. We'd let something precious slip through our fingers, and "Good Kid" was crying our tears for us.

The flight back to Milwaukee was a dreadful thing. Night flying never appealed to me anyway, but this was the night flight to end all night flights. It was an old propeller plane, a DC–6, I think, and I thought we'd never get to Milwaukee. No pioneers ever had a more miserable trip, even with the Indians on their backs.

There were no card games. A meal was served, but I never ate. Worst of all, I couldn't even sleep. You know, the Aaron who doesn't know what flying is like because he's asleep before the plane takes off and doesn't wake up until it lands? Well, Aaron the Sleeper didn't sleep that night.

I don't know what time we landed at Billy Mitchell Field —somewhere around three o'clock, I'd guess. There wasn't anything to remember about returning to Milwaukee that night. I assure you that no crowd of ten or fifteen thousand screeching fans was out to meet us. The terminal was cold, empty and without welcome. It made you feel like you were bringing a new disease into the city. Donald Davidson had our bus waiting for us to take us to County Stadium. There we all grabbed our bags and fled for home.

By this time I lived in Mequon. We had bought a home there in 1957, so when I reached Milwaukee, I was as good as home. Mequon is a suburb.

It was quiet at home, as you might imagine at about 4 A.M. Barbara said nothing. I went downtown to get a haircut the next day. Nobody in the barbershop said anything about it, not even the barber.

I beg your pardon, my barber did ask me one question.

"Who do you think'll win the World Series, the Dodgers or the White Sox?"

I didn't answer him.

14

I STILL HAD no feeling at the time of being a part of an empire that was in the state of collapse. After all, I was young and at the peak of my career. I was hitting. I was healthy. I was pulling my part of the load. I had to look at things on an individual basis, and, individually, my future looked bright.

If I am to believe history, though, the Braves' decline became a little more pronounced after we blew that play-off with the Dodgers. There's no question about it, the Braves were never the same again as long as they stayed in Milwaukee, and the fans never were the same toward the Braves again.

We finished second again in 1960, but we didn't make nearly such a fight about it. In other words, we weren't giving the Pirates anything to worry about right down to the wire.

There was something of a personal "disaster" that fell to me that season, too. It wasn't a bad year, understand. Any time you hit 40 home runs and drive in 126 runs and win the Golden Glove Award for fielding your position, I don't think you ought to go into mourning. But for the first time since I was a green rookie in 1954, I failed to hit .300.

I didn't like that. I don't like not hitting .300, and if I'm an old, tottering man swinging from a wheel chair, I'll still think I ought to be able to hit .300. It's significant, when it comes to "social stature."

When we played our first season in Atlanta my average dropped to .279. I still led the National League in home runs and runs batted in, but you had to look down among the reserve outfielders, platoon players and the rank and the file to find my name. No matter how well I did otherwise, those Southern baseball fans sort of thought I owed them something better than a .279 batting average, and nobody could have agreed with them more than Henry Aaron.

Every time I got asked about that average, I always said, "I'm swinging for the home run this season. The ball really flies out of Atlanta Stadium, and when I swing, I'm swinging to put it out of the park. Nothing thrills the fans like a home run, and it's our first season down here, so I'm trying to give them all the thrills I can."

A certain amount of that was true, and that amount that was fiction I began to believe myself after I'd said it a few times. But I'll tell you, man to man, I may have explained to the public's satisfaction why I wasn't hitting .300, but I couldn't fool myself.

After that '59 season, though, the retreat was on for the Braves. We dropped to second place the next year, then to fourth; then to fifth; then to sixth; then we got hung on fifth; and finally in 1967, arrived in seventh place. Managers began to come and go like a cleanup crew, and I never have been able to get used to that kind of change. All sorts of changes began to take place after the disastrous play-off with the Dodgers, beginning with the manager. Right in the middle of the World Series between the Dodgers and White Sox, Fred Haney resigned.

You remember that the Braves had hired Birdie Tebbetts and moved him in over John Quinn's head the year before, and that Quinn had moved to the Philadelphia Phillies, and that there were stories around that the Tebbetts-Haney team wouldn't last long because Tebbetts and Haney didn't gee and haw together? The two of them never let this side show to the players. Tebbetts stayed in the upstairs office where he belonged, and Haney kept to himself in the manager's office. The only cross fire I can remember between the two actually involved no personal contact at all. It was more a case of newspaper "matchmaking," and it had to do with Ed Mathews when he was in the midst of a terrible slump the first spring that Tebbetts was with the Braves, 1959.

Mathews had finished off the '58 season with a bad World Series. He had batted in only 3 runs and hit only .160 against the Yankees, and he opened up in spring exhibition games the same kind of way. It had to be one of the longest slumps anybody ever had. But Ed was never the kind to go around dragging his hindquarters, and he kept trying to fight his way out of it while everybody around him was giving the thing mouth service. This is where Haney and Tebbetts got engaged in a cross volley.

"I'm not going to let anybody tell Mathews how to hit," Haney told one newspaperman while the Braves were in Bradenton. "I've told him just to go up there and swing a bat."

Later the same day, some other newspaperman got hold of Tebbetts, and asked him what he thought was Mathews' trouble. Good ol' Birdie, he was never without a diagnosis for anything.

"He's holding the bat still now instead of jiggling it while the pitcher is warming up. That's his trouble," Birdie said.

The headline read: "Tebbetts and Haney Disagree on Cause of Mathews' Slump." They didn't disagree. They hadn't even talked about it, so you can see that that was manufactured.

There had been some news out in the summer that Haney wouldn't be back—win, lose or whatever. He'd indicated as much when he spoke at a luncheon in Los Angeles in June. This was his country, Los Angeles. This is where he had been big in minor-league baseball, and where he had his permanent home and where he really preferred to be—which he since proved, going back to run the Angels of the American League.

He sort of liked the Hollywood life, too. You'd see all

kinds of movie and television types coming in and out of his office when we were playing in L.A. Desi Arnaz was there more than any of the others. They were close friends. William Frawley was another, and Jack Webb, the "Dragnet" man, and Frank Lovejoy. Haney sort of reveled in the Hollywood limelight.

One time on a road trip into Los Angeles, Pat O'Brien visited the Braves in the clubhouse before a game with the Dodgers. O'Brien and Haney were close friends, too. I'm not too familiar with Pat O'Brien as an actor, except for those old films I see him in on the late shows, but I had heard that he played Knute Rockne, the famous football coach, in a movie about Notre Dame.

Well, before he got out of the clubhouse that night, Haney introduced O'Brien, and before the introduction was over, Haney had O'Brien standing on a trunk giving us the old "Gipper talk." He threw in a few changes, though, and wound up with the line, "Go, go, go, Braves!"

It didn't do a bit of good. The Dodgers beat us that night, 2 to 1. That happened in 1958, and we won the pennant, anyway, so you can't say that Haney's Hollywood influence did us any damage. Really, I think that if Haney had had his way about it, he would have been an actor, too.

It wasn't long before he was "on stage," in a sense. Leo Durocher left NBC about that time. He had been a commentator on the network's baseball telecasts. Haney got his job, at $50,000 a year. Don't think he made any sacrifices when he quit Milwaukee.

Durocher went back to the uniform. He rejoined the Los Angeles Dodgers as a coach, and guess who he succeeded? The next manager of the Milwaukee Braves, Charlie Dressen.

They began changing everything now but the pictures on the wall at County Stadium. The Braves had picked up several veterans down the stretch, trying to patch up and fill in on the bench. As soon as the season was over and Haney went, the veterans began following him.

Del Rice, who had been with us as a catcher for several

seasons, had been made a coach in August. He went. Enos Slaughter, Mickey Vernon and Ray Boone, three old-timers who had finished up with us, got their release. Stan Lopata, who had been brought in to back up the catching corps, went too.

That wasn't all, either. They began digging into the old-line Braves in addition to Rice. Andy Pafko was released as a player, but they remembered him with a coach's contract. Bob Trowbridge, a young pitcher, was sold to Kansas City. Casey Wise, a young infielder, was traded to Detroit.

That was just the beginning, though. The next December, at the winter baseball meetings, they really dug deeper into the roster. Joey Jay and Juan Pizarro went to Cincinnati in a trade for Roy McMillan. McMillan had played for Tebbetts. Birdie wanted him for shortstop. That meant Johnny Logan was on his way out. Believe me, when you've played around a guy as long as I played around Logan, you begin to love him. Johnny was great for team spirit, the most humorous man I ever played with. You knew darn well he wasn't going to be very funny riding the bench.

They didn't get around to hitting me a real lick, though, until December 7, 1960, and that date then began to have a meaning of double disaster to me. Bill Bruton and I went bird hunting with a friend of his up around Green Bay. We left before dawn and drove back to Milwaukee about six o'clock in the afternoon. They dropped me off at my house in Mequon, and Barbara was waiting for me at the door.

"Where's Billy?" she said.

"On his way home. Why?"

"Loretta's been trying to get him. She called here a few minutes ago. I thought you-all were coming in, or I'd have been out there waiting for you," Barbara said.

"Is something wrong?" I said.

"He's been traded," Barbara said.

I heard it a few minutes later on the radio myself. The Braves had traded Billy and Dick Brown, a catcher, and

Chuck Cottier, a second baseman, and Terry Fox, a pitcher, to the Tigers for Frank Bolling and Neil Chrisley. Bolling was a second baseman, and Chrisley was an outfielder, but Bolling was the fellow they wanted, and they'd paid a heck of a price to get him. As far as I was concerned, they had paid a lot too much. Any time they trade your roommate and a man who had meant as much to me as Bill Bruton had meant to me, they have traded too much.

I played for a number of years beside Bill Bruton, and I repeat that I considered him one of the greatest centerfielders in the business—Mays, Flood or anybody you want to consider against him. We got along well. More than that, I looked up to Bruton as a man. From the first time I saw him in my first spring training with the Braves I respected him.

It wasn't easy to get to know him. He wasn't that much outgoing. I had to respect him from a distance when I first came up in 1954 until I had been around the Braves a few weeks, even though we both lived at Mrs. Gibson's boarding house in Bradenton. Actually, I didn't get to know him very well until we broke camp that spring.

Bruton was sort of the "senior officer" among the Negro players. We were living separately from the white players in those times, at least until we got into the league cities and the season was on. We barnstormed our way north, and when we would arrive in a town, Duffy Lewis, the traveling secretary, would appoint Bruton to handle the money for cab fares and tips and other things that we might need, and Bruton would be in charge of our group until we joined up with the rest of the team again.

I wasn't saying much in those days. I was keeping my mouth shut and my ears open and swinging a bat. I guess Bill could tell I was a little nervous being among all those older players. Anyway, it seemed like he was sort of giving me a little extra attention.

We finally pulled into Milwaukee by train. I had never been to Milwaukee, of course, and I must have been looking like my usual "lost" self.

"You know where you're going, Aaron?" Bruton asked me.

"To the place that we're going to stay, I guess," I said. "Duffy Lewis said he'd have places for us."

"I don't know if they'll be ready for you tonight, or not," he said. "You come on home and have dinner with Loretta and me tonight, then we'll get you settled down later."

So I went to the Brutons and had dinner. He was the first player to invite me out, and I guess I sort of trailed him like a puppy dog after that, especially when the team was traveling. I knew he knew his way around. I knew he knew how to dress and the right things to say and the right things to do. If I watched Bill and did what he did, I'd be following a pretty good example, and so I did that. I'm certain that Bill never went to college, but he was one of the best-educated men I ever knew. He knew how to get along with people. I felt pretty special, I know that, when I finally got him as a roommate. The Braves had traded Jim Pendleton, who had been my roommate. Felix Mantilla roomed with me for awhile. Then John Quinn, who was still the general manager, moved me in with Bill because he thought the influence of an old player and one as stable as Bill would be good for me.

You must realize, then, that I felt pretty much disturbed when the Braves traded Bruton to Detroit. Then when they traded Jay and Pizarro a few days later, I began to feel for the first time that the old Braves were falling apart, that we'd never be the same again. Not *that* strong, I mean— not so strong that I felt we couldn't win again—but I felt the change in personalities. When McMillan came in, that indicated that the brass was unhappy with Logan at short-stop and that something was going to happen to Johnny. Schoendienst was already gone before the trade for Bolling. The Braves released him in October, right after the 1960 season was over. His days as a regular were over.

In other words, the Braves' personality was being changed to match the desires of the new personality of the front office: Tebbetts, McHale and Dressen.

I worked for the Braves during the off-season in 1962,

doing public-relations work, selling tickets and making appearances. I really didn't begin to realize what had taken place, and what was taking place between the team and the town until then. The former fans were still, two years later, talking about old deals.

"How could they get rid of Bruton?" people would ask me. "How could they trade Jay and Pizarro, just when they were about to become winning pitchers? How could they run John Quinn out of town? He was the fans' friend."

And when Jay went over to Cincinnati and won forty-two games in two seasons, and the Reds won the pennant the very next year, 1961, that didn't increase the happiness in Milwaukee, either. And when Pizarro went to the White Sox—the Reds traded him to Chicago for Gene Freese the same day they got him from the Braves—and became a big winner, that didn't increase the happiness in Milwaukee, either.

Once the club began trading, faces seemed to change every week. Players came and went like livestock. As the old favorites began disappearing, the replacements never really caught on with the fans, and if there was anything that Milwaukee fans liked to be reminded of, it was those good years when we were winning pennants. The new Braves couldn't bring back these memories, and the people who used to crowd County Stadium, fully equipped with ice chests filled with beer they'd bought at supermarket prices, began staying away from the place.

That was another thing. The Braves' management had put a ban on those coolers filled with beer, trying to force the fans to buy stadium-priced beer. Nothing could have made them madder. Those people in Milwaukee had been accustomed for years to coming to the baseball park toting their own buckets full of beer, and this seemed to them like they were being denied a constitutional right, or something like that.

Then Charlie Dressen coming in as the manager about this time didn't help matters any. Charlie and those fans didn't have anything in common, or at least they never seemed to fall for each other. They went their own way. They began to act as if a manager was a pretty unimportant part of the Braves, which brings up another subject: some of the managers I have known and played for and what they were like.

15

It was in the season of 1957—the year wo won our first pennant as the Milwaukee Braves—and we were playing the Giants in the old Polo Grounds in New York. They hadn't moved to San Francisco yet. That was the next year.

It was in the middle of the game. We had runners on first and second base. I was the batter. Ruben Gomez, a kind of "cute" right-hander, was pitching for the Giants. He tried to sneak a fast ball by me, and I hit a bullet to the shortstop, Daryl Spencer, and it was a double play— not a questionable double play, but a bang-bang double play because the ball was hit so hard.

I was disgusted, no doubt about it. If I had run as hard as I can run, I'd have been out before I was 20 feet from the bag. The point is, I didn't run it out. I sort of trotted down the line—"lallygagging," my mother would have called it— and turned for the dugout.

The next day, I got the only "chewing-out" I ever got as a baseball player.

Fred Haney was the manager, just to keep the history straight. He didn't say a word to me when I came into the dugout. He didn't say anything after the game. But the next day when I got to the ball park, he called a team meeting. He let me have it in front of everybody.

"I've called this meeting because I want to have a talk with Aaron," Haney said. "Henry, you mean a lot to this team, and everybody else is trying to win a pennant. You

135

didn't look like you cared yesterday, and I want you to know, by God, that I do care. You didn't hustle on that double-play ball. You loafed. Of course it was a double play, but suppose somebody had kicked the ball, what chance would you have had if you were jogging along halfway down the baseline? None. You might have stopped a rally. We won the game, but that makes no difference to me. You loafed."

In other words, Haney was making an example out of me in front of the whole ball club. I've always heard that this isn't the way to manage, that you call the player in and give him his "chewing-out" privately, but I guess there are times and places for everything.

What Haney was doing then was telling the rest of the Braves that Henry Aaron might be leading the league in home runs and runs batted in, and he might be a sweet, innocent kid who was going to become the Most Valuable Player of the year, but that he wasn't getting away without hustling. I didn't like it, but I think he had to do it, for the good of the whole ball club as well as my own good.

I never said a word to him about it, and he never said another word to me, other than what he had to say in front of the team. When he left the Braves, I hated to see him go, and the older players hated to see him go. I thought he was a good manager. I thought he had a touch with players; and I point out here the way he got everything out of "Hurricane" Hazle when he came in to fill in for Billy Bruton that season, and Wes Covington and Don McMahon that same season, and out of Mel Roach, when Red Schoendienst had to sit it out with tuberculosis in 1959. Haney may have been cold and he may have been standoffish in some ways, but in other ways, when he could see the need, he could get so close to a player that that player would play like he was trying to save his own house from burning to the ground.

I've always had my own attitude toward managers, though. It's nothing especially unusual. I read stories of players demanding to be traded because they can't play for

that mean old manager. I remember some players practically getting Johnny Pesky fired as manager of the Boston
Red Sox a few years ago. One of them was Carl Yastrzemski,
who is a great hitter. And there must have been some real
depth in the way he felt about it, because after Pesky left,
he really began coming out as a player.

Me, though, I've never really cared who the manager is.
I mean it doesn't bother me personally. I want some manager running the team who is going to be good for the team
as a whole, but as far as I'm concerned, the manager isn't
important to me—as a personality, I should say.

In other words, the manager isn't going to change the
way I play. I think I owe it to myself and to my family
and to the fans who believe in me to play as well as I can
play at all times, no matter who the manager is.

I think this has worked out in my favor over the long
haul. No manager ever fined me until 1967 (we'll cover
that later), put detectives on my tail or went to the front
office to get some help in keeping me in line. I've had only
the one "chewing-out," as I said, and that has been it. I've
been kicked out of only one ball game in my life.

That happened our first season in Atlanta. Tony Venzon
was the umpire. We'd had something going at the time,
anyway, and honestly, not one word was spoken until Tony
finally yelped, "Out!"

That was all. Just, "Out!"

The Braves were playing Pittsburgh in Atlanta Stadium,
and Bob Veale was pitching for the Pirates. Veale is so big
he looks like a vulture about to swoop down on you when
he releases the ball, and that night he was throwing nothing
but strikes. He was real hot.

He threw a curve that Venzon called, "Strike three!" I
was disgusted with myself, not the call particularly, and
just dropped my bat on the plate. The bat hit and rolled
toward Venzon's feet. Just as I started to walk toward the
dugout, Venzon kicked the bat at me. I kicked it back at
him. I glared at him. He glared at me, and that was all.

"Out!" he said, jerking up that right arm in the umpire's

motion that tells you your day's work is done, and I was out of the game.

So I haven't given any manager ulcers, and no manager has given me any, and I have played for a chorus line of "beauties," I might say. Some good beauties, some ordinary beauties, some who really didn't seem to care and some who were a lot more than just a manager to me.

When I broke in with the Indianapolis Clowns, a fellow named Buster Haywood was the manager. It's a funny thing, but I never felt that Haywood really cared to have me around. He had a bunch of older, experienced players that made up the nut of the team, and he just didn't want to be bothered with a new kid.

Everybody else had bench jackets. He never issued one to me, and it may have been May at the time in Winston-Salem, North Carolina, where we trained, but I'm telling you, some of those mornings were chilly.

We were walking down the street one day to the little café where we ate our meals in Winston-Salem. I hadn't been there more than a day or two. Ray Neal, the second baseman, was in the crowd. He had just been released by Cleveland. Nothing but older players and me. I mention Neal only because he later became my best friend on the team. They were talking about hitting the road in our bus and getting on with the season.

"It won't be long," Haywood said, "until we get rid of some of these green kids and get our team down to size and start hitting the big towns and seeing some sights."

And when he said it, he jerked his thumb in my direction, about like Tony Venzon did when he threw me out of the game.

Of course, when I started hitting over .400, his attitude changed. When the Braves were trying to sign me, he kept trying to talk me into staying with the Clowns, and I said, "No, Buster. You really ought to get rid of these green kids and hit the road and see some sights. Remember?"

I'll tell you the kind of manager Buster Haywood was.

I don't think anybody ever paid a lot of attention to this before, but I was a cross-handed batter at one time. When I joined the Clowns, I batted cross-handed. Buster Haywood let me keep on batting cross-handed. Never said a word to me about changing.

Of course, when you got a kid batting over .400, even if he has to stand on his head to bat, why monkey around with success? And the only thing Haywood was interested in was winning, and I was hitting over .400 and we were winning. He wasn't training me for the big leagues.

We get into Buffalo, New York, and now the scouting heat has turned from warm to hot. This was where the Braves sent in Dewey Griggs, one of their scouts, to look me over. The Clowns had had batting practice, then it rained and the game was held up. During the delay, Dewey Griggs called me over to the grandstand wall.

"Aaron," he said, "have you always batted cross-handed?"

"Yessir, I always have," I said.

"Well, I know you're killing this kind of pitching that way, but you'll never be able to play in the big leagues batting cross-handed," he said. "Those pitchers will knock the bat right out of your hands. Next time you come to bat, switch your hands and try the regular grip. See how that feels."

"I'll try it," I said. I wanted to play in the big leagues. I was willing to listen to anybody.

The first time I came to bat in the game, I used the regular right-hander's grip, right hand on top of left hand, and I swung. I hit the first pitch out of the park. You remember that I wrote I'd hit two home runs in the game, one over the right-field fence and one over the left-field fence? The first one cleared the right-field fence. I still wasn't as much at home with the new grip to get the bat all the way around, but the second time I did, and I gave the ball a ride. I never felt one bit of difference at all. It was great.

I never batted cross-handed again.

If I had only been thinking at the time, I'd have made one other change too. It would have made a lot of difference in my career, I'm positive of that.

I'd have kept the same cross-handed grip and moved to the other side of the plate, where it wouldn't have been cross-handed, and become a left-handed batter. It figures to have meant 10 or 15 more hits a season to me, being that much nearer to first base; and 10 or 15 more hits a season makes a lot of difference to a fellow's average. But then they never would have said that I was the greatest right-handed machine since Rogers Hornsby, whatever that may have meant to me. I was just a kid, then, and wasn't thinking. I was just happy to please Dewey Griggs.

One thing I've often wondered since then. Why didn't he say something to me about moving over to the left-handed side?

When I got to Eau Claire in the Northern League after I signed with the Braves, my manager was Marion Adair, known as "Bill," who was also the second baseman on the team, and who later was one of the Braves' coaches. At Jacksonville, I played for Ben Geraghty, who is dead now. He died of a heart attack in the early sixties. That winter I played for Mickey Owen, the old National League catcher, in the Puerto Rican League. Then in the majors I played for Grimm, Haney, Dressen, Tebbetts, Bragan and Hitchcock, and that brings me up to Luman Harris, who was Paul Richards' choice to manage the Braves in 1968. And so we have barely met yet.

16

IN MY TIME, the Braves have never had a manager whom the players liked more genuinely than Charlie Grimm. I've heard them make excuses for him and the way things were going until they sounded like defense lawyers.

When the bottom was dropping right out from under him in Milwaukee in 1956, we were standing around outside the clubhouse waiting for a ride one night, after we'd lost our tenth of the last thirteen games, and Johnny Logan was talking.

"We're just not getting any of the breaks. You've got to have a break once in a while, that's all. How can the fans quit on Charlie just because we're not getting any breaks?" Johnny said.

He was almost babbling, trying to say something good for Charlie, but not able to say a lot, other than "breaks, breaks, breaks," and that won't save any manager his job.

Most of us thought that Charlie had been saddled up in the spring and told, "Okay, we've been in Milwaukee long enough now. The honeymoon is over. You've been our manager all this time. Let's win one, or you'll be looking for a new job."

Charlie Root was the pitching coach. He and Grimm had been teammates on the Chicago Cubs when the Cubs were winning pennants. "I've known Charlie a long time," Charlie Root said one day, "and I've never seen him show tension

141

so much, and I noticed it the first day I checked in for spring training."

Well, we were in New York for a series with Brooklyn. John Quinn flew in. The papers hit the streets with the story and we had Fred Haney for a manager—which I have already covered in detail.

About the only thing I haven't covered on Haney has nothing to do with him personally. It has to do with the team situation when he became manager in 1956. The way I see it, he inherited a ball club that was just reaching maturity as a pennant contender, and any manager should have been able to win with it. It was a hand-tooled, custom-made, real, live championship club, and yet we won only two pennants when I have already figured for you that we should have won four.

You be the judge on where the manager's responsibility fits into that picture. I was too much in the middle of it to be able to see it clearly myself. I just hope that what I did clears me as one of the sinners.

I know that in '56, Haney was accused of taking such a conservative approach on offense that he became known as "Bunting O'Haney." That little title didn't originate in Milwaukee, but among some of the Eastern writers, who were insisting that the Braves bunted themselves right out of the pennant that year, when with all that power we had in our line-up we should have been swinging for the fences and big innings. That was the way the "Bunting O'Haney" group saw it, understand.

It left such a strong impression that when Dressen was hired for the 1960 season, the bunting subject came up pretty big in the first press conference at which he starred in Milwaukee. Dressen dug the hole a little deeper for himself.

"We're going to have an extra diamond built in Florida," he said. "We'll be able to send part of the squad out there for workouts, and they'll practice bunting against curve-ball pitching as well as the pitching machine. We'll hit-and-run, we'll bunt and we'll go for the extra base. This isn't the slowest club in the world. Guys like Ed Mathews and Hank Aaron can run, and I can't believe that Wes Covington isn't faster than he showed last season. Don't get me wrong, though. I'm not going to have home-run hitters like Mathews and Aaron stealing every base in sight."

I don't guess any manager ever knew any more baseball than Dressen. But he'd wear you out with his brilliance, which he seemed to value as a great asset to any team with which he was connected.

I'm not trying to indict the man. Heck, I'm not that smart myself. But the fact that he won only two pennants in his life as a big-league manager, and that, when he managed seventh- and eighth-place teams in Washington, he still finished seventh and eighth should have told him something.

As smart a manager as he may have been on the technical side, he didn't know how to handle the Braves, especially the older fellows, like Spahn, Burdette, Adcock, Crandall and those fellows. They had gotten along well with Haney, and then the switch to a personality like Dressen's was just about too much. He really got under Burdette's skin, and Lew was the kind of guy who didn't mind giving you a piece of his mind, if he had any to spare.

We were playing the Dodgers in 1960 and we'd been having a rough time with them. Of course, Dressen had managed the Dodgers, and had won his two pennants with them in 1952 and 1953, and some of the fellows were just bulling around one day, talking about how tough they were especially in that Coliseum in Los Angeles with the short left-field fence.

"Well, I wish somebody could tell me how to pitch to the Dodgers in that blankety-blank park," Burdette said.

"If you had a drop like Johnny Podres, I could tell you how to pitch to the Dodgers," Dressen said to Burdette.

I don't think he really meant it that way, but it cut Lew to the gizzard. His face clouded up and he could have bit a tenpenny nail in two.

It just happened that he was pitching against the Dodgers

that night and Podres was pitching against him. That was one game you knew that Lew wasn't going to lose, but to top it all off, he hit two home runs off Podres to boot.

After the second one, coming back into the dugout, he reached for a towel to dry himself off, and he made a point of walking by where Dressen was seated, and he said out of the corner of his mouth, "And that's what I think about Podres' blankety-blank drop."

Spahn and Burdette took great delight in pulling practical jokes on Dressen. Charlie talked so much and got so involved in what he was saying, he was easy game. One day Burdette set fire to his shoelaces, and Charlie started toward home plate for the pre-game line-up meeting with his shoelaces burning.

Their most publicized piece of arson, though, took place on a bus taking the team from the Pittsburgh airport into town, and that event got wide coverage. It was late at night. We'd played an afternoon game in St. Louis, and all of us were tired and sleepy. It's a long ride from the Pittsburgh airport to downtown Pittsburgh, and there were all sorts of irritating circumstances, such as a long wait for the driver to get started, and the club had been going bad—we'd lost three in a row—and Dressen was on fire inside already.

Spahn and Burdette were in the back of the bus. One of the players had bought a newspaper and was reading it. Spahn or Burdette—I don't know which—struck a match to the paper, then balled up part of it and started a fire with it. Now, it really wasn't much of a blaze, but it smoked up things and Dressen got a whiff of it up front, where the manager always sits on the bus, and he stormed back there yelping and bawling. Everybody else was laughing— or most everybody who had enough energy left to laugh. But Dressen was furious.

"I don't think that's so damned funny," he said, "particularly the way you guys have been playing lately. If you showed as much fire on the field as you show on the back of the bus, we might not be where we are. You bunch of clowns! That's another thing. If you put as much time on pitching as you do clowning around, we wouldn't be in fifth place. You act like a bunch of blankety-blank kids."

It wasn't long after that that Dressen was replaced by Birdie Tebbetts. Things were in a pretty big stew at the time, anyway. The general impression was that Dressen had lost control of the players, and I guess you'd have to say that was close to the truth. He'd lost their respect, at least, and that incident on the bus, childish as it may have been for Spahn and Burdette to have started that little blaze, had a lot to do with it. Then, too, Tebbetts and John McHale were both in the front office, and really nobody seemed to know who was boss. It was about this time that the deal was brought off between Lou Perini and Bill Bartholomay and his syndicate from Chicago, and the changes left a common, everyday player a little swimmy-headed.

McHale was one of the new partners—about five per cent, I've read—and he was going to do the general-managing for the new group obviously, and so it appeared that if there was going to be any place for Tebbetts, it was back in uniform. So back to the sweatshop for Birdie.

Frankly, I can take Birdie Tebbetts or leave him alone. He's not the kind of guy I'd die for. On the other hand, he was great with a young team, a lot of kids whom he could impress.

I don't think there's any doubt that one particular incident had a lot to do with the final impression I formed of Tebbetts, and I probably have let the thing wear a little too much like a tight yoke around my neck. But it burned me up then, and I still get hot flashes when I think about it even now, and that was in 1962.

The Braves were leaving for New York on a road trip. We had a chartered plane. I always picked up a young Puerto Rican kid we had with us for a while, Amado Samuel. Great fielder, but couldn't hit a medicine ball. He lived on my way into town, so it was easy enough to do. He was a rookie, didn't speak much English and didn't know his way around too well, so it was okay with me.

Well, on this particular day we have a flat tire. We get out and fix it ourselves, Samuel and me, and we push along, but it's thirty or forty minutes after take-off time when we get to the airport. Everybody is there and waiting, and we've held them up all this time.

Tebbetts is fuming. I tell him what has happened. "What the hell," he said, "haven't you ever heard of the telephone?"

"They don't have many on the freeway," I said. "Besides, that would have taken just that much more time to call you."

"Makes no difference, you could have done something," he said.

"I'm sorry, Birdie," I said. "That's all I can say. I didn't want to have a flat tire."

"It'll cost you," he said, and he turned to walk away, but not quite far enough not to let me hear his next line. "You'll learn that nobody's a star on this team."

It did cost me. He fined both Samuel and me. He was thoughtful enough of Samuel, though, that he fined him only half the amount he fined me.

Otherwise, life with Birdie wasn't too bad, except that we finished fifth with him in 1962, and that brought on Bobby Bragan the next year. Now there's a fellow who can stir up a conversation when his name becomes the topic. I don't suppose there have been more than two or three managers—say, Leo Durocher and maybe Harry Walker—who have created more controversy than Bobby Bragan. And you'll hardly ever run across two people in any group that have the same opinion of him.

But knock Bobby Bragan? Not me. I know that when he was fired as manager of the Braves our first year in Atlanta, the ball club was considered to be on the borderline of mutiny. But let me say this about him, and I want to put this on record. I thought the world of Bobby Bragan. He treated me just fine. He made me feel I was important. I don't mean that he put me on a pedestal and posed me and painted "Our Hero" on a sign and hung it around my neck. He made me feel my value to the ball club, that's what I mean.

In fact, I give Bragan all the credit for making me a complete ball player, and I assume that I am generally considered to be a complete ball player. Tebbetts once said, when Frank Robinson had just come up to Cincinnati as a rookie and was getting off to a great start, "I wouldn't trade Robinson for Aaron, for the long run, of course, but there's one thing Aaron's got that Robinson will never have, and that is versatility. He can play so many positions and do many things so well."

The first thing I remember Bragan telling me after he became manager was that he wanted me to be more aggressive as a base runner. It was during the first week of spring training. We had moved from Bradenton to West Palm Beach by this time. Bragan called me over to a corner of the dugout one morning before everybody got on the field.

"How many bases do you steal a season?" he said.

"Oh, about ten, maybe fifteen, if I get the chance to," I said.

"Do you think you could steal more?"

"Yep. I don't want to brag, but I think I can run with just about any player in the league."

"Tell you what I want you to do, then, Henry," Bragan said. "I want you to run the bases. I'm putting you on your own. When you see a chance to steal, steal. You've got the speed, and you ought to be putting it to use."

I had stolen fifteen bases the season before. The first season Bragan was the manager I stole thirty-one. I didn't go hog-wild. I wasn't going to push Maury Wills for the all-time record, but what I tried to do was steal when stealing would help the team and made sense. The seasons before, I had usually stolen only when I got the sign. One year I stole only one, the year we won our first pennant. I stole a few more after Dressen became manager, but I never cut loose until Bragan came in. Since then I have stolen an average of about twenty-two bases a season, and I'm right proud of the fact that I don't get cut down very often. In

1966, for instance, I didn't steal but twenty-one bases, but on the other hand, I didn't get caught stealing but three times—and I'll take that kind of average any time.

With Bragan and me, it would be sort of a mutual kind of respect. I'll have to admit that I developed a real fancy for his opinions when I picked up the *Milwaukee Sentinel* one morning and saw this headline: "Bragan Pins Million-Dollar Tag on Aaron as the Greatest."

Bragan was managing Pittsburgh at the time. I had hit 2 home runs the night before, and the Braves had taken the Pirates. The 2 home runs had put me 2 ahead of Babe Ruth's pace the year he hit 60, and Bragan, always the kind of fellow to let the quotes fall out of his mouth with a headline in mind, really laid it on for Lou Chapman, one of the *Sentinel* writers.

> He is more apt to hit .400 than any National League player since Bill Terry [the story said]. What's more, if anyone can break Babe Ruth's home run record of 60, this is the boy who will do it.
> Aaron is not only a good hitter, he's a great hitter. You'd have to put a million-dollar tag on him.

The Sporting News carried a story back in 1957 in which Stan Musial was quoted as saying I was an "arrogant hitter." He didn't mean it exactly the way it sounded, but he explained it this way:

> He thinks there's nothing he can't hit, but he'll learn there are pitches that no hitter can afford to go for. He still has something to learn about the strike zone.

Bragan was managing Pittsburgh then, and had no cause to defend me and my way of hitting at all. But he did.

"You don't try to change a hitter like Aaron," Bragan said. "In my book he's a better hitter than Willie Mays. He's going to get better too. He's the one to beat for the batting championship for ten years or more."

I never could understand why my cap didn't fly off my head every time I ran—like Willie's—unless I've got a better fit than he's got. And I don't know why somebody in

Milwaukee didn't coach me to say something clever like, "Say Hey," when I first came up—like Willie—then I would have been everything that Bragan said I was, plus some.

Naturally, after such a display of brilliant judgment, you might say that whatever move Bragan made after that, I bought. Only trouble is, I never did hit .400—and I've gone into that—and Roger Maris was the guy who broke Ruth's record.

More seriously and to the point, though, I had no complaints with Bragan. I'm sorry to say that several of my teammates couldn't say the same.

Bragan had a little way of humiliating a player, not really meaning to, I think. Sometimes he'd do it when he was peeved, and sometimes he'd do it in the clubhouse when he was only meaning to kid somebody.

One night during our first season in Atlanta, Joe Torre struck out with the bases loaded, and Joe was going good at the time, hitting about .315. Of course it was tough to take, because the strike-out just about broke a rally. Well, Bragan gets up from the bench, puts his hands in his hip pockets and starts striding along the dugout, and he gets this ugly look on his face, and he says, "Joe Torre is a ——— hitter! He can't hit good, big-league pitching."

It was said so that everybody on the bench could hear it. Joe didn't. He heard about it later. You can imagine what that did for his attitude toward Bragan.

Denver Lemaster, the left-handed pitcher, gets knocked out of the box, and they walk in from the mound together, Bragan and Lemaster. They start down the dugout steps. Bragan looks at Lemaster, and says, "You'll never be another Lefty Grove."

What's the point?

One of the coaches, Grover Resinger, said that Bragan had been associated with so many great players that he expected a lot from his own players. One of the Braves, and I'm guessing it was Gene Oliver, said, "Any guy who spends most of his big-league career in eighth place with the Philadelphia Phillies and has a lifetime batting average of .240 hasn't seen too many great players."

Ed Mathews just didn't get along with Bragan at all. Before the 1966 season, our first in Atlanta, Bragan said he had an announcement to make one day. Photographers showed up. Television cameramen showed up. Sports reporters came out.

The event took place in the dugout. Bragan and Mathews came out of the clubhouse runway together. "Gentlemen," Bragan said, "I want you to meet the new captain of the Braves, Captain Mathews."

The Braves hadn't had a captain since Del Crandall. Crandall had been Haney's choice. Crandall and Dressen didn't get along, so Dressen dropped the title. Bragan was bringing it back and pinning it on Mathews, hoping to win him over.

It didn't work. It didn't change the way Mathews felt about Bragan. Eddie was a slugger, and when he wasn't hitting home runs, he felt like he was in a slump. It boils down to the basic fact that Bragan simply didn't care for Mathews' style of play or his attitude. But there was never any incident between the two. It was just a situation that was constant, and neither man ever changed his opinion of the other.

But Lemaster, oh, man, how he could tell you about Bragan! And Rico Carty! Rico had a rippet with him in 1966. Rico was late for a game with San Francisco. Bragan laid him out. Rico claimed that Bragan had given him permission. Bragan said he hadn't. They never had a reconciliation.

Lemaster and Bragan came apart in May of that first year in Atlanta. Denver had a heck of a game going with Jim Maloney of Cincinnati, and the fifth inning came up and the score was 3–2, Cincinnati. We had nobody on base, but Bragan lifted Lemaster for a pinch-hitter. Well, sir, Lemaster blasted Bragan in the papers the next day.

"How's a pitcher ever going to be able to get the job done if he isn't allowed to stay in the game?" Lemaster

A typical spring-training pose when I was a green rookie with the Braves at Bradenton in 1954.

Fred Haney, on my left, meant pennants to the Braves when we were in Milwaukee. We won two but should have taken four. (Wide World)

The highest moment in my life, when my teammates carried me off the field after I hit the home run that beat St. Louis and won the pennant in 1957. (Wide World)

Mickey Mantle and I cross bats before the World Series between the Yankees and the Braves in 1957. (Wide World)

Here is the picture sequence taken during the third game of the 1957 World Series that raised the question of whether or not I made the catch of Gil McDougald's sinking line drive. I don't care what the pictures might show—I know I made that catch! (Wide World)

National League president Warren Giles presented me with a silver bat for leading the league in hitting in 1959. My teammate and pal Ed Mathews received the Mel Ott plaque as the National League home-run king. (Wide World)

One of the few miscarriages of justice that provoked me to vocal protest. I have just been called out by Ed Vargo on a tag by Cincinnati's Willie Jones in 1960. (Wide World)

My brother Tommie and I in spring training, 1962. (Wide World)

My two sons, Larry and Henry, Jr., on Father-Son day in Atlanta, 1966.

Robert Winborne of Atlanta caught No. 700 and won himself 700 silver dollars. (Wide World)

No. 700: Thank you. (Wide World)

The year is 1968 and that's No. 500 off Mike McCormick. No one believes it. (Wide World)

Hitting one out in the playoffs against the Mets in 1969. Jerry Grote, catching for the Mets, knows it's gone. (Wide World)

My daughter Dorinda is eleven. Here we're loosening up prior to our annual fathers-kids game. (Wide World)

Out goes the first ball of the 1973 World Series between the A's and the Mets. (Wide World)

The morning after No. 700. Only fifteen more to go. (Wide World)

Up, up and away: No. 713. (Wide World)

I enjoy playing the outfield. This picture was taken during a game against the Phillies. (Wide World)

said. "How can the guy take me out, the way I'm going? Who's he got in the bull pen that's going to improve on it? It's enough to ruin your confidence."

Denver's a moody sort of guy anyway, has a pretty quick temper, but usually he gets mad at himself more than at anybody else. His disposition didn't improve after he left the game, when the Reds ganged up on his relief and won the game 8–2, and he was the losing pitcher.

Bragan closed his office door and had a conference with Lemaster the next day, but one of the first guys who cheered when Bragan was fired in August was Lemaster. They never got together after that episode in May.

Somebody asked me the day the news got out that John McHale had fired Bragan and replaced him with Billy Hitchcock, if I had expected Bragan to be fired.

I told the man, "I expected him to be fired *before* this. In fact, I expected him to get fired about the All-Star Game break."

What really turned out to be the last straw was a game in St. Louis in late July. The Braves got out ahead by 7 runs in the first inning. We got the bases loaded and Torre hit a home run, and we were off and flying. The Cardinals kept nibbling away at Tony Cloninger until they tied it up. We got a second chance in the seventh inning. Torre hit another home run with one man on base and we took the lead again 9–7, but the Cardinals climbed all over this kid pitcher, Arnold Umbach, in the twelfth inning and we got beaten finally 10–9.

This was the last deadly blow to the Braves' morale. We'd gone into St. Louis on a five-game winning streak. I mean, we had the spirit. On the bus coming in from the airport, passing by that big arch the city has built along the Mississippi River waterfront, Torre pointed and said, "Remember that, men. Remember that funny-looking thing as the sign of the town where the Braves got their move on for the pennant."

It became the sign of Bragan's disaster.

Things go your way sometimes, so that nothing you do

comes up wrong. When you're on a good streak, everything goes against the loser. We'd even had a repeat of the Nippy Jones "shoeshine" incident on our streak.

Remember Nippy Jones, the hit-batsman from the 1957 World Series with the Yankees, in an earlier chapter?

The series before we moved into St. Louis, we played in Cincinnati. The Reds took the lead twice, but two times we came back. The second time, Tony Cloninger is at bat and Billy McCool throws one that breaks low and into the dirt, but Cloninger claims that the pitch hit his foot. He and the umpire are arguing, then Tony gets the ball and shows the umpire the shoe polish. The umpire waves him to first. Felix Millan runs for Cloninger, and scores the winning run on Mathews' single.

This is the way it is when you're on a good streak. When it started going bad, everything we did went wrong. It wound up getting Bragan in the end, though Atlanta fans were pretty positive they didn't want him way back in June.

No man ever took over as manager of a big-league baseball team on a wider plane of public appeal—and demand —than Billy Hitchcock. It happened on August 9, 1966. We had really hit the bottom two months before—the Braves' bottom for the season, I mean. Almost any other man but John McHale, who was president of the Braves then, would have made his move earlier, played to the fans and changed managers, because the fans were asking for nothing less than Bragan's head on a platter.

McHale, though, was not that kind of man. He had compassion for another human being. He felt he owed Bragan a debt. He said this to a very close friend of mine:

> Bragan went through the throes of hell that last season in Milwaukee. He came to Atlanta with us and did a good job of selling the Braves and the new movement in the South. He has a personality that got through to the people in a public-relations capacity. I know he's stubborn, almost to the point of arrogance. I've told him of specific changes that I wanted made, moves that I

didn't want him to make, and he has gone right out and, almost as if in utter defiance, done the exact opposite of what I had told him.

For instance, we made a trade with Boston last winter for Lee Thomas. We thought that Thomas might be our answer at first base. The Braves have had a problem there since Joe Adcock was traded to Cleveland.

Bragan was starting Thomas, but when a left-handed pitcher would come in, or maybe it wouldn't involve a pitching change at all—he'd just get entangled in a flurry of line-up switches—out would come Thomas. We couldn't determine if he might be our first baseman or not.

Obviously, the Braves decided that he wasn't. Thomas was traded to the Cubs for Ted Abernathy, a submarine ball relief pitcher, in May.

I finally called Bragan in and told him to leave Thomas in the line-up. Just leave him in, no matter what. That very night we're playing Houston, Bragan goes into a line-up juggling act when Houston changes pitchers, and out comes Thomas again, almost as if he's looking up at my box in the Stadium and saying, "Okay, now do you get the idea of who's in charge here?"

Yet McHale bore up under this—and I know what I'm talking about—until it had a lot to do with his authority in the Braves organization. He protected Bragan, and allowed him to go beyond what some of the other members of the executive board felt was a reasonable deadline, and there's no point in avoiding Bill Bartholomay's name here. I think that Bartholomay felt that Bragan should have gone earlier, and that this disagreement in thought is what led to McHale leaving and joining Commissioner Eckert as his assistant later that winter.

I mentioned "hitting the bottom." It happened in the standings on June 3. We were playing the Cardinals in Atlanta. I had a triple and a home run off Bob Gibson—and against Gibson, that's a great day for me. But we lost,

3–2. The defeat dropped us into ninth place. Even the New York Mets were ahead of us. It was June 3, and we were already twelve and a half games out of first place.

That really shook us up as a team. The next day we played a double-header. We were running short of pitchers, so Bragan gambled with Umbach, a soft-spoken Southern kid who had signed a contract for $100,000 but never had come through. On that day, though, Umbach came as near to repaying his debt to the Braves as he ever did. He held the Cardinals to one run until the ninth inning, and Bragan finally had to take him out. Abernathy came on with two men on base and struck out Phil Gagliano and got Bob Skinner on an infield out. We won the game in the bottom of the ninth, 2–1.

Tony Cloninger hadn't pitched a full game since opening night, when he had gone thirteen innings against Pittsburgh in the first regularly scheduled National League game ever played in Atlanta Stadium. In the second game of that double-header on June 3 he beat the Cardinals 4–1, and went all the way.

In other words, ninth place scared the hell out of us, and we put on a move for a little while. Five days later, in fact, I had the biggest day with the bat I'd had in three years. We went to work early on Jack Fisher, who was a big, right-handed pitcher, and beat the Mets in Shea Stadium. The first three Braves got on base, and when I came to bat, I hit Fisher's first pitch over the left-field fence.

It was more than just an ordinary grand-slam home run, if there is such a thing. It was the tenth one I'd hit in the big leagues, and tied me with Ernie Banks for the lead among active players.

The next time I came up I singled, and the time after that I hit another home run. For the day, I drove in 6 runs with the 3 hits, and we needed every one of them to win 7–6. After it was all over, though, and the excitement settled down, a good look at the standings in chilly dawn of the next day showed that we were only in sixth place, eight and one-half games behind the Giants, who were leading the race at the time. We settled back in our old rut, and by the middle of June we were twelve games behind again, and it was pretty certain by that time that the Braves weren't going to knock anybody out of a pennant in 1966.

When Bragan finally got fired, we were on a winning streak—two games. We'd beaten the Dodgers twice in a row, 10–9 the night before McHale called a press conference and announced that Hitchcock was the new manager. Bragan didn't show. Grover Resinger came by, but only in order to resign himself. He was the one coach Bragan had been allowed to hire. The others—Whitlow Wyatt, Ken Silvestri and Hitchcock—he had "inherited."

Paul Richards had just joined the club a couple of weeks before in a sort of an indefinite capacity as McHale's assistant. Bragan said something significant at the time:

"When Richards came to the Houston club, I was soon on my way out. It'll be interesting to see how long I last here now."

Bragan didn't have to spend much time in suspense. He threw out his challenge and he got his answer.

Hitchcock got off to a great start in one of the most emotional games I've ever seen in my life, especially for a ball club in seventh place and going nowhere. A crowd of 52,270 came out to the stadium on the night of August 9 for his debut, but I think the fact that Sandy Koufax was pitching for Los Angeles had more to do with the size of the crowd than Hitchcock's debut. Koufax and Lemaster tied up in a great pitching battle. Until Jim Lefebvre hit a home run in the eighth inning, Lemaster had a no-hitter going. The most remarkable thing about the game was that most of the crowd sat there through a rain delay of two and a half hours, if you can imagine that. It was sort of like they were watching some big history being made, and they weren't going to quit until they got a final result.

When the game started up again, Lefebvre hit his home run. We went into the ninth inning with a tie, 1–1. Felipe Alou had hit a home run leading off the first inning, which seemed like day before yesterday by that time. Alou flied out to open the ninth, and Mathews came up. It had been Bragan's habit to platoon Mathews. He considered him an "out" against left-handed pitching, but Hitchcock stuck with him—as much as anything else, I'd guess, to show that a new policy came with a new leader.

Mathews looked at a ball, then fouled a pitch into the netting. The third pitch he got hold of, and pulled it hard and true down the right-field line and into the stands for one of the most dramatic home runs I've ever seen—and at the ungodly hour of 12:30 in the morning.

The game was ours, 2 to 1.

As a manager and a man, Hitchcock was nothing but a gentleman to me. Peculiar that I should even put it that way, I guess, he being white and me being colored, and both of us being from Alabama. Twenty years ago nobody would have cared what a colored player from Alabama thought about a white manager from Alabama. I say this about Hitchcock though, he and Tebbetts were the only managers who ever fined me. Hitchcock fined me for an incident that took place on a flight from Houston to Los Angeles in the 1966 season.

The plane had just got leveled off, and some of the players—Rico Carty, Mike de la Hoz, Mack Jones and another one or two, were getting a card game set up. I don't even know how I came to get involved in the thing, except to say that I wasn't going to play. Carty said something to me. I said something back, and then he called me the particular kind of S.O.B. I don't choose to be called and I took a punch at him.

It was the kind of thing that was over as quick as it started. Some of the other players broke in and Hitchcock showed up in a flash, and that was it—except for the damage it did to my pocket book.

Hitchcock fined both Carty and me $250. I didn't think it was justified, but then I'm not the manager and he was, and I guess he had to let it be known that he had taken some kind of police action.

It was soon after that, it seems, that Hitchcock began losing some of the respect of the players, and I tell you now that he had come in on a wave of the highest respect. From where I sat on this particular thing, I could see him shrink up before the eyes of a lot of the Braves.

It had to do with one of the players talking back to him in front of other players in a way that no manager should have to stand for. Hitchcock did nothing about it, at least not to the knowledge of the other players.

I've never talked back to any manager. (And that's about the best term I can use for it—"talking back.") The manager has got to be the boss and he's got to let everybody know who's the boss. When Hitchcock let this player get away with that kind of behavior, it cost him in respect.

My personal relationship with Hitchcock was always good. If we ever had any difference at all it was based on something that should have flattered me, I suppose you'd have to say. Hitchcock just never seemed to realize that I could get tired. I think he should have given me more rest at my age, thirty-three, and if he had, I believe I'd have had an even better season than I did in 1967.

He finally did break down in August and let me sit out a couple of games on a hard, ten-day road trip to Los Angeles, back to Houston, then to San Francisco, which is a schedule disaster every National League team has to face each year. If it hadn't been for Bob Kennedy, one of the coaches, I don't think I'd have gotten a rest then.

I was having trouble seeing the ball in Dodger Stadium. It must have been obvious, because Kennedy said something to me about it.

"Is your side hurting you again?" he said. I'd had some pains in my side for a year or two.

"No, I just can't see the ball clear," I said. "It's blurry. I'm just plain tired."

"You mean you're *that* tired?" Kennedy said.

"I'm *that* tired," I said.

"You want me to talk to Billy about it? I can tell him you need a little rest. When?"

"'Now," I said. "Right now. It'll be cooler when we get to San Francisco and I ought to get my vigor back again. I'm just tired all over. I'm thirty-three years old, man.'"

"Henry, I know how old you are, but I'm not going to break out a wheel chair for you yet. I'll talk to Billy."

We lost the first game of the series to the Dodgers. Then Kennedy talked to Billy. The third game was a day game. That morning Billy called me into the little office the visiting managers use in L.A.

"Is your side hurting you again?" That same old question. He couldn't accept the idea that I might be tired and needed some rest. To him it had to be something physical.

"No, Billy, my side isn't hurting me," I said. "I'm tired. Fatigued. That's all."

Really, I hadn't wanted to make too much of it. I remember all the fuss they had in San Francisco when the Giants would let Willie Mays sit out a game. I didn't want that kind of thing buzzing around my head. They'd think I was getting old ahead of my time. So I wasn't going to sit there and point-blank ask Hitchcock for a rest. He made it pretty hard for me to pass the buck back to him.

"Well, I'd rather have a tired Henry Aaron than anybody else in right field," he said. He was really nailing me with psychology, right where my pride lives.

"Anything you say, Billy," I said.

He was quiet for a minute. He sucked on that pipe he always smoked. "Tell you what," he finally said. "I want you to play against Osteen today. You hit Osteen too good to sit this one out. You play against Osteen, then we'll see how it's going. If you still want to rest, I'll give you a rest."

Osteen beat us. I was 1 for 4. The "1" was a home run, but I left several runners on base who could have won the game for us.

The next night Hitchcock rested me. We flew back to Houston. The first game in the Astrodome he rested me. After that I went back into the line-up.

I want you to understand that I wasn't goofing off. At that time I had played more games than any other Brave. I had been in 129 games. Alou had been in 128. Clete Boyer had been in 127. Denis Menke had been in 123. So, at my age, I think I had a right to be tired, especially with such an energy-sapping road trip as that eating away at me. The wear and tear of playing is not so bad. It's those nights of no sleep, or at best, restless sleep sprawled out in a seat in the tourist section of an airplane; then arriving at the next stop at four or five in the morning and not getting to bed before daybreak. That's where the real fatigue comes in. And the older you get, the more you feel the late hours and the loss of sleep. And the less likely, as I pointed out before, that anybody in this game of baseball on the present day scale is to bat .400 in the major leagues.

During the 1967 season, when the Giants were draggling in mid-August, the magazine *Sports Illustrated* carried a story on Willie Mays, who was thirty-six years old by that time and having his troubles at the plate, and they turned on the age theme pretty strong. I'll never forget the description of Willie's condition in the opening paragraph:

His eyes were like road maps—route 1, from San Francisco to Santa Cruz—and the circles beneath them said Willie does not sleep too well at night any more . . . the vigorous "Say Hey" is only a memory. . . .
"These kid pitchers," Willie was saying, "they're so big and strong and throw the ball so hard they make you feel old too soon."

Oo-o-o-o-o-o-o! That's the way the story went, and it made me shudder. I think that maybe that story, that one thing alone, that picture of poor, tired, old, red-eyed Willie, did more to make me conscious of age than anything else, anything that I have seen, done or endured. It made me more conscious of being tired, and so when I felt it I didn't think there was any reason I should apologize for it. So when they asked me, I told them.

The heck of it was, I thought they'd never ask me.

Well, that covers Hitchcock. Now, let me tell you about the best manager I ever played for, and I think he deserves a chapter all his own.

17

BEN GERAGHTY HAD A FACE that came out of a John Wayne western. You know, one of the leathery types who's always standing or sitting in the background in the saloon scenes. Maybe I'd describe it better by saying that it looked like Stan Laurel (of Laurel and Hardy) with a Western accent.

It was a long face, and it came to its end at the point of a big Irish chin. I think that writers would describe him as lantern-jawed.

He had played parts of three seasons in the major leagues, but the way he got started as a player is probably the most interesting thing I know about his past. He was in college at Villanova in Pennsylvania and just disappeared one spring. The next thing his coach knew about him was as the sensation of the Dodgers in spring training in Florida. He opened the season as Brooklyn's regular shortstop, and they tell me he was hitting over .400 at one time.

Pretty soon the pitching caught up with him, though, and his honeymoon was over. That was in 1936. He played a few games during World War II years with the Braves when they were in Boston.

You may remember the crash of that baseball team's bus out West several years ago, when several players were killed and a lot of others were injured? Geraghty was one of the players hurt. He had just reported to the team in Spokane, Washington, to observe and later take over as manager.

160

The people who owned the club were dissatisfied with the manager they had. The manager was killed in the wreck, and this was where Ben got his start as a manager himself, when the team was reorganized.

He had an amazing capacity for beer. The players used to kid a lot about it. "Ol' Ben's keeping the Schlitz brewery working late tonight," they'd say. It did seem to keep one brewery busy to keep Ben supplied with beer. The unusual thing about him, though, was that he never seemed to show the effects of it at all. And above all else, he was a good manager, the best I ever played for.

Maybe I say that because I was so young. I was eighteen when I played for him at Jacksonville in 1953. Maybe I didn't know a good manager when I saw one. Maybe it was because he was so fair and so decent and so concerned with me. Maybe it was because I had a tremendous year playing for him, and any manager would have looked like a good manager. You always remember how great the year was, and everybody concerned with it, when you win a pennant, lead a league in the big things and are the Most Valuable Player. But I've got to believe Ben Geraghty was a good manager, a fine manager.

More than anything else, he knew how to communicate with his players. He was able to handle punishment without causing a rebellion. If you should ask me the first thing that comes to my mind about Ben Geraghty, it would be something that involved punishment.

One night against Savannah, our center-fielder, Horace Garner, and I pulled one of those Alphonse and Gaston acts, as they say on the sports pages. Jacksonville was leading, 5–2, in the eighth inning, and one of the Savannah hitters raised a pop fly back of second. (Remember, I was a second baseman then.) I called for it. Horace called for it. We both kept running, me backing up, Horace coming in like a runaway truck. He was a long, tall guy with two bad knees, but he could run.

We both must have stopped about the same time. The

ball fell in. Two men were out and the bases were loaded, so everybody was running and three Savannah players scored. Eventually, we lost the game 6–5.

When we got inside the clubhouse, Geraghty was waiting for Garner and me. He didn't yell. I can't repeat the language he used in this book, because this is supposed to be for family consumption. But Horace and I heard some choice words that night.

What it boiled down to was that one of us should have caught the ball. "Aaron, any time you have to back up on a ball, and you've got an outfielder who can make the catch coming forward on it, always let the outfielder have the ball," he said, and I am using certain refinements, I guess you'd say. "He can see what kind of play may be in front of him. You're backing up with your head in the air and you can't. You've got to stop and get your bearings. In this case, that wasn't even involved. All we wanted was to get the ball caught and we're out of the inning. But no! You've got to play it like a couple of dumb billy goats."

By the time he was through, he had taken two hours to explain to Garner and me how the play should have been made. Everybody was gone but us and the trainer, Harvey Stone—who, by the way, is now the trainer with the Braves.

That wasn't all. The next day Geraghty had Garner and me out to the park early practicing our co-ordination on pop flies. It made an impression, such an impression that all these years later—that was 1953—it's still sticking in my mind when the name of Geraghty comes up.

It wasn't any easy year for me or for either of the other black players, Mantilla and Garner. We were breaking the color line in the Sally League, and we've gone into that before. The white players lived out around town in Jacksonville, and the black players lived in a boardinghouse—in an opposite section of town, of course.

Ben would come to visit us at our boardinghouse from time to time, just drop in to see that we were living all right. Now and then he'd have a beer with us, and he'd sit and talk. He never talked anything but baseball. Made no difference to me what he talked about. The fact that he was the manager, and the manager had dropped in for a visit with us, meant a lot to me.

One other thing I won't forget about Ben. The Sally League didn't wait until the end of the season to elect the Most Valuable Player. The league sports writers association voted on it in the last weeks of the season. When I got the news that I had been voted the man, the club was playing in Macon.

On the bus back to Jacksonville, Ben slipped into the seat beside me and shook my hand.

"I just wanted to congratulate you again, kid," he said. Sometimes he'd call me "kid" and sometimes he'd call me "Aaron." "Surprised you, huh?"

"Yeah, sure did, Skip," I said.

"Didn't surprise me. I knew it couldn't be anybody else," he said. "You've got a long way to go, Aaron. You've got a great future. You've got a chance to be a real big leaguer. I just want you to know that I believe in you, and that I think you're going to make it all the way. Now, go on and get some sleep." Then he went on back to his seat.

I didn't go to sleep for a while. I looked at the ceiling of that bus, and wondered if Ben ever had any screaming memories of that Spokane bus tumbling down the mountainside as we rode through the South during those long summer nights.

Geraghty never did get to the big leagues to manage. I don't know why. Maybe I was too young to know, and then maybe I wasn't too young and maybe I did know, too. Maybe he didn't wear his clothes too well. Maybe he could have put on a Brooks Brothers suit and still have looked like he had just stepped out of Robert Hall. Maybe he just didn't look like a big-league manager.

He almost made it as a coach. One winter, the Braves decided he ought to be on Fred Haney's staff, but before he ever got there somebody changed signals.

"Ben's great with youngsters; just look at what he has done with our farm clubs in Jacksonville." (Honestly, this guy had a pennant winner or a team that was up there every year, no matter what the Braves sent him to work with. I will admit this: since Atlanta couldn't use blacks in the Southern Association at that time, he did get the advantage of getting all the good black players in the organization.) "It would be a shame to deny the young players in our system the chance to play under him. Therefore, we are promoting him to our triple A farm club at Wichita in the American Association as manager rather than to the less significant post as coach of the Braves."

That's what the announcement said when Ben was transferred from Jacksonville up the ladder. He died in 1962 of a heart attack, in the place that loved him most—Jacksonville. Heart attack or heartbreak?

18

SOME PLAYERS REMEMBER things that happened to them in their careers which make tears run down their cheeks. Me, too—the All-Star Game. When I think of the way I've played in the All-Star Game sometimes it makes me feel so bad I could cry.

Up until 1971, when I hit a home run I had never had an extra base hit in an All-Star contest and that's going back an awful long way. The truth is I played my first All-Star Game in 1955. When it takes you sixteen years to get an extra base hit you have to wonder. If I had to depend on my lifetime All-Star average to get me into the Hall of Fame, I couldn't get inside the city limits of Cooperstown. I've been picked eighteen years running now and the fact that my average in those games is less than .200 is a little disturbing.

This thing never really got to me very much until the first time the game was played in Busch Stadium in St. Louis. The stadium was brand-new. In fact, the Braves had played the Cardinals in the dedication game that year, 1966.

Some of us were in the airport at Lambert Field after the All-Star Game. We had a pretty good wait for our plane, so Donald Davidson, the world's smallest traveling secretary, had decided we might as well go straight to the airport from Busch Stadium and have our dinner there. Everywhere we went, see, even to All-Star games, the Braves sent Donald along as our guide and protector.

It was late afternoon. We had a table by the window, and we could watch the planes take off and land. And we could watch the heat. That's what I mean, watch the heat. It was so hot that day that you could see the heat waves rising from the pavement. I never knew a hotter day in my life. The official temperature was 105. Down on the field it was 116. The St. Louis newspapers said the next day that over four hundred people were treated in the Busch Stadium first-aid room from heat prostration or exhaustion.

I must have been the coolest thing in the place. Once again I managed to un-distinguish myself. I was 0 for 4 again. The National League won the game, 2 to 1, but the only run the American League scored . . . well, I'll let you read it from *The Official Baseball Guide* for yourself:

> With one away in the second, Brooks Robinson smashed a line drive to left field. Aaron had trouble locating the ball against the background of white shirts in the stands. Starting in late, he slipped and the ball skipped by him for a triple.

Robinson scored later.

Now we return to the account in *The Official Baseball Guide:*

> The Nationals caught up against Jim Kaat of the Twins in the fourth inning. Mays led off with a single, his 22nd hit in All-Star competition. Clemente followed with a single, Mays stopping at second. Aaron fouled out. . . .

That was the way it went that day for Aaron.

Maybe the white shirts did bother me. I wasn't conscious of it if they did. It was strange enough to me to be in left field—and I'll get around to that later—and in a strange stadium. I did hesitate, I know that. I can't say why I hesitated.

Anyway, we reached the airport and the blessed air conditioning inside the terminal. We had drawn a pretty good crowd around our table. The only players were Joe Torre and me, the two delegates from the Braves. John McHale was with us, Donald Davidson, of course, some sports writers, and Gabe Paul of the Cleveland Indians just dropped into a chair to say hello.

One of the sports writers pulled out a record book and started thumbing through it, and naturally he came to my record first, and that's one time that having a double-A name is of no advantage.

"Henry," he said, "you don't like All-Star games, do you?"

"What do you mean?" I said.

"Well, I hate to bring up unpleasant subjects, but your lifetime average in the All-Star Game, it says here, is .184," he said.

"It was before I went o for 4 today. Why are you bringing me all this joyful news right now?" I said.

I knew I hadn't done too well in the All-Star Game, but it never really bothered me before. From that time on, though, it has. It has bugged me. It bugs me now. I don't understand it. I don't have jinxes, I don't have slumps. What I mean is, I don't have slumps that get sports writers to wondering if I'm ever going to get another hit and cause everybody in town who ever swung a baseball bat to write letters about secret "cures." If I don't get a hit after a few times at bat, I don't let it throw me into panic.

One of the few slumps I can ever remember, I remember in association with the All-Star Game. It wasn't really what I'd call a slump, but the newspapers did.

It happened in 1958. We were World's Champions. We were supposed to play like World's Champions, but I had a slow time getting out of the box. At the time of the All-Star balloting, I was hitting exactly .258. Yet I was voted onto the All-Star team as a starter.

I hadn't even expected to win a berth as a reserve, and here I was a starter. This was when the team was being selected by players, coaches and managers, and so the vote had a meaning for me. It meant, really, for the first time to me, that I was an established major-league star. I had enough stature at last to be recognized as a baseball player by the men who saw me play every day and knew me best, even if I wasn't getting all the hits that I was supposed to be getting.

The Braves were playing a home stand in Milwaukee at the time I was elected. I didn't get the news until I got to County Stadium that night. Everybody was congratulating me around the clubhouse and out on the field. Fred Haney walked up, put out his hand and said, "Congratulations, All-Star. How do you feel?"

"Surprised as hell," I said. "I couldn't have been more surprised if I had had triplets."

"It shows you what the rest of the league thinks about you, Henry," Haney said. He never said many serious things like that to me, never wasted his time on such sentimental things.

I thought about that. It made me feel good. I know it had something to do with getting me out of that . . . well, call it a slump, then. Anyway, I started hitting like a mad man. I got 11 hits the next thirteen times I went to bat. Three of the 11 hits were home runs. One of them was a grand-slam homer that beat the Dodgers. I was off and flying again.

This shows you that making the All-Star team means something to me. Some players resent it because they could be taking a vacation those three days. Not me. I'm honored to be there. I get keyed up for the game. In fact, maybe I get over-tensed. I feel that on this one occasion every eye in the world is on me.

That line drive that Brooks Robinson hit in the game in St. Louis wasn't really that hard to see. I never thought about white-shirt background until I saw it in *The Official Baseball Guide*. A guy who played left-field regularly would have caught it. I was out there because Walter Alston—he was manager of the National League team that year because the Dodgers had won the pennant the year before—asked me.

Alston came to me before the game, and asked me if I would be willing to play left-field. I said okay, I would, without thinking. Now I wish I hadn't, because of something that came up in Atlanta during the season in 1967. It had to do with Roberto Clemente of the Pirates and me.

The Braves 400 Club, which is a club of baseball boosters, was having one of its regular luncheon meetings at the Marriott Hotel in Atlanta in May. The Pirates were in town for a series, and Clemente was one of the guests. He was sitting on the dais. Sportscaster Milo Hamilton, who is known as the "Voice of the Braves," was the master of ceremonies.

Milo was introducing all the people at the head table. When he came to Clemente, he said, "We all know how great Henry Aaron is, and what he has done, but when it comes to making the All Star team . . . He paused here. Then he went on again.

". . . well, you see who the right fielder was. Here he is, Roberto Clemente."

I wasn't in the audience that day. If I had been, I don't think Milo would have said it. I guess he was sort of like a pitcher trying to slip a gambling pitch by some hitter.

It's over now, and I'm past being irritated about it, but I was burned up at the time. The next day in the *Atlanta Journal,* Wilt Browning, the *Journal's* baseball writer, had this to say about it:

> Henry Aaron was the starting left-fielder for the National League in last summer's [1966] All-Star game, and he's not apologizing to anyone about it.
>
> The Atlanta right-fielder was doing a slow burn before Friday night's game with the Pittsburgh Pirates when he heard that Atlanta play-by-play announcer Milo Hamilton had brought up the subject while introducing Roberto Clemente at Friday afternoon's 400 Club luncheon.
>
> Hamilton referred to Clemente, who started the All-Star game in right-field for the National League, as the greatest in the game today.

Man, in your own town that's pretty tough to take. Milo came to me later and tried to explain it to me.

"You know how I respect you, Henry," he said. "It wasn't

nearly as bad as it was blown up in the newspapers. It was just the way they blew it all out of proportion."

No matter how it was blown up, the words were still there, and I know they did sting. It's true, I didn't start in right field in the game in St. Louis. I've explained that. I could have if I had wanted to. I got more votes than any other player for right field, but when Alston asked me if I minded starting in left field, I didn't mind switching. Same thing happened in the game played at Anaheim in 1967. Alston asked me if I minded starting in center field this time, so he could have an outfield of Lou Brock of the Cardinals, Clemente and me.

You notice who's missing? Nobody less than Willie Mays. Willie was having an off year, and he didn't get any ballots. You think the Giants' announcers were saying in San Francisco that I am the greatest center-fielder in baseball because I was starting and Mays wasn't?

The way I look at it, being asked to play left field or center field has got to be a compliment to me. He didn't ask Clemente. He asked me. That seems to indicate that Alston believes I'm a versatile sort of fellow who can play all three positions better than some others. At least I'm going to accept it that way.

There's another coincidence that hurt some, too. The year on which my first $100,000 salary was based, the year of 1966, I didn't make the seasonal All-Star team. Right field went to Clemente, though I hit 44 home runs and drove in 127 runs. What killed me with the voters at the end of the season was my batting average. That .279 just didn't look like All-Star stuff to them. Clemente won the "Most Valuable Player" ballot. Clemente was the right-fielder.

At the time when Milo Hamilton had his say at the boosters' luncheon, I said some things I wish I hadn't said. I told Wilt Browning, "I wish I'd been there. I would have had to stand up and defend myself, I think."

Well, I wouldn't have, of course. In the first place, that's not my way, and in the second place, I'm not that stupid.

Clemente, in my book, was a great hitter. He had no weakness. He had all the tools, the big bat, the good glove and the great arm. He'd fool you as a hitter; he was a lot stronger than he looked.

He had a batting style that was a little peculiar. He had a little crouch in his stance, and when he swung at the ball, his rear popped out and he looked like he was almost jumping at the ball. He always got a lot of the fat part of the bat on the ball, though, and he hit more and more long balls at the end of his career.

I had an entirely different batting style. I'm more what you'd call a "free swinger"—less than I used to be, but still a "free swinger." When I first came up I was such a "free swinger" that I'd swing at anything that moved and was anywhere around the plate.

Edd Roush, an old outfielder who led the National League in hitting one time himself, and later was voted into the Hall of Fame, spent his springs in Bradenton when the Braves trained there. He worked around the scoreboard and just dabbled around the ball park at odd jobs. He was a great guy and loved to sit and talk baseball.

Right after I first came up, one of the Milwaukee papers talked to Edd Roush about me, the "wild rookie" swinger.

"I've never seen a player with Aaron's ability to swing at bad pitches and convert them into hits," Roush said. "He hits the ball where it's pitched. High over his head, 'way outside or inside, practically in the dirt. I don't believe he knows where the strike zone is."

I'm still a "free swinger" to some extent, but not nearly like I used to be. A pitcher can't be as "dishonest" with me now as he could when I was younger. He's got to get the pitch to me. I'm more willing to take a base on balls than I used to be. When you're not willing to wait, or shop for your kind of pitch, is when you're not getting your base hits. I'm not going to say "slump," because I've already told you I don't believe in that word.

If I've got to make one admission, I've got to say that the only time I've ever really been stirred up about not getting my hits was early in the season of 1966, the Braves' first year in Atlanta. I was struggling. My average slipped to .214. In Milwaukee, it wouldn't have made too much difference, but we were new in Atlanta and people were coming to the park from all over the South expecting Henry Aaron get some hits.

The Houston Astros were in town when I finally broke out of it. We were in a seesaw ball game. The Astros had just tied the score in the top of the ninth inning. In the bottom of the ninth we got something going, and Grady Hatton, the Houston manager, went to his bull pen for a young relief pitcher named Carroll Sembera.

I was the next batter. At the time, I had two hits to show for my last twenty-four times at bat. These people were beginning to wonder if I was a myth, or just the product of some friendly official scorers.

I don't think Sembera took me very seriously, either, because he threw me one of the nicest, fattest fast balls you ever saw. I hit that ball high up in those blue seats in Atlanta Stadium, and from that time on I was out of the ditch. That kid just thought he was going to be able to slip a pitch by me and get out ahead with a strike. It'll happen that way, when you're not getting your hits.

I'm the kind of hitter who depends on his wrists and co-ordination. I hit a ball on top, and it rotates and gives it distance. Willie Mays, on the other hand, swung up on the ball and put the thing in orbit.

Willie was a different kind of hitter, of course. He was a lot stronger than people think, had big, strong shoulders and overpowered the ball. He was a tremendous curve-ball hitter. So was Clemente, with that style of his.

However, the most powerful hitter in the National League, though, is Willie McCovey of the Padres and Giants. He can hit a ball farther than anyone else, but he can be pitched to, also.

I'm not able to stand up for my All-Star Game record, though, I regret to say. I said before that I feel a real tenseness in the All-Star Game, feel all those eyes on me, and

I feel the impressiveness of being there with all those great players in both leagues. I want to make it clear right here, though, that the All-Star Game isn't a "choking" game to me. I don't quit hitting when the moment is big and the issue is pressing, and I think I can prove that to you.

I'll use my World Series record to make that point. My lifetime batting average in the World Series is .364. I've played in fourteen games, hit 3 home runs and driven in 9 runs and never made an error, playing both center field and right field, and I think that's defense enough of my record under pressure.

19

New Year's Eve came on a Saturday in 1966. One of my neighbors, Joe Kennedy, a schoolteacher, was driving into Milwaukee to the GEX store to pick up some things for a party. I went along just for the ride. On our way out of the store, he picked up a copy of the afternoon paper. He got a glimpse of Eddie Mathews' picture, and said, "Say, there's Mathews. Wonder what he's done?"

Then he answered his own question. "Holy mackerel! He's been traded!"

I was shocked. "Traded!" I said. "You're kidding me. They wouldn't trade Mathews."

"Well, they wouldn't but they have. See?"

He handed me the paper. There it was:

Atlanta, Ga.—(AP)—Third baseman Eddie Mathews, dean of the Atlanta Braves, was traded to the Houston Astros today for pitcher Bob Bruce, outfielder Dave Nicholson and a minor league player to be named later.

The trade took everybody by surprise, including Mathews himself. He learned the news when telephoned in his Milwaukee home by an Atlanta newspaperman for his reaction. Paul Richards, who is President John McHale's special assistant, made the announcement from Dallas, Tex., near his home in Waxahachie. . . .

I couldn't believe it. "They didn't even let him know he was going to be traded," I said to Joe.

He was driving the car. I sat and watched the street

markers go by—West Chestnut, Lovers Lane, West Capitol, North 76th and on toward Mequon. I sat and watched the street markers and, man, try as hard as I could, I couldn't imagine the Braves without Eddie Mathews. We'd been together a long time, from 1954 to 1966.

I remembered the first time I really ever heard much about him. It was during that winter I played in Puerto Rico. Bob Buhl pitched on the Caguas team with me, and he was Mathews' roommate on the Braves. Buhl came into the dugout one day when some of the American players were talking about wrists and hitting, and he said, "You talk about wrist action, you never saw any wrist action until you see Mathews. This guy has such snap in his wrists he can make up his mind to swing at the last minute and pop one out of the park."

Buhl wasn't talking to me, but I was listening and thinking. I just wanted to be up there in the big leagues some day with that guy, meaning Mathews. That's what I was thinking.

There was something that came to make it seem like home to me, seeing that "41" on his back in the batter's box before me, or in the waiting circles back of me. This was an act that had been going on for a pretty good while with pretty good results.

Our best act was the home run. I wish I knew how many times we have hit them one after the other. I do know that late in the season of 1965 we established a peculiar home-run record together. We hit our 794th home run as teammates, and that was one more than Babe Ruth and Lou Gehrig hit as teammates on the Yankees. The National League record was 745, held by Gil Hodges and Duke Snider when they were Dodgers.

Funny thing about that Ruth-Gehrig record: we broke it sometime early in the month of September, 1965, but it was right at the end of the season before somebody discovered it. I never have seen in print which one of us broke it, when he broke it or who the pitcher was. But I know we've got it. I know that I hit my last 2 that season off Juan Marichal in the same game, and that Mathews and I both had 32 for the season. When he left for Houston, we had 864 home runs between us as teammates, and that's where the record stands until our paths cross again, and heaven knows I don't want that to happen unless he becomes a Brave again.

I'll admit, when he was traded, it gave me a lot of things to think about. I thought about a lot of them as Joe Kennedy and I drove along that afternoon on the way home from the GEX store.

"Why hadn't they called Mathews in and given him a chance to make a deal for himself?"

"If they didn't want him for third base, then why not give him a chance to play first, pinch-hit and fill in maybe as a coach? After all he had been to the Braves, from Boston to Milwaukee to Atlanta, didn't he deserve better treatment than this?"

"And what would happen to a certain right-fielder named Henry Aaron when the time came that the Braves decided they couldn't use him any more?"

Some of the thoughts made me shudder. I want to finish my career as a Brave, and I want the organization to know that I want to finish my career as a Brave. I don't want to wake up one morning and find the papers carrying a big, black headline that says, "BRAVES TRADE AARON."

Fans associate a player with a certain team after he has played with that team for so many years. Can you imagine Stan Musial as anything but a Cardinal? Or Mickey Mantle anything but a Yankee? Well, I don't want anybody imagining Henry Aaron as anything but a Brave. I remember last winter, after he'd won the Triple Crown in the American League his first year as a Baltimore Oriole, people would start talking to me about Frank Robinson, and they would say, "Oh, he had a great year for Cincinnati, did he?"

To them, Frank Robinson was still a Cincinnati player because he had been a Red so long.

Trades are a part of baseball, and I recognize that as one

of the risks of the business. But there are some players you just don't trade. The Cardinals would never have traded Musial. The Red Sox would never have traded Ted Williams. I hope that by this time I'm pretty close to the same status with the Braves. Not an "untouchable" exactly, but a fellow who's established such an identity with the team that when people think of the Braves they think of Henry Aaron.

During the summer of 1967 the Braves signed a young pitcher from Charlotte, North Carolina, named Gary Hill. The kid came to Atlanta to work out with the big team before he reported to a farm club, and his father came with him. He wanted to meet me.

You know what he told me? "I've been a traveling man all my life," Mr. Hill said. "The Braves have always been my team, and when I think of the Braves I always think of Spahn, Mathews and Aaron."

I liked that. It made me feel good. It made me feel like a part of the image. But of course I couldn't help remembering what had happened to those other two names, Spahn and Mathews. There's a story that goes with both of them, though.

Spahn had every chance to stay with the Braves, first as one of the team radio broadcasters, then as a roving pitching coach. The way it came to me, John McHale offered him a job when the Braves thought it was time for Spahn to retire. After all, he was forty-three years old and he had had a record of 6 and 13 with an ERA of 5.28 the season before, and when a fellow has reached the age of forty-three, I'd say he has given it a pretty good run, it's time to hang it up, and when you are given the chance to move into something soft like Spahn was, you can't lay too much blame on the club. I think the Braves were fair with Spahn. I think he blew it himself. His record the next season with the Giants and Mets proved the Braves were right. He was through.

Mathews? Well, after I cooled down some and got to thinking about it with some of the details clear in my mind, it didn't come out as bad as it did the first time I got the news. If nothing else, the Braves gave Eddie a chance to play out the last dregs of his career indoors, on a carpet under the Astrodome in Houston. His salary, about $60,000, was protected. He was going to get a chance to play first base, and that ought to add some years to his baseball life. That wasn't too bad a fate, the more I thought about it.

Finally, about two weeks after the deal, I telephoned Eddie.

"Hello, Astro," I said.

"Who the hell is this?" he said.

"Hank." He always called me Hank, and I called me Hank when I talked to him.

"Oh, how are you doing, Hank? I thought I'd have heard from you before now."

"I'm doing all right. How you doing?"

"The shock has worn off now, Hank, but It was a real shock at first," he said. "'The Houston club has offered me the same contract I had in Atlanta, and they've told me they'll play me at first base. So I feel pretty good."

"First base?" I said. "Man, that's a rocking-chair job. That's where they put those fielders they can't hide, isn't it? That's a lazy man's job."

Eddie just laughed. By the time we finished talking I was pretty certain that he wasn't ripped up about it any more. That's when I quit feeling sorry for him and reasoned, after all, that it probably was for the best. He'd get a chance to play regularly in Houston. He wouldn't have in Atlanta, because the Braves had already traded with the Yankees for Clete Boyer.

As it turned out, all the rhubarb turned into roses for Eddie. He was traded to Detroit during the season, and wound up in the middle of the American League pennant race until the last day of the season.

Nevertheless, I still want to wind up my playing days as a Brave. Then what?

That's a question I've been asking myself a little more often lately. Hardly anybody else ever asks me about it. I guess they think I can go on playing forever. During the winters now I have been selling insurance around Milwaukee. I worked for the Prudential Life Insurance Company, and I've done pretty well at it. I led my division in sales the first year I was with the company. I've qualified for a license to sell insurance in Georgia since then, but a lifetime of selling insurance isn't for me.

Some ball players make investments during their playing years that set up careers for them when they're through on the field. Ernie Banks owns a Pure Oil service station in Chicago. Tim McCarver took a page out of Stan Musial's book and is part-owner of a big restaurant in Memphis. Duke Snider went into land investment in California and now has a big avocado grove—or orchard, or whatever you call a bunch of avocado trees—out there. Warren Spahn kept buying up property in Oklahoma until he now has a big ranch out near Hartshorne. Smoky Burgess invested in an automobile agency in North Carolina.

My personal experiences in outside investments haven't been very many or very good. In the first place, I'm not the thriftiest guy in the world. I'm no spendthrift, but I'm not the kind with the magic touch. I'm not always coming up with something that's going to turn my money into more money. The only outside property I own now is forty acres of land down in Alabama, close to Mobile. My brother Tommie has twenty acres of land adjoining my forty, and we talk about some day doing something with it.

I've been approached since I've been a major-league ball player by all kinds of characters with all kinds of investment schemes. Most of them are interested in using my money and my name, and they'll generously furnish their brain and donate some time to a project that "simply can't miss."

I learned my lesson early about that sort of thing, and I paid a price for it. In the first place, I don't want my name hanging over some saloon or bowling alley or even a restaurant, unless it's something of quality. I didn't take a stand on that principle soon enough, though.

During my second year in Milwaukee, this fellow came to me with a proposition. He wanted to open a lounge to be called "Hank Aaron's Place."

"It won't cost you a penny," he said. "All I want to do is use your name and you'll have a share in the business and you'll get a share of the profits. We'll decide later how we'll cut up the profits."

It sounded as easy as picking up money on a sidewalk to me. If I had been older, though, I would have known better. I would have known that somebody on a sound business basis just doesn't come offering you something for nothing. Anyway, just a few days before "Hank Aaron's Place" was supposed to be opened, John Quinn called me in to the Braves' front office.

"What's this about you going into business?" he asked.

"That's right, Mr. Quinn. This fellow"—we'll call him Tom—"and I are going to open this lounge," I said. To show you how thorough I had been about it, I couldn't even tell John Quinn the address.

"How well do you know this man, Henry?"

"I just met him at the ball park. He came out to see me one day and we talked about it."

"Have you signed any papers?"

"Yeah, I signed something. I don't remember what it was."

"You mean you didn't read it? You didn't consult a lawyer about it? You didn't talk to anybody about it?"

"No. This guy looked all right to me."

Quinn threw up his hands and then let them plop on his desk top. "Henry, in the first place you owe it to the ball club to check out such things as this, and in the second place, you owe it to Henry Aaron to check it out. Now, give me this man's name and how I can reach him."

Quinn got in touch with Tom. It turned out that this place

that was about to become "Hank Aaron's Place" had been raided two or three times under other ownership. That was the reason it was available. It had a bad name and was, in short, a "joint." Quinn moved in and cut the whole thing off at the pass, but the contract was still there and I would have been stuck except for one thing. "Hank Aaron's Place" didn't open on the day it was scheduled to open, violating one of the clauses, and when Tom's end of the contract was broken, Quinn found a way out of it for me.

That wasn't the one I paid the price for in hard cash, though. That one came a little while later, and in my own hometown, Mobile.

In Mobile, Davis Avenue is known as an "exclusive black residential district." I had this idea—all on my own—of going into this building that I had seen vacant for several years and establishing a shoe outlet on Davis Avenue. I signed a five-year lease on the property, but I signed too soon. I couldn't get a contract with the shoe company I wanted. Then I decided to switch to a laundromat. Everybody was going hot for laundromats in those days, and all the reports were that they were becoming fabulously wealthy. Then I found out there was a lot of fiction involved in those tales. Then I decided I wasn't going to live in Mobile, anyway, but that I was going to settle in Milwaukee, so I dropped the whole thing.

There was just one little item left hanging—the five-year lease. The man who owned the building wrote me and wanted his money. I still wasn't too smart about business affairs, and I wrote back that since I wasn't going to use his building and it was vacant anyway, I didn't think that I owed him any money.

Well, the next time I visited Mobile, I also had a visitor. This deputy sheriff showed up at our house with a notice for me, telling me to pay up or else. My mother was horrified. I was scared. I called a lawyer who was a great friend of the Braves while we were in Milwaukee, Harry Zaidens. The man was asking $15,000 settlement. Harry took over from there and finally got it down to $5,000.

That's what it cost me, $5,000 to settle out of court, and I swore then and there, no more get-rich schemes for me, at least not until I had a lawyer check everything out for me.

There's no doubt about what I'd like to do in the future, the way I'm thinking now. I'd like to stay in baseball and I'd like to stay with the Braves, either as a hitting instructor, or a coach, or anything that would keep me in uniform. No indoor stuff for me. No front office. None of that politics. I've seen too much of it to want to get involved.

I'm not going to try to show a great big bundle of gratitude and say that I want to stay in baseball because it has been good to me, and because of what it has done for me, and because I think I owe the game something. We've gone this road together, baseball and me, and it has done something for me and I think that I have done something worthwhile for baseball, and anything else that I would try to say would be a lot of hogwash. I want to stay in baseball because I love it, because it is the one business I know, and because the living is good in baseball.

Undoubtedly, the question will come up about my ambitions as a manager. The answer is: yes, I'd like to manage.

I've thought a lot about it. I haven't talked a lot about it because hardly anybody has ever asked me about it. It's in the back of my mind, though, and has been the last few years to the point that I've been paying closer attention to the managers I've played for, the way they handle a ball club and the mistakes they've made. They say that the best way to learn to manage is on losing ball clubs. That way you can learn more about what not to do. I've not been underprivileged along that line, I must say.

I don't know if I'm smart enough to be a manager or not. Men a lot smarter then I am have failed at it. As I said before, I don't think I've ever seen men who knew more baseball than Bobby Bragan or Charlie Dressen, and they always seemed to be looking for a job. On the other hand, I've seen men who weren't nearly as smart as they were succeed as managers, mainly because they knew how to get along with players and handle men. This is something I'd have to find out about myself.

I've always been able to get along with the other players. I can't think of a real, full-fledged, twelve-gauge enemy I've got in the world.

I can think of only one ball player who doesn't care a lot for me, but that doesn't put me in a class by myself. He never appeared to like a lot of other people, and the feeling apparently was mutual.

Our mutual dislike grew out of an incident that took place when we were teammates and the Braves were playing in Philadelphia a few years ago. We were waiting out a rain delay by playing some cards in the clubhouse. This fellow, a big outfielder no longer in the National League, accused me of cheating. I don't cheat in the first place, and in the second place, you didn't have to cheat to beat him. He just wasn't a good card player.

I finished the hand and quit the game. I wasn't going to sit there arguing when the intention was to have fun, mainly, and to kill time, anyway. I started out of the clubhouse and all of a sudden this Coca-Cola bottle splattered around me. He had thrown it at me from across the clubhouse.

Well, naturally, something further developed. I laid into him. Some of the players later swore that I yanked his tongue out of his mouth so far that it looked like he was wearing a red necktie. I wasn't conscious of it if I did. Somebody ran for Charlie Dressen, who was our manager then, and he came in and broke it up. I wasn't fined, which appears to establish my innocence in the proceedings.

Having or not having enemies, I grant you, doesn't say you are or are not managerial material. I think that the ability to get along with others is basic. I'd surely start off in the minor leagues, anyway, and get plenty of practice at getting along with men before I ever got a chance in the majors—if I ever did.

I don't think my color would have anything to do with

my success or failure as a manager. I honestly feel that. Athletes accept or reject another athlete or a leader on the basis of what he can or cannot do, not on any peculiarity about his physical being or his color.

20

I don't go up there swinging for the fence every time I go to bat. I like the feel of a home run. It does have a special feel, too. You can almost tell when one leaves your bat. Not every time will the feel be true. Sometimes you hit a "home run" that hangs in the wind and gets caught, or "hooks" like a golf ball and goes foul. But you still get the feel that when it left the bat it was a home run.

I never really got home-run conscious until the Braves moved to Atlanta. Then I think newspaper talk had something to do with that. The winter before we played our first season in Atlanta, John McHale, who was president of the Braves then, called a press conference to announce that I had signed a contract for $75,000 for 1966, the most any Brave had ever made up to that time.

As baseball men will do on occasions like this, they'll say what a great man the player he has just signed is. I remember when I was fresh in Milwaukee I went to a baseball writers' dinner during the winter. I had been voted the Braves' Rookie of the Year, and Lou Perini made the presentation.

You never heard such a mess of adjectives. I was beginning to wonder if he wasn't about to introduce the father of our country. Or Booker T. of the Washington clan, at least.

"This young man is one of the bright new stars of the game," he said, "one of the great right-handed hitters. He

185

is an all-around player, one we're proud to have in our Braves organization. . . ."

And he went on and on. I hadn't signed a contract for the next season yet. I had played the first season for $8,000. That was a lot of money to me, but listening to Mr. Perini I began to think of bigger figures. Charlie Grimm was sitting next to me, and I turned to Charlie and said, "Does he mean all that before I sign or after I sign?"

In the Atlanta press conference, John McHale mentioned that the Braves valued me highly and were proving it, and then threw the floor open for questions. One of the first was about home runs.

"Henry, knowing how the ball carries in Atlanta Stadium, do you expect to be swinging more for the home run down here?" Dave Moffitt of United Press International asked me.

I gave him a stock answer. "I don't ever go up there swinging for home runs. I swing to meet the ball. I want a base hit. If it goes out of the park, then I got a real good base hit. If it goes over the bag at second base, I got me a real good single." That kind of answer.

But that question got me thinking. "These people down here are expecting me to hit home runs," I said to myself. And when the season started I went to bat thinking that these people expected me to hit home runs. I don't think there's any doubt that to a fan the biggest thrill in baseball is the sight of a home run traveling out of the park. We were moving into a new territory. We needed to give the new fans all the thrills we could, and if I didn't hit a lot of home runs, I'd be a flop to them. They expected me to hit home runs, so I swung for home runs.

I hit home runs, but it cost me. I started the season in a slump . . . oops, forgot. Anyway, I started the season not hitting well at all. I don't have to look at the averages to tell when I'm hittting the ball the way I like to. I look at my right shoe. It's worn from dragging it when I move into the ball the way I should.

I never got my average back up to where it should be. But I did accomplish something I wanted to accomplish my first season in Atlanta. I wanted to lead the league in home runs and runs batted in, and I did. I drove in 127 runs—the seventh season I've had 120 or more—and I hit 44 home runs, which ties my own personal record. But that average, I couldn't get it up to save my soul, and I was never anybody's threat for the Triple Crown.

Of all the home runs hit in Atlanta Stadium—207 flew out of there by actual count during the regular 1966 National League schedule—one that was hit by another Aaron has more historical significance than any of mine. My younger brother Tommie hit the first home run in the history of the place.

The Braves, while still in Milwaukee, stopped in Atlanta on the way north in the spring of 1965 and played Detroit three exhibition games. In the first inning of the first game ever played in the new stadium, Tommie hit one of Hank Aguirre's pitches into the left-field stands. Tommie got his peculiar kind of place in history, but he never has been able to get a break with the Braves, and that brings up about the only real, lasting disappointment I've ever had in baseball.

Tommie is about four and a half years younger than me. We were never particularly close when we were little boys because of the age difference. Then I left home when I was still a child, and after that, all I've been doing is moving about, so I hadn't seen much of him until the Braves signed him to a contract in 1958 and sent him to Eau Claire, Wisconsin, where I broke in.

Since that time I've looked forward to the day that we would play together on the same team in the major leagues. There aren't enough of us Aarons playing baseball to threaten the Alous' act—Felipe, Jesus and Matty—but there would be a lot of family pride in knowing that two of the Aaron family members are capable of being big-league ball players. For a season, it was so. Tommie worked his way up from Eau Claire to Jacksonville, then to Cedar Rapids, Louisville and to Austin, and finally made it to the Braves in 1962. He played in 141 games but was in and out of the line-up.

Occasionally we roomed together, but you know how brothers are. You want to know the other one is around, but you don't want to be too close, unless there's trouble. Then you get as close as the fur on a cat's back. In fact, the only time I can remember that we roomed together, trouble developed.

The Braves were in St. Louis at the Chase Hotel. Tommie had already left the room to check out. I heard this "poof!" noise, saw smoke coming out of the air conditioner, and all of a sudden the room was on fire. I barely had time to get his bags out of the room. A lot of my clothes were still unpacked and were damaged. Something in the air conditioner blew up. I never stayed around for a full report.

Afterword

In the six seasons that have passed since this book was first published, Henry Aaron has lived another lifetime. To be impeccably up-to-date, he is no longer "rf" but has since been "1b" and now is "lf," having removed himself to this outfield haven in deference to an arm that is now forty years old and fading.

He is, as this is written, boring in on the Holy Grail of baseball, Babe Ruth's lifetime record of 714 home runs. His face has become one of the most familiar in sport, his name one of the most often spoken. His personality, once concealed beneath a natural layer of blandness, has been squeezed out, like toothpaste from a tube, onto sports sections, magazine pages, television screens and radio frequencies.

Those whose name and fame overshadowed his have now been overshadowed. Willie Mays, Joe Namath, Mickey Mantle, Muhammad Ali, Wilt Chamberlain, Arnold Palmer, Johnny Unitas, Jack Nicklaus, and the old ones who have passed out of view before them, such as Ted Williams and Stan Musial.

The new portion of Aaron's story would probably best be entitled "The Emergence." Without the instrument of the home-run record he would have gone through his major league career admired, applauded politely, interviewed infrequently, exercised in the proper successions of grooming

189

for the Hall of Fame at Cooperstown, but always the kind of whom it is written and said, "How sad it is that he couldn't have played in New York." In the agony of assuming his position in the respect and the adulation of Americans and non-Americans, the most refreshing reward is that they have come to know him as he really is. Not a Willie Mays running out from under his hat, making the catch with a toreador's flourish, talking incessantly in the locker room for the scrounging interviewers, flashing the smile and doffing the cap for a stadium filled with spectators gushing back. Through it all, the intrusions and the discourtesies of the brash, Aaron has remained constant, unflappable, accessible and pleasant. Perhaps as remarkable a feat as the record-crashing chase itself.

The New York Times dispatched a general news reporter to Atlanta to flush out the unflushed sensations that *The Times* in all its pompous wisdom reasoned must surely lurk somewhere back there in the recesses of Aaron's life. The reporter spent several days, enjoyed the privilege of visits to Aaron's apartment, nearly lived in his pocket, on field and off, and then reached a humbling conclusion.

"This man is a helluva man. He is really what he seems to be."

At one stage of Aaron's career, Mickey Mantle spoke of him with a certain reverence. "Aaron was to my time what Joe DiMaggio was to the era when he played." It sounds a little heavy for Mantle, but things are different now. DiMaggio became a hero in the age of the hero. Aaron has defied the age of the anti-hero and become one anyway.

The door to Room 216 was wide open. A blur of noises came forth with voices, punctuated by laughter and the slap of playing cards against a background of the Supremes, who were still in their original form in March, 1968. Ramada Inn on the Golf Course was spring training headquarters for the Atlanta Braves, no more than a short jog from West Palm Beach Municipal Stadium.

Henry Aaron was the registered tenant in 216, and his

room somehow became a gathering parlor each spring for the young black Braves, some who were rookies, others who had been around a little, like Tommie Aaron and Ralph Garr. The door seemed to be open always and Henry made them feel welcome, never holding court, never monitoring, only offering his company and the use of a tape deck. The guests gathered on one of the beds and played cards. Hearts was their game.

When the 1968 season began Aaron had hit 481 home runs, and 714 seemed an infinity away, but even then calculating minds had him aimed on a collision course with the ghost of Babe Ruth. Comparisons were beginning to spring forth.

Based on tales handed down of the big man, it was impossible to imagine him holding open house in his spring training room. Take yourself back forty years, to St. Petersburg, Fla., where the New York Yankees took their spring purging. Try this imaginary scene! The door flung open, Ruth sprawled across a bed, surrounded by younger Yanks and some rooks—Ben Chapman, Dusty Cooke, Jimmy Reese, Lyn Lary or Joe Glenn—playing cards, rollicking about and listening to the latest dance tunes of Eddie Duchin and his orchestra on a Victrola, or maybe by remote control broadcast direct from the Casino on the Park at the Essex House in New York City.

It would not happen. In 1968 the lines of comparison between the two men were faint, but they were already being drawn, the one whose home runs had "saved" baseball and the one who was encroaching on his lifetime record. Ruth and Aaron were alike only in that both were born under the astrological sign of Aquarius, both played baseball, both hit home runs in abundant numbers and both played right-field. (Ruth began as a pitcher and Aaron later would be a first baseman and a left-fielder.) Otherwise, they were as dissimilar as east and west, black and white.

Resentment of anyone, Aaron in particular, welled up later as he homed in on the figure of 714, but mainly in the

breasts of old-timers who insisted that the Babe should re-
main immune to such effrontery.

"Look at how many more times he has been to bat than
Ruth," the protestors would write. That's true. Through the
1973 season Aaron had batted nearly 3,000 times more
than Ruth. Are points not allowed for durability and clean
living?

"Ruth wasted five years as a pitcher," was another familiar wail. "Wasted" is hardly the word. He won 92 games
and for many years held the record for most consecutive
scoreless innings pitched in the World Series.

One fellow resorted to whimsy. "If Aaron hits 715 home
runs, let him hit 715 home runs," he wrote. "He'll never be
another Babe Ruth. He won't win 92 games pitching."

Aaron himself made a valiant attempt at placing it in
perspective. He seemed uneasy in this situation in which he
found himself cast as the villain. "Babe Ruth will still be
the best, even if I pass him," he said. "Even if I'm lucky
enough to hit 715 home runs he will still be known as the
greatest home-run hitter who ever lived."

Nothing, however, would ever put the issue to rest, even
as the great moment approached in 1973.

The seasons between 1968 and 1972 brought one high
moment to the Braves as a team. In September, 1969, they
charged out of a lethargy that became characteristic of their
behavior in their new surroundings of Atlanta and crashed
into the National League playoffs, winning the Western
Division title by three games. Otherwise, their existence
could be justified only, it seemed, in that they provided a
stage for Aaron. Some resentment festered on this point.
How dare this man Aaron go on hitting home runs while
the rest of the Braves slopped along in a mire of sloven fin-
ishes? That was the preposterous attitude of the snipers.

As the seasons moved on, and as Aaron systematically
clipped off one record after another, from "Most Years Appearing in 150 Games or More" to "Most Total Bases," he

began to congeal before the public in his proper image. Aaron had always played in the shadow of the flamboyant Willie Mays, who filled in what personal career gaps needed filling in by his own naive charm.

Only grudgingly did Mays give ground to Aaron, the man whose supremacy was not going to be denied by anything short of injury or poor health. Once, when Aaron was within approximately 15 home runs of Mays' lifetime total a reporter asked Willie:

"Do you think Aaron can break Babe Ruth's record?"

Eyes snapping, Willie fired back: "He's got to catch me first."

It was inevitable and Mays knew it, but he wasn't surrendering one jewel out of his crown. Aaron breezed by him in the summer of '72, striking 34 home runs while Willie hit but eight. At the end of the year the gap was 673 to 654, Aaron's favor.

"All that did, when Willie said 'he's got to catch me first,' " Aaron said, "was give me a little added incentive. I was in no fight with Willie. I wasn't after anybody's record. All I wanted to do was do the best I could for Aaron. After he said that, though, I was consciously trying a little harder."

Try as hard as he could in 1968, Aaron could NOT get his home-run machinery tuned up and humming. It was a near disaster as one looks back now and relates it to the campaign for 715. He stole almost as many bases (28) and he hit home runs (29). Only once since his third season in the major leagues had he fallen before the figure of 30, and even that year, 1964, his average had held up to an elegant .324.

He played long and hard, 160 games, 606 times at bat, but drove in only 86 runs, his lowest total since his rookie season in Milwaukee, and his batting average slipped to .287, virtually a slum area in the records of Henry Aaron.

"Did you have an idea you were seeing the caution light?" I asked him. "You know, the warning that you were peaking out?"

"Playing 160 games? Stealing 28 bases? "After all, I was only thirty-four years old. I could still run. I could still throw. What happened was, I was a sitting duck in the batting order that season. Rico Carty missed the whole season with tuberculosis. Clete Boyer had an off year. He had hit 26 home runs the year before and he followed that up with four. Joe Torre hit only 10 and Felipe Alou only 11. We all seemed to have gotten together and decided to have bad years at the same time."

It was not a season of total waste, however. Another of his milestones was reached in the oppressive heat of Sunday afternoon, July 14. After being hung up on No. 499 for a week, Aaron finally lifted his 500th home run over the left-field fence off Mike McCormick of San Francisco with two runners on base in the third inning. It was more than merely a blow for legend. It also won the game, 4–2.

Throughout the week, Bill Bartholomay had sat ready in a box by the Braves dugout, a trophy in hand to present to Aaron commemorating the occasion. At each game the president came, and at each game he sat and waited, and as Aaron finally trotted around the bases while the message board flashed "500" "500" "500," the club's chief executive got the chance to move into his act. He met his most treasured employe at the plate, and as they met Aaron said apologetically, "I'm sorry, Bill, I kept you waiting so long. I know there are other things you need to be doing."

"Can you imagine that?" Bartholomay said. "Apologizing for being late with his 500th home run."

There was little celebration afterward. Aaron has the lowest party average in the major leagues. There was even a touch of remorse. Aaron's father, Herbert, a shipyard employe in Mobile, Ala., had been in the park three days waiting for the moment. He'd left for home Sunday morning, went back to his job, and missed his son's feat.

There was a touch of class for which to be grateful. Mike McCormick had won the Cy Young Award the year before. Aaron was happy he'd hit the shot off a pitcher of prestige.

"Somehow it means a little more when you hit it off a Cy Young winner."

If the wait for No. 500 was agonizing, the wait for No. 501 was twice as bad. Twelve days passed before he finally hit that one off Grant Jackson in Philadelphia. Home runs then became scarcer and scarcer. By the All-Star break he had hit 19. He finished up with 29. He couldn't remember a more miserable finish.

One of the Braves' pitchers who had a reputation for popping pills and throwing so hard he fell on his face slipped up to Aaron and asked him, "How'd you like to pop a greenie or two, Henry? It might snap you out of it?"

Aaron laughed. "I'm scared of those things." He thought the pitcher was kidding.

"You might find out where your long ball has gone."

"Look," Aaron said, "I tried those things one time in my life. One pill. You know how hot it is in St. Louis? We were playing the Cards at old Busch Stadium. I thought just one little pill might pep me up on one of those miserable Sunday afternoons.

"I popped it. I went out for batting practice. I started feeling so bad I thought I was having a heart attack. My heart started beating so hard I could see it through two shirts."

So much for drug abuse.

The natives refused to be downhearted or spiteful for Aaron's futility. On August 23 they rallied around him. Atlanta turned out for a "Henry Aaron Day" at Atlanta Stadium. The family gathered around him, Gaile, Henry Jr., Larry, Dorinda and his then wife, Barbara, and many flattering remarks were made and gifts were passed; after which the guest of honor showed proper appreciation by hitting home run No. 504 off Rick Wise of Philadelphia.

The 1968 season opened another door to Aaron. One of opportunity and self-preservation, it may have seemed. All of his major-league life he had been considered in terms of right-field. That was his personal kingdom. As previously established, he resented any infringement by Roberto Clemente, or any other man carrying a bat and wearing a glove. He had come to the Braves a second baseman, played one whole World Series in center-field (because Billy Bruton was injured), but "Aaron, rf" was the man's baseball trademark.

First base became a plagued position with the Braves that season. It was like a revolving door at rush hour. They had traded the previous winter for Deron Johnson, giving Cincinnati outfielder Mack Jones, later the rage of Montreal, ultilityman Jim Beauchamp, later to help the New York Mets to the 1973 pennant, and pitcher Jay Seay Ritchie, a journeyman who spelled out his initials, for a twenty-nine-year-old who only three seasons earlier had led the league in runs-batted-in. It seemed they were about to cure what ailed them at a position which had given them trouble ever since they had arrived from Milwaukee.

They hadn't. Johnson hit less than .200 for most of the season. Desperately, manager Luman Harris turned in all directions. Tommie Aaron, Henry's younger brother, tried it. He could handle the glove fanciiy, but his bat was not meant for daily play. Tito Francona, the old American Leaguer, had a few flings. Joe Torre was perfectly at home there, but was needed behind the plate. That was no solution either, for Torre, who did not get along with general manager Paul Richards, was on his way out of Atlanta in the first decent exchange that could be made, which turned out to be for Orlando Cepada of St. Louis the next spring.

On August 15, Aaron was given an audition at first base when the Braves played an exhibition game with their farm club at Richmond, Va. On August 28, playing the second game of a doubleheader against the Phillies, Aaron's name appeared on the lineup card as the first baseman.

"Not bad," he said in the clubhouse after the game. "I may like it over there. I know I've got a lot to learn. You know what they say, that the legs are first to go, and this ought to be easier on the legs and the wear-and-tear."

Aaron played 14 games at first base that season, but with

Cepeda in town playing a dramatically slashing first base and hitting well, the project was put aside the next two seasons. As the 1971 season came around, Cepeda's old knee problems recurred and the Puerto Rican, following his finest season as a Brave, was healthy only about half the time. Aaron was the first baseman in 71 games. He would never make the world forget Hal Chase, or even Ferris Fain.

During the off-season Aaron's new future jelled. "We've got several young outfielders, Henry," Paul Richards told him, "Dusty Baker, Ralph Garr, Mike Lum and Oscar Brown, and Carty should be ready to play again." (Carty had been recovering from a dreadful accident to his knee that cost him another full season.) "We'd like for you to consider playing first base next season. We don't know what Cepeda's condition is going to be. Either one of his knees is liable to go any day."

Aaron went for it. Bill Bartholomay didn't, not with any enthusiasm, but consented, with reservations to allow his $125,000 investment—Aaron's salary had increased after the expiration of the $100,000 contract—to take up the new station. It was a move that fell just short of disaster. Not to mention that it created a breach between Aaron and Cepeda, who was later traded to Oakland.

"I don't know whatever gave me the idea I was a first baseman," Aaron said, "And I don't know who ever thought first base was a good place for an old man to retire to. A fellow can get killed playing there, and I damn near did.

"Sonny Jackson throws a ball that slides from shortstop. One day he was trying to throw out Don Money and Sonny's throw kept sliding, kept sliding and I kept following it right into Money's path. Money is a big man. Just a little bump from him and I'd have been knocked into right-field. Instead, he was kind enough to dodge me, but even then I tripped and fell.

"When I got up I thanked him for saving my life. The Phillies' first-base coach, Billy Demars, was looking me over pretty anxiously, wanting to know if I was all right.

" 'I'd feel a lot better if you were back out there in right-field,' Billy told me.

"I was the next season, but then I found out I couldn't play right-field any more, either. I'm not kidding myself. I can't throw any more. It doesn't embarrass me. When you get my age something's got to go."

The transition, then, as it worked out, was not back to right-field, but to left-field. It was easily made. By this time, 1972, Eddie Mathews, another of the 500-home-run hitters and an old Braves teammate, had been made manager.

"It wasn't difficult to handle," Mathews said. "I only told Henry I wanted to save his life. I never had to finish. He knew what I wanted. He was as anxious to go back to the outfield as I was for him to go."

After a few stabs at the old preserve in right-field, Aaron's name suddenly appeared on the lineup card as the left-fielder. It was another compromise with age. The throw is less demanding from left-field, and then there isn't that gutting peg to be made from right-field to third base which separates the average right-fielder from the great one.

"The ball was leaving my hand just as fast," Aaron said, "but it was traveling slower and dying faster. Base runners were taking advantage of me. It was hurting the team. Nobody had to beg me to go to left-field. They had Mike Lum for first base, and they had Ralph Garr for right-field, so I wasn't leaving any gap to be plugged."

As demeaning as it may have seemed, Aaron rode handsomely with his physical rejections. In contrast to Mays, who ranked at any suggestion he was an "old-timer," Aaron accepts the fact of age gracefully. He feels his age has bestowed upon him a complimenting maturity, surely a kind of confidence he never knew before.

"I have an appreciation for things in life that I wasn't capable of appreciating before. I'm not afraid to speak out, and I was before.

"If I had walked into a store 10 years ago and found something I didn't like, or been treated discourteously, I'd have gone on and said nothing. Now I don't mind saying what I think, or making a complaint."

Since Mathews had been traded after the 1966 season, the Braves had functioned without a team captain. Just before the 1969 season began, a new dimension was added to Aaron's stature. Luman Harris called the press around and Henry in and said, "Gentlemen, I want you to meet the new captain of our team." It was a gesture that originated, no doubt, in the walnut-paneled office of Bill Bartholomay, but in whatever manner, it was a popular one, though the captaincy consists of little more than the title and the duty of occasionally delivering the starting lineup to the umpires.

It was a season that seemingly should have been pleasant to look back on. But somehow, in retrospect, it seems best forgotten. The playoffs developed into flushed face embarrassment. The ex-lowly New York Mets blew out the Braves in three straight games, averaging nine runs and treating Atlanta pitchers as if they were chimney sweeps.

Aaron had a very fine season of 44 home runs and 97 runs batted in and an average of even .300. In the big drive, though, during which the Braves moved into first place on a 10-game winning streak, he was not the big factor. Rico Carty was. He batted .390 and drove in 25 runs the last month of the season. "The Beeg Mon," as he was known—whether for his ego or his body is a question—never let anyone forget it. "If ever one mon carry a baseball team, I do," he said later. "The other players, they do not like me for I speak out, but I do for that is Rico."

Quietly and with dignity, Aaron took his place to the rear. He studiously gave the big outfielder wide berth. As the playoffs came, though, the load fell to Aaron again. He hit a home run in each game, batted .357 and drove in seven runs, but even that performance wasn't enough to overcome the Braves' poor pitching.

At least the Braves had known the pop of the corks, the rancid odor of the mixture of sweat and champagne, and the morning after. It was their one sweet moment in Atlanta, their first brush with the elegant class since they blew the pennant of 1959 in an unscheduled playoff with Los Angeles. And probably Aaron's last chance to make a World Series in uniform.

Aaron arrived at the plate for his first time at bat in 1970 before the home crowd on April 13. He ran through his exercise in muscle-flexing, not a very demonstrative one, almost in slow motion. It has been the same for many seasons, lofting the bat gently with the swinging grip just outside the batter's box, then stepping in as gingerly as a lady testing the bath water, tapping the plate with his bat.

Frank Reberger, tall right-hander from Idaho was pitching for San Francisco and there was something about his delivery that Aaron liked. He whipped the bat into one of Reberger's fast balls and only the upper deck of the stadium caught it, three flights high, at least 500 feet from where the ball had been launched. It was the first time any Brave ever planted a ball in that section of the stadium, was surely the longest home run ever hit in Atlanta, but more than that, it signaled the beginning of what was to become his most significant season to that time.

As the season began, Aaron needed 44 hits, matching the number he wears on his back, to become the eighth major league player of this century with 3,000. Cap Anson had done it in the early years of the game, but with a scoring aid that considered bases on balls as hits. With his 3,000th, Aaron would move into some classic and exclusive company. Only Tyrus Raymond Cobb, Honus Wagner, Eddie Collins, Nap Lajoie, Tristram Speaker, Paul Glee Waner and Stanley Musial had made it before him. (Roberto Clemente accomplished this feat on September 30, 1972.)

Consider for a moment just a few of the great ones who never crossed the 3,000 line, all of them rattling around in the Hall of Fame at Cooperstown. Ruth himself didn't. The Babe retired 127 hits short. George Sisler, the first baseman with the perfect form, didn't. Among others who fell short:

Ted Williams, Joe DiMaggio, Harry Heilmann, Rogers Hornsby, Mel Ott, Al Simmons, Wee Willie Keeler, Heinie Manush, Kiki Cuyler and Mickey Mantle. When Aaron crossed the line, Willie Mays was still 43 hits away, which had to give Aaron some pleasure. It was at this point, and not until then, in fact, that Aaron at least finally began drawing even in the public eye with the idolized Giant.

It had been anticipated as the season opened that Aaron would hit the 3,000 level sometime around mid-May. He was right on schedule. It wasn't a shot heard around the world. In fact, it was barely heard in Crosley Field, where the Cincinnati Reds were still doing business on Sunday, May 17, 1970. Facing a rookie right-hander, Wayne Simpson, in the first inning of the second game of a doubleheader, Aaron beat out an infield grounder, and that was No. 3,000. For awhile, or until Mays made the grade, he was the only man in history who had a collection of 500 home runs and 3,000 base hits.

For those of the sentimental nature and those who believe in omens, there had to be some special feeling that Aaron had been destined to complete his cycle at Crosley Field. This is where his major league career had begun, where he had played his first game as a Milwaukee Brave in 1954. It contributed nothing to his 3,000 collection. He went hitless.

Bowie Kuhn had been a lawyer in a New York firm at that time. Charles Feeney had been a carefree member of Uncle Horace Stoneham's court of the New York Giants, and "Chub" was his form of address. Peculiarly, the Commissioner of Baseball and the President of the National League, in that order, were on the scene in Cincinnati on May 17. Also on hand was Stan Musial, the only other man with 3,000 hits still alive.

"Congratulations, Henry," Musial said, "it was getting lonely in the club."

The Cardinal vice-president, leaping the low railing at Crosley Field, ran out on the field to shake Aaron's hand as he stood on first base doffing his cap to the standing applause of the spectators. Leaving the park early in a police car, someone said to Musial:

"I'll bet you don't remember No. 3,001."

"Sure, I remember it," he said. "It was a home run."

The radio was tuned to a broadcast of the Reds-Braves game. Just about the time Musial finished his sentence, Aaron stepped up to bat again, and the broadcaster ranted, "It's going, it's going, it's out of here!"

Henry's No. 3,001th also had been a home run, a drive over the center-field fence, the one he'd have preferred for No. 3,000.

"Go get 'em, Henry," Musial said softly, sinking back in the seat.

If there was ever an actual crossing of the barrier, of Henry Aaron the excellent and renowned but passively accepted baseball player to Henry Aaron the living legend, this in time would become recognized as the occasion. There were home runs yet to be struck and hits yet to be made and records yet to be broken, but to Henry Aaron himself this was his personal moment of highest achievement. Of course, the matter of the Ruth record came up that day, and was becoming ritual.

"Sure, catching Ruth would be a thrill," he said. "But, making 3,000 hits is more important because it shows consistency. I've studied the list of men who made 3,000, and the one that's unbelievable is Ty Cobb. Can you imagine making 4,191 hits?"

Peculiarly, perhaps even to the point of some question in some minds, even as he stood on 713 and holding, Aaron persisted in this feeling. After the 1973 season he fielded the question again: "You said you felt more of an achievement in making 3,000 hits than you would breaking Ruth's record at the time of your 3,000th hit. Is that still true?"

"That is still true," Aaron said, and regardless of challenging questions he would not be jarred loose from his position.

"I felt that was quite an achievement for me [the 3,000 hits]. I look back now and 700 home runs look like a lot of home runs, and it is a lot of home runs. I realize that I'm the only player who has made it besides Babe Ruth, too. But to make 3,000 base hits you have to be mighty consistent. In order to accomplish anything you have to hit the ball first.

"There've been a lot of guys who've played this game that might of hit 700 home runs. Might of, you understand. But for some reason or another they'd never have been able to make 3,000 hits.

"I'm pretty proud of putting them both together. Another record I'm right proud of is one of Stan Musial's that I broke last year. (On September 2, 1972, Aaron hit two home runs against Philadelphia and passed Musial in total bases. The record was 6,134. By the end of 1973 Aaron had run it up to 6,424.) I was talking to Stan and he told me that before I was through he thought I'd make a record that would never be broken.

"Of course, that's what everybody thought about Babe Ruth's record."

Aaron ran down another record of Musial's during 1973. Fifty-three extra-base hits—doubles, triples and home runs —elevated his total to 1,393. Both Musial (1,377) and Ruth (1,356) were between Aaron and the record at the start of the season.

Still another record of Ruth's, and one by which the productiveness of a hitter is measured, should fall to Aaron in 1974. Ruth drove in 2,209 runs in his career. Aaron went into the season of '74 needing 76 to catch him, and only in his rookie year has he failed to drive in that number of runs.

Baseball makes a great hullaballoo about its Triple Crown, the batting championship, the home run championship and the runs-batted-in championship. With 77 RBI's in '74, Aaron would become the Quadruple Crown champion of all time, exclusive of the department of batting averages. He would become the all-time champion in home-run hitting, total bases, extra bases and runs-batted-in, and that, it must be engraved on the minds of those who know and worship the baseball idol, would establish Henry Aaron in a realm out of the reach of any man who has played this game, including Cobb, Musial, Lajoie, Williams, Ruth, DiMaggio or any other man whose residence has been established in the Hall of Fame.

The Braves were quick to respond to Aaron's arrival at the level of 3,000 hits. Within the week after the club returned home from Cincinnati a combination "day" was set aside to honor him and to honor Hoyt Wilhelm, the forty-seven-year-old relief pitcher who had just set a record for appearing in major league games for pitchers. The solemn old fellow had been a main cog in the drive that set the Braves up in the playoffs the previous season. On May 23, both Wilhelm and Aaron were awarded plaques, and somebody showed up at the park with a poodle pup for Aaron. Not being the poodle type, Aaron posed with the dog and passed it on to some unknown party.

As was becoming habit then, and a tiring one to Aaron, Ruth and the home-run record again came up as a topic of discussion in the locker room as the placid man sat on his metal folding chair in front of his locker and considered where he stood in relation to time and history that was cascading down and around him.

"The way I see it," he said, "this year and next year are going to be the critical ones if I'm going to catch Babe Ruth. I'd almost have to hit 50 in one of those seasons, I think. I'd need one big year, I know that."

A prophetic man, he turned out to be. The Big Season was just ahead of him. Not that 1970 was a season to be swept under the rug. He batted .298, drove in 118 runs—after two seasons of less than 100, this was a joy to the man and his beholders—hit 38 home runs, scored 103 runs. Rico Carty led the whole major leagues in hitting. Carty and Orlando

Cepeda also drove in over 100 runs. The pitchers pitched more shutouts, struck out more batters, accumulated more complete games—but threw more pitches that became home runs. And the team as a whole led the National League in defense. Still, with all this the Braves fell from first to fifth in the Western Division, won only 76 games, finished 26 games behind Cincinnati and, in general, became through some mysterious evolvement the worst of the teams fielded since the transfer from Milwaukee in 1966.

It was a season of deep disappointment to Henry Aaron.

Worse was yet to come. It was personal. Family-rending. The trauma of Aaron's relatively untraumatized life. His marriage to Barbara Lucas Aaron, whose brother William is farm director of the Braves, creating a rather awkward entanglement of front-office and personal affairs, came apart.

What triggered the final separation has remained one of Atlanta's best-kept secrets. Lawyers and the court, through some delicate manipulation, were able to keep it hidden from the newspapers and broadcast media, and it was months after Judge Osgood Williams awarded the divorce decree in February, 1971, that news of it leaked out. Aaron was spared making a court appearance through mutual arrangement between his and Mrs. Aaron's attorney. Details of the settlement have been kept as much a secret as the cause of the split.

Aaron has discussed the divorce only as it related to the children. "It's hard to make them understand. How do you explain it to four children who love both their parents? How do you tell them of things that happen in a marriage, that you don't just get a divorce for the sake of getting a divorce, or because she didn't get up in the morning and fix you a cup of coffee?

"There's more to it than that. Things happen and you don't know why they happen, and the more they happen the farther apart you get. Things kids wouldn't understand. Being a baseball player I was away a lot, and the kids were with their mother. A mother can put a bad taste in their mouths toward you. . ." His voice trailed off. You knew the discussion had ended. More than anything else, and especially for the children's sake, Aaron is thankful that the handling of the breakup was such that the gory details were never smeared across the front page. He moved into the Landmark Apartments in the heart of the city and Mrs. Aaron retained the residence in Cascade Heights, with custody of the children.

Aaron's response was an artistic explosion. To forget his marital problems he lost himself in baseball. "I threw myself into baseball to get my mind off it," he said. "The kids were always on my mind. There were times when I'd really be depressed."

These depressions were never apparent to the pitchers of the National League. In 1971 he hit a lifetime high of 47 home runs. Four times before he had stopped at 44 and once had gone as high as 45. He drove in 118 runs and batted .327.

He also went to bat for the 10,000th time and his embarrassing All-Star Game complexion began to clear up. He hit a home run off Vida Blue into the upper deck at Tiger Stadium in Detroit, though the National League eventually lost.

On April 27 he hit home run No. 600 off Giant Gaylord Perry. There's a sign on the left-field wall in Atlanta Stadium commemorating it. Now, No. 714 seemed to be within view of everybody but Henry.

"That's still a long way off," he said.

One afternoon as he arrived at the stadium there was a note that he should contact Bob Hope, the Braves' publicity director.

"Can you appear on the 'Today in Georgia' show?" Hope asked him. That's a morning studio guest-talk show on WSB-TV in Atlanta.

"When is it?" Aaron asked.

"Next week," Hope said.

Aaron said. "I liked what I saw of her and I thought we

207

"I mean, what time?"

"Nine o'clock in the morning. You wouldn't have to get up before eight," Hope said.

Aaron didn't know anybody got up as early as 8 o'clock in the morning. "Man, that's early. Tell 'em I'll try, but I won't be there if it's one of those games that runs on into the morning."

Twice he was scheduled and twice he canceled, but the third time he made it, to discover happily that his hostess was a very lovely lady named Mrs. Billye Williams, in her mid-thirties, with an attractive figure and manner, obviously intelligent and full of charm. Mrs. Williams was a widow. Her late husband, Dr. Sam Williams, had been pastor of Friendship Baptist Church, and a member of the civil rights movement in Atlanta. He had died of a lung ailment not long before.

Billye Williams was a Texas native who had come to Atlanta as an educator. She had been an assistant professor of English at Morris Brown College before her husband died, but struck out to make a place for herself in television. "I want to become a part of and involved in television in an area in which I can be of service," she wrote on her application.

"She had gone through the same kind of loneliness I had," Aaron said. "I liked what I saw of her and I thought we could share some time together. I asked for a date and she turned me down.

"I thought that over. It had been a long time since I'd done any courting, and I had been a boy then. Now I was a man, and being a man I wasn't going to let it go at that. I asked her again. This time she accepted. We went out to dinner, and it started with that."

News of their engagement leaked out on the "Today in Georgia" show late in the summer of 1973. Mrs. Williams' third finger, left hand, broke out with a big stone, and on November 12, 1973 Mrs. Billye Jewell Suber Williams and Henry Louis Aaron Jr. were wed in Jamaica.

Aaron had played 71 games at first base in 1971 and made only three errors. It was still new to him. There was some excitement in it. He had the incentive to make it work, for he knew that his days as an effective right-fielder were short. He tried to sound happy.

"I really like it at first base," he said. "I find that I'm more involved in the game. I'm in the middle of it, and I like that."

In 1972 it became a full-time job. Cepeda's knees were gone and early in the season he was traded to Oakland for another fallen idol, pitcher Denny McLain.

He did find himself more involved, but with plays he'd never had before, and situations that caught him in his worst posture. Sometimes he looked like a kid in finishing school. It became increasingly obvious that it was unfair to an immortal to be placed in such a humiliating situation, and equally as unfair to the Braves, who were dreadful enough as a team.

Paul Richards was still general manager—or, vice-president in charge of baseball, if you insist on the Braves' terminology. His unseating didn't take place until June. Desperation was closing in on him, I suppose, the day he discussed the prospect of trading Aaron; I'll admit, it did not come as any great shock to me.

"He looks like he's over the hill," Richards said. "He can't play first base. He's a miserable first baseman. He can't play right-field. His arm is gone. He's not hitting. He's making $200,000 a year. The gate attraction that he is, I ought to be able to make a helluva deal for him now."

The Braves trade Henry Aaron? The Baltimore Colts traded Johnny Unitas. The New York Yankees traded Roger Maris. The San Francisco Giants even had the heartlessness to trade Willie Mays. Babe Ruth wasn't even traded. The Yankees coldly closed the door and hung out a shingle that said, in effect, "No Vacancies."

I never was able to determine how serious Richards was. I learned that the matter had been discussed with the Chicago Cubs. Joe Pepitone had freaked out again. There was a need at first base. But if Aaron couldn't play first base for the Braves, he couldn't play first base for the Cubs.

"He'd have all those daylight games at Wrigley Field," Richards said. "In a way, it would be a great break for him."

Richards knew Bill Bartholomay would never sanction the deal. Aaron was Bartholomay's private immortal. It was he who always handled his contract, never Richards. Aaron, to Bartholomay, was the incarnate Braves. The fact that Richards would even nibble at the fringe of the subject indicated the bind he was in.

The season had begun with the player strike. ("Can you imagine," Richards said one day, "a man making $200,000 a year being on strike?") This cost Aaron eight games of the season. Richards and Luman Harris, his manager, had their orders in hand: Produce, or start looking for work. This was their last chance.

The season began like a last chance and ended like one. The Braves were never around the lead. They set an even pace—to the rear. Aaron marched to the same drummer.

Only one other first baseman in the league made more errors—Willie Stargell, a stranger in the land himself. The burden of the job seemed to rub off on Aaron at the bat. It was his worst season in the major leagues, except that he did manage to hit 34 home runs. He batted only .265. He drove in only 77 runs.

At the same time he was revising the history book of baseball. Records seemed to fall every time he went to bat.

He started the season with 639 home runs. On June 10 he hit No. 649, far behind his usual clip, but with it he moved past Willie Mays into second place behind Ruth. It was also a grand slam, tying him with Willie McCovey and Gil Hodges for the National League record at 14.

He moved into second place ahead of Lou Gehrig when he drove in run No. 1,199 on June 28.

He knocked in his 2,000th run on July 3.

He hit his 660th home run on August 6, a record for most home runs ever hit by a player with one team.

He extends a family record every time he hits another home run, obscure though it may be. He and Tommie Aaron, now a manager in the Braves' farm system, hold the major league record for most home runs hit by brothers. Tommie hit 13.

The season achieved its peak, emotionally and artistically, when the annual All-Star game was played in Atlanta Stadium on July 25. Before a full house, Aaron faced Gaylord Perry, now of the Cleveland Indians, in the sixth inning and delivered one of his pitches to the same general area where he had parked No. 600 the previous season. Nearly 54,000 people arose and cheered him all the way around the bases, and for a couple of minutes afterward.

"That has to be the most dramatic home run I've ever hit," he said, "for two reasons. I've never had good luck in the All-Star game, and I was able to hit before my own fans. They can talk about the fans here all they want to, but people in Atlanta have been great to me. I'm just glad I could hit this one for them."

Unquestionably a gesture of magnanimity in a moment of moving sentimentality, but here again Henry Aaron, good guy, came through again as only his nature directed him.

Only one player has aroused Aaron to the point of lowering his guard and speaking out. The same player aroused him to the point of exchanging blows in a widely publicized fight that took place as the Braves flew from Houston to the West Coast one summer. His name: Rico Carty, the outfielder from the Dominican Republic. Unlike Will Rogers, Aaron cannot say that he never met a man he didn't like.

"I didn't dislike Carty. I resented the way Carty manipulated people, the things the public didn't see. He gave the public one side of him, but in the clubhouse it was a different Carty," he said. "He was a trouble-maker. Carty would see something in somebody's locker he wanted, he'd take it.

"He was the 'Beeg Boy' to the people in the stands, smiling that toothy smile, waving and signing autographs. He could have been a very good politician. But I didn't think he was good for the team. And the club, Richards, Harris and those people, let him get away with it.

"One year Carty led the league in hitting. He hit over .360, and that's some average. I never hit .360. But what irritated me, Carty would come to bat in the late innings and we'd be behind by a run. Now, here was a man capable of hitting 35 or 40 home runs. What we needed was a run, not a single. He'd move up on the handle of the bat and try to punch out a hit, anything to protect his average. He doesn't try to hit out, to get his team back in the game.

"They'll be saying, 'Okay, Aaron, why didn't you do more of that?' Well, it's not my nature. I've got to give it a full swing. Go for it all. When you're a run behind and time's running out, what good's a single?

"Carty's never been able to get along with anybody anywhere, Texas, Chicago, any place. He hadn't been in Chicago a week before he was criticizing Ron Santo."

Shortly after Eddie Robinson, the old American League first baseman, succeeded Richards as overseer of the baseball operation, his first move in the off-season was to dump Carty. He took some backlash from the public and the press for it, trading a batter who had led the league one season before for a journeyman pitcher from the Texas Rangers named Jim Panther. Aaron's appraisal of the departed party only adds to the justification of the deal.

The 1972 season saw another move out front that went Aaron's way. Eddie Mathews was appointed to succeed Harris as manager on August 7. Aaron and Mathews had been teammates and close friends at Milwaukee. Together they broke the record Ruth and Gehrig held for most home runs by teammates. Aaron liked the man and the move.

"Eddie's gonna take some time," he said, "but he's gonna make a fine manager."

"Is it going to be sort of uncomfortable, adjusting to an old teammate being your boss?" he was asked.

"Eddie?" he said. He laughed heartily. "Of course not. I've been friends with a lot of my bosses."

As their relationship worked out in 1973, it was unquestionably a boon to Aaron to have Mathews for a manager. Mathews not only made the move that rescued him from first base, but also allowed him to dictate his own playing schedule.

But wasn't the first base situation a delicate one? Hadn't Aaron expressed his life's desire to finish his days there? Hadn't he thought he was doing a reasonably good job?

"It wasn't tough at all," Mathews said. "I called Hank in and we talked about it. I started by saying, 'I think you'd be happier back in the outfield.'

"That was all I needed to say. He jumped at the chance. He realized first base was no place for him. It was no problem. Hank and I will have no problems."

Even as the spring of 1973 came around, Henry Aaron still knew very little about Babe Ruth, the man and the legend now within his range. "Why should I have read a lot about a man playing a game that I couldn't get into?" he said.

What he didn't know, he was about to learn, willing or not. From the time National and American League teams reported for spring training Ruth became as topical as the weather. Old writers who had known and covered the Babe found themselves in business again. Mrs. Ruth, now living in an apartment in Manhattan, found herself in the eye of a new storm of interest and curiosity. At first, it was refreshing, revitalizing to her. She professed her interest in the story that was developing, but she was devout in her loyalty to her husband, now dead twenty-five years. When reporters began to close in on her as Aaron closed in on the record, she notified the world she had reached her saturation point. She told an Associated Press reporter, "I don't care how many home runs Mr. Aaron hits. I just want to be left alone."

The Resurrection of Ruth brought back memories of another age. Old teammates came out of oblivion:

Guy Bush, the pitcher who served his 714th home run; Waite Hoyt, now a retired broadcaster, but once a teammate and close friend, and, ironically, the winning pitcher for Pittsburgh the day Ruth hit his last home run; Ben Chapman, who had been a kid outfielder in Ruth's fading days as a Yankee; Jumpin' Joe Dugan, third baseman and drinking pal of the Bambino's Yankee days; roommates, playmates, old reporters, hotel managers, anybody who had a tale to tell of Ruth was in demand.

Spring training at West Palm Beach was calmer than you might have expected. There was still, for that matter, the question of whether Aaron would be able to play capably enough and long enough to get close to the record. There was the negative evidence left by the 1972 season. He had not played well and he was still 42 home runs short. And Aaron had taken to the bench at times with back trouble and knee trouble, though none of it had been serious.

Aaron's arrival in the Braves 1973 camp was an unpretentious one. He flew in, suited out, met a few cameras and went stoically about his work. In the glare of Florida sun he looked somewhat more plump than I had remembered him in the past.

"You look as if there's a little more of you this spring," I said, picking my way cautiously.

He laughed. "Whatta you mean?"

"Your face, it seems filled out, which I suppose is nothing more than one would expect of a gentleman of advancing age."

"You putting me on?"

There were other developments which kept part of the limelight off Aaron. A new general manager, a new manager, several trades to evaluate. Earl Williams, and a minor league infielder had been traded to the Baltimore Orioles for second baseman Dave Johnson, catcher Johnny Oates, and two pitchers, Pat Dobson, a fearsome fellow with a hair style traceable to the Shakespearean Age, and Roric Harrison, a nice, clean-cut and intelligent lad. Two more pitchers, Gary Gentry and Danny Frisella, starter and reliever in that order, came from the New York Mets in exchange for sec-

ond baseman Felix Millan and southpaw George Stone. It
turned out to be a bad deal for Atlanta. Millan and Stone
helped the Mets into the World Series. Gentry and Frisella
finished the season on the bad-arm list.

New manager Mathews respectfully allowed Aaron to be
his own trainer. "Nobody knows better how to get Aaron in
shape than Aaron. Hank is on his own."

He was, until the afternoon that Mathews caught him on
the field after hours, horsing around in a pickup game with
a bunch of young players. Mathews sped to the trouble spot
on his golf cart.

"What are you trying to do to yourself?" he yelped.
"You're not supposed to be out here. That's for the other fellows to get in some extra work. Get on in before you get
hurt."

Obediently, Aaron left for the clubhouse.

Spring training came to a conclusion with a barnstorming trip. The Braves cut out of West Palm Beach for a few
days on the west coast of Florida, then wrapped it up with
games in Birmingham, Ala., Savannah, Ga., and Richmond,
Va. By this time, Aaron had fielded the question of Ruth's
record time and again with remarkable patience. Basically,
all his answers, when summed up, amounted to this:

"I plan to play two more seasons. If I can't hit 42 home
runs in two seasons, I'm going to be mighty disappointed.
Of course, it all depends on good health and not being injured. I'm not going to bat looking for a home run every time
I swing. But if one falls in, I'm going to be pleased."

The Braves' season opened against Houston on April 6,
and Aaron played right-field, but his season was a long time
starting. He got away to a miserable start. He couldn't make
himself comfortable in his old position.

"I charge a ball to get in position to throw," he said, "because I have to have that little edge now, and I can't find
the handle on it, or, it goes all the way through to the fence.
I feel all right running, but I can't seem to cover the ground
I used to. I'm running just as hard, but it's more in one
place."

His batting average was anemic. By the first of May he had only eight hits but five of them were home runs. His critics took notice of this ratio early. The daily mail brought in a stream of protests that he was only swinging for the fences, not playing for the team. He looked out of shape. He looked fat and played fat. Mathews had gone too far with leniency in the case of his old teammate, said the letters to the sports departments. "He'll never be a manager. He manages Aaron one way and the rest of the Braves another. And neither of them very well."

Mathews was sorely concerned. "I hate to take him out of the lineup because he needs to play, but I hate to keep playing him because he's hurting the team," he confided. He wavered, but never varied from the arrangement he'd made with Aaron: To play or not to play was Aaron's decision.

Team performance was erratic. The Braves beat themselves as often as they were beaten. The new pitching wasn't producing. Attendance was dreadful, and after a season in which they had drawn barely 750,000, management could ill afford another such catastrophe. They had counted on interest in Aaron's home-run progress. It never developed.

He was assailed one night as the Braves played at home by a clot of males gathered in seats near his station in right-field. The same group had harassed Aaron two or three nights in a row, and as the harassment went on, grew bolder in their racial tones. Attendance was so bad that every word echoed throughout the stands.

"Hey, nigger, you're no Babe Ruth!"

"How come a nigger sonofabitch like you can make so much money and strike out so much?"

"Hey, you black *******"

"This had gone on long enough," Aaron said. "If I strike out and somebody hollers I'm a bum, that's part of it. I can take the normal amount of razzing. But these guys got personal, vicious, obscene, and I'd had all I was going to take."

As he trotted in from his position during a game with the New York Mets, Aaron stopped and engaged his tormentors vocally, but security attendants raced down through the stands and broke up the exchange. The spectators were escorted from the stadium. The next day the story circulated across the country. News leaked out of the volume of "hate" mail Aaron had been receiving.

Now he admits to receiving any number of threatening letters. "Threatening me, my family, warning me not to hit any more home runs. It got to be routine that they were all turned over to the FBI," he said.

One threat was not written off so easily. It demanded ransom money in advance, or else some member of his family would be harmed. The letter was traced to Nashville, Tenn., where his oldest daughter, Gaile, attended Fisk University. Gaile reported that she had been receiving strange telephone calls, and students on the Fisk campus had been accosted by a man inquiring of her and her habits. She was kept under surveillance for some time. The watch eventually was relaxed after a long period of no further contact, and the case was only revealed to me over matter pertaining to this book.

Aaron felt somewhat embarrassed at finding himself in the center of such a harangue as took place during the game with the Mets. "All I want," he said, "is to be treated like a human being. I've said it until it's tiresome: I'm not trying to be another Babe Ruth. All I'm trying to do is play the game and earn a living and be a part of my team.

"But I'll tell any fan this much: This kind of abuse isn't going to stop me. The more they push me, the more I want the record."

Howard Cosell, the mordant wit of ABC, later was quoted as saying, "The Commissioner tells me that Aaron is receiving 5,000 letters a day, most of it hate mail."

Untrue. The mail volume did pick up immensely after the Mets game incident, but it was overwhelmingly pro-Aaron. Fans rallied to his support, both by letter and by response at the stadium. The matter eventually drifted into oblivion.

A short time afterward, in mid-May, Aaron was quietly transferred from right to left-field. This aroused speculation that Mathews was moving him out of target range of the old grandstand snipers. "I'm moving him because of his arm," Mathews said. "He simply can't make the throw from right-field any more. It's easier all around for him in left-field."

After all those seasons in right-field, it would seem that a proper ceremony would have been in order. Aaron laughed at the suggestion. "No way," he said. "It's not the same any more. They've done something to right-field while I've been playing first base. It don't play like it used to. Just let me get to left-field as quick as I can and I don't want to look back."

Performance did improve, but slowly. All the while his home-run pace had been holding up. It developed into a race for No. 700 before the break for the All-Star game in Kansas City on July 24.

It was near twilight on Saturday, July 21, when Robert Winborne settled into his seat in the lower left-field stands. He was no average run-of-the-comic-book baseball fan. He opened a copy of *Point Counterpoint* by Aldous Huxley and read. He had recently been graduated from Westminster School, an exclusive academy on the exclusive northwest side of Atlanta, and was the son of a University of North Carolina alumnus who had played on the same football team as the late George Stirnweiss, who became a New York Yankee and once led the American League in hitting.

Robert was attending the game with a lively group of pals. The previous night Henry Aaron had hit the 699th home run of his career off Wayne Twitchell of the Philadelphia Phillies. The Braves were offering a bounty of $700, one silver dollar for each of Aaron's 700, to the fan who retrieved the 700th. About 6 o'clock, five minutes before the first pitch, Robert put down *Point Counterpoint* and prepared himself for the mission.

Aaron's first time at bat developed nothing more than an out. The scrounging and the shifting about for position had turned the section into a cattle car. "I'm surprised somebody don't get hurt," an usher said. "I know one thing, if cussing had a sharp edge, they'd be a bunch a people bleeding and dying in there."

Robert held his ground in the same seat as Aaron came to bat in the third inning. The crowd was relatively small, but it made much more noise than 16,236. A left-handed pitcher, Ken Brett, was working for the Phillies. The count became 1-and-1 and Brett unwisely tried to slip a fast ball by the best fast-ball hitter of the modern era. The ball took flight toward the left-field pavilion. Robert Winborne never moved, frozen there as he watched the white thing fly toward him. He sat there and the ball took one bounce through, around and over the scramblers, who were canceling out each other's savage effort, and into his hands. No one seemed to notice. He looked furtively about, tucked the prize under his shirt and waited until he spotted a clearing in the mass. He jumped from his seat and fled, *Point Counterpoint* left behind, eventually arriving at the press-box door, and later the Braves' dressing room after the game to meet, be photographed with and talk with the man who had hit the ball. And to collect his 700 silver dollars.

"Did you make a clean catch of it?" Aaron asked.

"No, I had to scramble a little," he said. "Hey, by the way, that son Hank of yours is going to be some kind of a football player. I've seen him. I can tell you that."

Suddenly, something flashed through his mind. "Hey, my book! Really, I've got to get my book back. Will you 'scuse me, please?"

And so the eighteen-year-old boy who fielded Henry Aaron's 700th home run raced back to the left-field pavilion in search of *Point Counterpoint* by Aldous Huxley.

Just two days before home run No. 700, news of Aaron's engagement to Billye Williams had surfaced. Then came the historic clout, only the second time in baseball history a 700th home run had been hit by one man. The All-Star game was three days away in Kansas City. Though he had been restored to right-field several weeks before the season opened, Aaron had gone on the official ballot drawn up by Commissioner Bowie Kuhn's office as a first base candidate. His batting performance had improved as had his fielding since the transfer to left-field. He was hitting only .251 at the time of the All-Star game, but it was inevitable that he would play. He was the opening first baseman for the National League, the position he had learned to despise.

Telegrams and calls and letters of congratulations had flooded the Braves clubhouse after the 700th home run. A glaring name missing among the correspondents, however, was that of the Commissioner himself. Kuhn hadn't been in Cincinnati for the 3,000th hit. Now this.

"I don't understand it," Aaron said. "When Ford Frick was Commissioner he took time to wire me. He told me he was fining me $25 for talking to players on the other team." That was the famous occasion when Aaron, then a mere youth and uninformed of baseball's hierarchy, looked blankly while being told he'd been fined by Ford Frick, then said, "Who's he?"

He knew Bowie Kuhn well enough to feel he'd been snubbed. The Commissioner, however, was only waiting to extend his congratulations personally in Kansas City. "I just wanted to wait and tell you face to face, Henry," he said. "Furthermore, I want you to know that when you hit 714 and 715, I'll be there in the stands ready to jump out on the field and congratulate you."

It was all right with Henry now.

Another relic of a home-run craze had been reclaimed from the obscurity of a beer distributorship. Roger Maris, retiring as a St. Louis Cardinal, had come into an Anheuser-Busch agency in Gainesville, Fla., and was living in affluence and as an established and respected member of the community. Aaron's feats, however, sent inquisitive reporters to his doorstep asking him to compare notes of pressure and moments of exhilaration with Aaron's experiences. Aaron was a beauty of simplicity and coolness through the furor, which was only beginning to hit its upbeat. Maris marveled at him. He was visiting Atlanta on business and spent some of his evenings in Atlanta Stadium.

"I watch Henry and I sit here and think about it. I'd handle the press differently if I had it to do over again," he said. Of course, there was a difference in types of pressure. If Aaron didn't get 714 in 1973, there was always 1974. With Maris, it was 61 home runs in a season, 1961, as it was, or the chance was out the window.

He had been a bombastic man, snapping back at his interviewers, curling his lip and giving them the sneer. Hiding out. Dressing them down. A man with a load he didn't know how to handle.

The view was from the heights of another age, in 1973. "There were people always wanting something from me. It became personalities. I remember all the incidents. They're all still inside, but I don't talk about them.

"I would have interviews for three or four hours after a game. Writers would drift in late and ask the same question over again, or just get half the story. The next day the headline would make me look bad. People got on my back."

He had no advice for Aaron. "The way he's handling it, he doesn't need any. Ain't he beautiful? I'll be glad when it's over for him, then things will cool off for me again."

The respect that Aaron had coveted now had gone far beyond that into adulation, very nearly a state of reverence among the ball players of the National League. I remember a reserve outfielder of the Cincinnati Reds, Larry Stahl, pausing to speak to him one evening behind the batting cage. There was a tone of awe in his voice, and as he spoke he removed his cap and as he finished and moved on, he replaced the cap. I can't say that it was an act of respect, but there was something about it that made it stick with me.

The All-Star exposure had brought national attention zeroing in on him. He tried to get a couple of days of leisure down home in Mobile after the game. When he went fishing with some friends on Mobile Bay he found about as much privacy as if he had rented Times Square for an exhibition. As their little boat bobbed around, three or four other boats closed in, loaded with photographers and newsmen.

Newsweek magazine hit the market in August with the Aaron swing on the cover. So did *Ebony*. NBC announced that it was sending in a crew to do a documentary on Aaron and the home-run crusade. NBC also announced that once he reached 712 it would have a crew on the scene until he hit 714, at which time it would interrupt its programming to show the historic moment on its national network.

Privacy while the Braves were traveling became more and more a problem. Donald Davidson, the little traveling secretary, began registering Aaron as "Victor Koplin." Carla Koplin was the girl employed by the Braves to handle Aaron's correspondence and other such affairs. All telephone calls to Aaron were channeled by hotel switchboards through Davidson's room. Once, a rumor broke loose in Houston that Aaron had been shot. Calls flooded Davidson.

"I'm sure," he said, "that if Henry had been shot, he'd have called and told me."

As the Braves took off from Los Angeles late in the season, the pilot of the plane came on the intercom with the usual routine about keeping the seat belt loosely fastened and how high they would fly.

And as addenda, he said, "I'd like to welcome aboard Henry Aaron and the rest of the Atlanta Braves."

"Henry Aaron!" a woman passenger said. "On this flight with all these people? I thought he flew in his own private plane."

Out for a stroll one day in Los Angeles, Aaron was confronted by a young woman who said, "I know who you are. You're the home-run king."

"No, not me."

"Oh, c'mon now, you're kidding me. You're the home run king."

"No, you're looking for Davey Johnson. He's upstairs in his room asleep."

Johnson was leading the National League in home runs at the time, another of the miracles of the season. Before it was done, Johnson, Aaron and Darrell Evans, the third baseman, established a three-man major league record. Never before had three men on the same team hit 40 home runs.

Bowie Kuhn made further amends. He announced that Aaron was being invited to throw out the first ball for the first game of the World Series. It didn't stop any presses, but it was the first time any active player had ever been so honored.

"As bad as my arm is," Aaron said, "they ought to let me hit it out."

September arrived with Aaron standing on No. 706. Preachers were preaching sermons on him. Teachers were teaching about him. He was constantly on the television screen, and the press was absorbed in saturation coverage of every move. The Braves hauled out for the West on September 19, their last road trip of the year. On the previous Monday, September 17, Aaron had hit No. 711 on a rainy night before a meager audience in Atlanta off a young San Diego pitcher named Gary Ross. Nine games were left on the schedule and the fever was rising.

Back in Houston on September 22, the Braves opened a two-game series with the Astros. The press box was beginning to fill now with added starters, writers and columnists attracted to the scene to look in on the countdown. The group was swelled somewhat by those who had covered another sports event that had the country babbling, and had stayed over. Thursday evening, Bobby Riggs and Billie Jean King had played the mixed-sex singles match to settle the monstrously overblown issue of male chauvinism versus female pride. Could a fifty-five-year-old man beat the best woman tennis player in the world? He couldn't, but they attracted many sports writers who stayed in town to watch Aaron hit the 712th home run of his major league career off one of the better left-handed pitchers in the major leagues, Dave Roberts. It came in the sixth inning at the Astrodome with two Braves on base Saturday night, the 22nd.

They screamed "We want Hank!" on Sunday. He maintained his program. He didn't play. Sunday night the Braves flew home to Atlanta to finish the season. Columnists came in droves, and men with tape recorders, and television cameramen. Commissioner Bowie Kuhn was there, as he had promised, prominently exposed in a special box that had been erected near the Braves dugout. Henry's father, Herbert Aaron, Sr., had come from Mobile for the occasion. The dapper little man, neatly dressed and full of conversation, was a retired shipyard employe. He had been with his son earlier in the month and, drinking in fully the glamor of the moment, had enjoyed his finest hour when Henry hit No. 712 off Gary Ross.

Just a moment before the blast, Herbert Aaron had leaned toward a newspaper man sitting near him, Mike McKenzie of the *Atlanta Journal*, and said, "Watch him. This time he's going to hit one."

Henry fouled off the first pitch. "Be ready for 711," his father said. "See him shake his head? He liked that one and he knows he should have hit it out."

The next pitch Henry dispatched to the left-field bull pen and his father burst into a high-pitched laugh.

"See! Didn't I tell you! I know my son. I never mentioned it before, but as soon as he hits No. 714 I'm going to tell his secret to hitting."

Aaron could hardly make a move without bumping into someone. NBC cameras recorded his coming and his going. Before they were through, they would shoot thirty miles of film. From the time the Braves returned to Atlanta on the night of Sunday, September 23, it was like a circus with no clowns and few laughs. This is how the diary of the final week ran:

Sept. 24—Off day. Henry visited young Hank at Marist College. Tidied up a few loose ends of business with Frank Menke, an attorney who was handling his local affairs.

Sept. 25—The Dodgers opened a three-game series. Thursday was an open date on the schedule, but it was being used as a rain date. Don Sutton, a Southerner from Pensacola, Fla., who won 18 games, started for the Dodgers. Commissioner Kuhn, his aide, Henry Fitzgibbon, Henry's father, and a few loyal fans chosen by the Braves, including Jerry Fields, president of the Braves 400 Club, and Pearl Sandow, an elderly lady who actually had never missed a game in the stadium, sat in the jerry-built box.

Sutton's first pitch to Aaron was a ball. Boos rang out. The second was a strike. Aaron fouled the third, then grounded out. "Throw him a strike, you bum!" some fan yelled.

This was to be the mood of the week. The crowds were small, arousing the critiquing spirit in visiting journalists, but they came to see Aaron hit home runs. They made much noise about it when any pitch wasn't down the pipe.

Sutton threw strikes the second time and Aaron fouled out to the catcher, Joe Ferguson.

In the fifth inning, Sutton struck back at Aaron. His low liner reached Aaron in left-field about knee high. Aaron juggled it, slapped it in the air with one hand, bounced it off his body and finally made the catch, the crowd howling.

Bill Russel lined a shot at him later and Aaron made what appeared to be a trap catch. Umpire Jerry Dale shot up his hand, indicating a catch. The Dodgers didn't howl. You don't upstage an immortal in such immortal times.

Aaron drove Willie Davis to the center-field fence in the seventh and crowd reaction swelled and died with the flight of the ball. He was kneeling in the waiting circle in the eighth inning when Darrell Evans popped up just when it seemed Sutton would walk Evans, filling the bases. It was a dry night for Aaron. When he popped out in the ninth, most of the 10,000 got up and left.

Hoyt Wilhelm, another holder of records, dropped in to visit after the game. Aaron was escorted to a special interview room.

Some visiting writers complained sorely in their dispatches of the small crowd, 10,201. I checked the figures of Pittsburgh in May, 1935, when Babe Ruth hit No. 714 off Guy Bush. Attendance at Forbes Field had been 10,000.

the game and let well enough alone!" I sa...
son. We sat in the general manager's booth.

"I wish he would," Eddie said. "That's somethin...
left to Henry all season."

Settle for .300? Not on your life. Aaron sh...
He dropped a single into left-field. Three f...

He popped out to Tommy Helms...
average stuck at .301.

It began to well up, gradually...
ward left-field. It spread with...
come a crescendo by the tim...
Henry Aaron stood there in...
hand on his hips, as 40,5...
him for a full five minut...
then took it off and h...
down upon him.

It was, in all m...
seen for any man...
out to second ba...

Most of the ...
lost their 85th gam...
come a downpour by...
concluding the season. A...
home run, they had seen L...
major league game. The next da...
manager.

"I'm sorry I couldn't hit one for them,...
and all," Aaron said in the big interview roo...
for the home run. I wasn't trying to hit singles....

"And that applause, I guess that's the biggest...
moment I've ever had in baseball. I guess I didn't realize...
people cared that much."

There was one delicate moment during the interview session. A man with a tape recorder asked, "What have you done for baseball?"

Aaron looked puzzled for a moment. "I don't get what you mean."

Sept. 26—A downpour struck downt... afternoon after threatening all day. The gam... until 9 o'clock while the ground crew put the fi... condition. There was much interest in other ga... treal beat New York, Pittsburgh beat Philadelphia,... ing the race in the National League East.

The game was wild and badly played, matching the...eld conditions. Evans hit his 40th home run. Johnson was al... ready in the 40s. Now only Aaron needed his 40th to make it a party. Aaron had a single and drove in two runs, but no cigar. Twice he faced a young flame-throwing right-hander, a Dodger rookie from Warner Robins, Ga., Eddie Solomon, being vigorously cheered by a small clot of hometown ad- mirers. Solomon retired him once, walked him the second time to a deafening chorus of boos, most unnerving to the rookie's following.

Sept. 27—The rained-out game was rained out again. The field was like a marsh. Ground crewmen futilely tried to sweep the water off, but succeeded only in moving it around. After a second squall struck about 8 P.M., big Tom Gorman, the Irish umpire, stepped out on the field and dra- matically signaled that the game was being called off. It could not be rescheduled. The Dodgers were due in San Diego the next day.

Aaron sat in front of his locker hearing questions.
"Are you really enjoying all this?"
"That question," he said, "I'd really rather not answer."

Over one hundred newsmen milled around the premises. Before the cancellation, he had said, "If I don't hit one to- night, you guys might as well go home. It won't happen this year."

Nobody went home. He said he would an- nounce Saturday his new affiliation with the William Mor- ris Agency.

Sept. 28—Off day. More business.

Sept. 29—Houston at the stadium for the two last games of the season, a modest crowd of 16,000. Jerry Reuss, a tall left-hander with stringy blond hair and a good record of 16

against
electronic
took off and
out of the dugout, a m
ticket offices to buy se
Aaron added two sing
dreadful start. He had picked up
was closing in on .300, a
All-Star game.

Sept. 30—Last day. The setting could
perfect had it been contrived. Box offices op
Lines had been forming since early morning. Tick
40,517 at the game, 32,000 of whom bought tick
day. It was the busiest day in the history of Braves'
office. It urged attendance over 800,000, a face-saving level.
By noon, two hours before the game, streets leading to the
stadium seethed with scurrying people, mothers struggling to
small children and tugging others, fathers carrying
keep up. Traffic was stacked up in all directions and far beyond the state capitol, whose gold dome glistened in a bright
sun. That lasted only a short time. Clouds began moving in
during batting practice, increasing the pace intermittently, never
really ceasing. In the second inning rain came,
first in a drizzle,

Dave Roberts, who had served No. 711, started for Houston. Aaron beat out a topper down the third-base line, driving in a run the first time up. He arched a single to center-
field the second time, and officially his batting average
reached .300 for the first time during the season.
Rain was coming down harder. It was a dismal, and a
dangerous day for a thirty-nine-year-old immortal to be
sloshing around in the outfield. "Why doesn't he get out of

"Well, when Babe Ruth hit his home runs he saved baseball. He brought it back from the throes of trouble. He gave it a new face and it became stronger than ever. What have you done for baseball?"

Unfair a question as it was, tense as the moment became in the press room, Aaron paused for thought.

"Well, that's a new question," he began. "Maybe what I've done is create some new fans for baseball. At first there was a lot of mail from people, older people who didn't want me to break Babe Ruth's record. The younger generation took notice of that and came to my support. I think they wanted me to relate to, to see me have a record in their time, not somebody their granddaddies had seen play. That's about all I can say I've done for baseball, I guess."

There was a brief silence, then a short burst of applause.

Percival Wentworth Ford, a moon-faced little Bahamian who writes a column for a Nassau newspaper in the off-season, had been the Braves' starting pitcher that day. He was a rookie just in a few weeks from the farm club in Richmond. He had pitched more like a columnist than a pitcher. By the second inning he was gone.

He stood in the crowd outside the interview room when it broke up. He carried a bag. He had been in the center of the field before the 40,000, pitching in front of Henry Aaron. Now he seemed lost, a face in a sea of faces. Aaron moved near him as he left. Wenty Ford looked into his face. He said nothing. He stood there a moment, holding his bag, in frozen idolatrousness. Then he turned and started walking, to Nassau, I guess.

Inside the locker room, Aaron pronounced his final benediction to 1973. "I'm thankful it's over and that it came out as well as it did," he said. No. 714 was for 1974.

—FURMAN BISHER
December 1973

Appendix

LIFETIME BATTING RECORD

Bold face figures indicate led league or tied for league lead.

Year	Club	League	G	AB	R	H	TB	2B	3B	HR	RBI	SB	Pct.
1952	Eau Claire	Northern	87	345	79	116	170	19	4	9	61	25	.336
1953	Jacksonville	So. Atlantic	137	574	**115**	**208**	338	**36**	14	22	**125**	13	**.362**
1954	Milwaukee	National	122	468	58	131	209	27	6	13	69	2	.280
1955	Milwaukee	National	153	602	105	189	325	**37**	9	27	106	3	.314
1956	Milwaukee	National	153	609	106	**200**	340	34	14	26	92	2	.328
1957	Milwaukee	National	151	615	**118**	198	369	27	6	**44**	**132**	1	.322
1958	Milwaukee	National	153	601	109	196	328	34	4	30	95	4	.326
1959	Milwaukee	National	154	629	116	**223**	**400**	46	7	39	123	8	**.355**
1960	Milwaukee	National	153	590	102	172	**334**	20	11	40	**126**	16	.292
1961	Milwaukee	National	155	603	115	197	**358**	**39**	10	34	120	21	.327
1962	Milwaukee	National	156	592	127	191	366	28	6	45	128	15	.323
1963	Milwaukee	National	161	631	**121**	201	**370**	29	4	**44**	**130**	31	.319
1964	Milwaukee	National	145	570	103	187	293	30	2	24	95	22	.328
1965	Milwaukee	National	150	570	109	181	319	**40**	1	32	89	24	.318
1966	Atlanta	National	158	603	117	168	325	23	1	**44**	**127**	21	.279
1967	Atlanta	National	155	600	**113**	184	**344**	37	3	**39**	109	17	.307
1968	Atlanta	National	160	606	84	174	302	33	4	29	86	28	.287
1969	Atlanta	National	147	547	100	164	**332**	30	3	44	97	9	.300
1970	Atlanta	National	150	516	103	154	296	26	1	38	118	9	.298
1971	Atlanta	National	139	495	95	162	331	22	3	47	118	1	.327
1972	Atlanta	National	129	449	75	119	231	10	0	34	77	4	.265
1973	Atlanta	National	120	392	84	118	252	12	1	40	96	1	.301

Major League Totals .... 20 Yrs. 2964 11288 2060 3509 6424 584 96 713 2133 239 .310

HANK AARON'S HOME RUNS

No.	Date	Inn	On Base	Opp	Pitcher	No.	Date	Inn	On Base	Opp	Pitcher
		1954 (13)				18	May 8	2	0	at StL	Haddix
1	Apr 23	4	0	at StL	Raschi	19	May 10	8	2	Pit	Surkont
2	Apr 25	5	0	at StL	S. Miller	20	May 12	2	0	Bkn	Erskine
3	May 21	8	1	at Chi	Jeffcoat	21	May 19	2	0	NY	Hearn
4	May 22 (2ndG)	1	1	at Chi	Hacker	22	May 28	6	0	at Chi	Hacker
5	May 25	5	1	at Cin	Wehmeier	23	Jun 7	2	1	at NY	Antonelli
6	Jun 15	1	1	at Bkn	R. Meyer	24	Jun 17	4	0	NY	Antonelli
7	Jun 17	1	0	at Bkn	Podres	25	Jun 24	3	2	Bkn	Erskine
8	Jun 22	4	0	at NY	Antonelli	26	Jun 28	6	0	Chi	S. Jones
9	Jun 26	4	0	at Pha	Roberts	27	Jun 29	4	1	Chi	Andre
10	Jul 2	7	1	Cin	Valentine	28	Jun 29	6	0	Chi	Andre
11	Jul 8	3	1	at Chi	Hacker	29	Jul 2	7	1	at Cin	Collum
12	Jul 29	10	0	at Pit	Hetki	30	Jul 8 (2ndG)	1	1	Cin	Minarcin
13	Aug 10	1	1	at StL	Raschi	31	Jul 14	6	0	at Pha	R. Miller
		1955 (27)				32	Jul 16	8	1	at NY	Maglie
14	Apr 17	7	0	at Cin	Staley	33	Jul 21	4	0	at Pit	Donoso
15	Apr 27	8	0	at NY	Wilhelm	34	Jul 22	6	0	at Bkn	Craig
16	Apr 30	9	0	at Pha	Kipper	35	Jul 24 (2ndG)	8	1	at Bkn	Roebuck
17	May 7	9	0	at StL	Moford						

HANK AARON'S HOME RUNS (Continued)

No.	Date	Inn	On Base	Opp	Pitcher	No.	Date	Inn	On Base	Opp	Pitcher
36	Aug 7(1stG)	8	1	Pit	Donoso	85	Jun 19	3	0	NY	Gomez
37	Aug 9	4	0	StL	L. Jackson	86	Jun 26	5	0	Bkn	Newcombe
38	Aug 19	3	1	Chi	Hacker	87	Jun 29	6	2	Pit	O'Brien
39	Sep 4	1	1	Cin	Klippstein	88	Jun 30(1stG)	1	0	Pit	Law
40	Sep 4	6	0	Cin	Black	89	Jun 30(2ndG)	4	0	Pit	Trimble
	1956 (26)					90	Jul 1	1	0	at StL	Dickson
41	Apr 17	6	0	Chi	Rush	91	Jul 3	1	1	at Cin	Jeffcoat
42	Apr 22(2ndG)	3	0	at StL	L. Jackson	92	Jul 4	7	1	at Cin	Gross
43	May 7	5	0	Bkn	Roebuck	93	Jul 5	9	0	Chi	Elston
44	May 22	2	0	Bkn	Erskine	94	Jul 12	6	0	at Pit	Law
45	May 30(1stG)	1	0	at Chi	R. Meyer	95	Jul 16	1	1	at Pha	Haddix
46	May 30(2ndG)	6	0	at Chi	Hacker	96	Jul 25	4	0	Pha	Roberts
47	Jun 6	1	1	Bkn	Newcombe	97	Aug 4	6	2	Bkn	Erskine
48	Jun 27	2	0	at Pha	Haddix	98	Aug 9	3	1	at StL	McDaniel
49	Jul 4(2ndG)	8	2	StL	Wehmeier	99	Aug 15	1	2	at Cin	Jeffcoat
50	Jul 6	7	0	Chi	Kaiser	100	Aug 15	7	1	at Cin	Gross
51	Jul 16	4	0	Pit	Kline	101	Aug 22	1	2	at Bkn	Maglie
52	Jul 17	7	2	NY	McCall	102	Aug 23	4	0	at Bkn	Koufax
53	Jul 20	1	1	Pha	S. Miller	103	Aug 24	4	0	at Bkn	Podres
54	Jul 22(1stG)	8	0	Pha	Flowers	104	Aug 31	1	1	at Cin	Nuxhall
55	Jul 26	1	1	at NY	Antonelli	105	Sep 3	8	2	at Chi	Littlefield
56	Jul 30	7	1	at Bkn	Lehman	106	Sep 10	4	0	Pit	Douglas
57	Aug 5	3	2	at Pit	Kline	107	Sep 17	8	0	NY	Barclay
58	Aug 19	8	1	at Cin	Acker	108	Sep 22	4	0	at Chi	Drott
59	Aug 23	5	0	Pha	Simmons	109	Sep 23	11	1	StL	Muffett
60	Aug 26	3	1	Bkn	Craig	110	Sep 24	1	3	StL	S. Jones
61	Sep 1	3	0	StL	Mizell		**1958 (30)**				
62	Sep 3(1stG)	4	0	Cin	Klippstein	111	Apr 20	7	0	at Pha	Roberts
63	Sep 3(1stG)	7	0	Cin	Klippstein	112	Apr 22	4	2	at Pit	Kline
64	Sep 3(2ndG)	8	0	Cin	Lawrence	113	Apr 24	3	0	at Cin	Lawrence
65	Sep 13(2ndG)	11	0	at Pha	Roberts	114	Apr 24	5	0	at Cin	Rabe
66	Sep 15	7	2	at Pha	R. Miller	115	May 13	4	0	at Pha	Roberts
	1957 (44)					116	May 31	1	0	at Pit	Kline
67	Apr 18	6	0	Cin	Jeffcoat	117	Jun 3	4	0	at SF	Gomez
68	Apr 22	2	0	Chi	Rush	118	Jun 3	9	0	at SF	Grissom
69	Apr 24	3	2	StL	Wehmeier	119	Jun 8	5	0	at LA	Podres
70	Apr 27	1	0	at Cin	Hacker	120	Jun 10	3	2	at Chi	Drott
71	May 3	6	2	at Pit	Friend	121	Jun 20	8	3	StL	Muffett
72	May 5	4	2	at Bkn	Bessent	122	Jun 27	4	0	LA	Koufax
73	May 11	7	0	at StL	Schmidt	123	Jun 28	7	0	LA	Erskine
74	May 12(1stG)	4	1	at StL	Dickson	124	Jun 29	6	3	LA	Drysdale
75	May 12(2ndG)	3	1	StL	Wehmeier	125	Jul 12	6	1	at SF	Antonelli
76	May 18	3	0	Pit	Law	126	Jul 15	2	0	at StL	Maglie
77	May 18	4	2	Pit	R. Smith	127	Jul 15	4	0	at StL	Maglie
78	May 27	8	1	Cin	Klippstein	128	Jul 16	5	0	at StL	Stobbs
79	Jun 4	3	1	at NY	S. Miller	129	Jul 18	6	0	at Chi	Briggs
80	Jun 9(1stG)	7	0	at Pit	Friend	130	Jul 19	1	1	at Chi	Drabowsky
81	Jun 9(2ndG)	7	0	at Pit	Kline	131	Jul 25(2ndG)	7	0	Chi	Elston
82	Jun 12	9	0	at Bkn	Roebuck	132	Jul 27	1	1	Chi	Hillman
83	Jun 14	6	2	at Pha	Cardwell	133	Jul 31	4	0	LA	Podres
84	Jun 15	2	0	at Pha	Haddix	134	Aug 2	7	0	SF	Monzant

HANK AARON'S HOME RUNS (Continued)

No.	Date	Inn	Base	Opp	Pitcher
135	Aug 6	1	1	at Pit	Law
136	Aug 19	7	1	at LA	Podres
137	Aug 21	4	0	at LA	Koufax
138	Aug 24	10	1	at SF	Worthington
139	Sep 12	3	2	StL	Mabe
140	Sep 21	7	1	at Cin	Acker
1959 (39)					
141	Apr 11	3	0	at Pit	Law
142	Apr 18	7	2	Pit	Law
143	Apr 23	9	0	at Pha	Semproch
144	Apr 26	4	0	at Cin	Jeffcoat
145	Apr 29	6	0	at StL	Blaylock
146	Apr 30	4	0	at StL	Kellner
147	May 3	1	0	SF	Antonelli
148	May 3	4	0	SF	Antonelli
149	May 16	3	2	at LA	McDevitt
150	May 16	9	0	at LA	Koufax
151	May 17	5	1	at LA	Drysdale
152	May 20	6	0	at SF	McCormick
153	May 22	1	1	at Pha	Roberts
154	May 30	6	0	Pha	Cardwell
155	Jun 3	7	0	SF	Worthington
156	Jun 10	1	0	at StL	Kellner
157	Jun 21	1	1	at SF	Antonelli
158	Jun 21	6	1	at SF	S. Miller
159	Jun 21	7	1	at SF	G. Jones
160	Jun 24	1	2	at StL	Ricketts
161	Jun 25	3	1	StL	Mizell
162	Jul 3	8	1	at Pit	Witt
163	Jul 11	7	0	LA	Drysdale
164	Jul 14	6	0	at Chi	Henry
165	Jul 29	1	1	Chi	Hillman
166	Jul 29	3	0	Chi	Hillman
167	Jul 30	3	0	Chi	Ceccarelli
168	Jul 31	8	0	StL	Jeffcoat
169	Aug 1	6	0	StL	Broglio
170	Aug 12	5	0	at Cin	O'Toole
171	Aug 17(1stG)	8	0	LA	Labine
172	Aug 18	6	0	LA	Drysdale
173	Aug 18	11	0	LA	Drysdale
174	Aug 28	4	0	at Chi	Buzhardt
175	Aug 29	4	0	at Chi	Henry
176	Aug 29	9	0	at Chi	Elston
177	Sep 2	6	1	Pha	Roberts
178	Sep 7(1stG)	1	1	Pit	Friend
179	Sep 20	1	0	at Pha	Roberts
1960 (40)					
180	Apr 14	1	1	at Pha	Simmons
181	Apr 16	6	2	at Pha	Gomez
182	Apr 22	3	0	at Pit	Friend
183	Apr 27	1	0	at Cin	Hook
184	May 5	6	0	at LA	Podres
185	May 13	4	0	Pit	Friend
186	May 15(1stG)	7	0	Pit	Haddix
187	May 15(2ndG)	1	2	Pit	Daniels
188	May 17	2	0	LA	Drysdale
189	Jun 2	4	0	at Pha	Gomez
190	Jun 3	3	0	Cin	Hook
191	Jun 4	5	0	Cin	Newcombe
192	Jun 12	9	0	at SF	Byerly
193	Jun 20	2	0	LA	Drysdale
194	Jun 20	6	0	LA	Drysdale
195	Jun 21(1stG)	4	1	SF	McCormick
196	Jun 24	1	1	LA	Koufax
197	Jun 29(2ndG)	2	0	at Chi	Anderson
198	Jul 1(2ndG)	8	2	at StL	Simmons
199	Jul 3	4	0	at StL	Kline
200	Jul 3	7	0	at StL	Kline
201	Jul 4(1stG)	8	1	Pit	Friend
202	Jul 7	6	0	Pha	Short
203	Jul 8	4	0	Cin	Hook
204	Jul 19	8	1	StL	Kline
205	Jul 20	4	0	StL	Broglio
206	Jul 22	8	1	at Chi	Elston
207	Jul 23	9	0	at Chi	Cardwell
208	Aug 4	9	0	at StL	Sadecki
209	Aug 5	8	0	Chi	Morehead
210	Aug 16	4	0	at Cin	Hook
211	Aug 17	8	1	at Cin	Brosnan
212	Aug 23	6	0	at LA	Roebuck
213	Aug 30	8	2	StL	Bauta
214	Sep 8	1	0	SF	McCormick
215	Sep 9	4	1	LA	Williams
216	Sep 10	1	2	LA	Craig
217	Sep 21	6	0	Cin	O'Toole
218	Sep 30	1	1	at Pit	Law
219	Sep 30	8	1	at Pit	Olivo
1961 (34)					
220	Apr 14	7	0	at Chi	Anderson
221	Apr 30	1	2	SF	Loes
222	Apr 30	6	0	SF	Loes
223	May 12	1	1	at SF	S. Jones
224	May 13	1	2	at SF	Marichal
225	May 21(2ndG)	4	1	at Cin	Maloney
226	May 26	8	0	LA	Farrell
227	May 28	3	1	LA	Craig
228	May 31	8	0	at Pit	Gibbon
229	Jun 8	7	0	at Cin	Maloney
230	Jun 18	3	1	LA	Drysdale
231	Jun 20	6	0	SF	McCormick
232	Jun 22	3	0	SF	Marichal
233	Jun 23	4	0	Chi	Curtis

HANK AARON'S HOME RUNS (Continued)

No.	Date	Inn	On Base	Opp	Pitcher
234	Jul 1	6	0	Cin	Hook
235	Jul 2(1stG)	3	1	Cin	O'Toole
236	Jul 4	7	0	LA	Farrell
237	Jul 5	1	1	Pha	Mahaffey
238	Jul 7	1	2	Pit	Haddix
239	Jul 7	3	1	Pit	Haddix
240	Jul 21	1	1	at Pit	Friend
241	Jul 21	6	0	at Pit	Friend
242	Jul 23(1stG)	6	0	at Pit	Haddix
243	Jul 25	4	0	Cin	Hunt
244	Jul 26	6	0	Cin	K. Johnson
245	Jul 28	2	0	StL	L. Jackson
246	Aug 2(2ndG)	7	3	at Chi	Anderson
247	Aug 4	7	0	at SF	McCormick
248	Aug 4	9	0	at SF	McCormick
249	Aug 12	6	1	Chi	Cardwell
250	Aug 15	6	1	Pit	Gibbon
251	Aug 25(1stG)	4	1	at Pha	Buzhardt
252	Sep 3(2ndG)	3	0	at Chi	Ellsworth
253	Sep 25	1	0	StL	Washburn
1962 (45)					
254	Apr 15	7	0	at LA	Koufax
255	Apr 18	1	0	at SF	Sanford
256	May 3	1	0	at Pha	Mahaffey
257	May 3	9	1	at Pha	Baldschun
258	May 12(2ndG)	5	1	at NY	Moorhead
259	May 18	2	0	NY	Craig
260	May 25	1	0	at StL	Simmons
261	May 25	7	2	at StL	Washburn
262	May 28	9	0	at Chi	Hobbie
263	May 31	6	1	Cin	Purkey
264	Jun 12	2	0	LA	Ortega
265	Jun 14	1	1	LA	Williams
266	Jun 15	7	3	at Pit	Olivo
267	Jun 18	3	3	at NY	Hook
268	Jun 20(2ndG)	3	1	at NY	Hunter
269	Jun 20(2ndG)	6	0	at NY	Hunter
270	Jun 25	5	1	at LA	Moeller
271	Jun 30	1	1	Chi	Ellsworth
272	Jul 3	4	1	at StL	Gibson
273	Jul 6	4	0	at Chi	Cardwell
274	Jul 8(1stG)	9	2	at Chi	Ellsworth
275	Jul 12	9	3	StL	McDaniel
276	Jul 17	4	1	SF	O'Dell
277	Jul 19	2	0	SF	McCormick
278	Jul 20	2	0	at Pha	Mahaffey
279	Jul 22(1stG)	6	0	at Pha	W. Smith
280	Jul 26	2	0	NY	Anderson
281	Jul 29	4	1	at Cin	Purkey
282	Jul 29	6	1	at Cin	Purkey
283	Aug 7	3	1	Chi	Koonce
284	Aug 14	7	0	Cin	Wills
285	Aug 19	2	0	SF	O'Dell
286	Aug 19	3	1	SF	O'Dell
287	Aug 24	2	0	at Chi	Buhl
288	Aug 25	4	1	at Chi	Cardwell
289	Aug 29	3	0	at SF	O'Dell
290	Sep 7	4	0	Pha	Bennett
291	Sep 9	6	0	Pha	Short
292	Sep 10	7	0	at NY	R.L. Miller
293	Sep 18	3	0	LA	Podres
294	Sep 22	8	1	at Pit	Sisk
295	Sep 23	1	0	at Pit	Friend
296	Sep 23	4	2	at Pit	Friend
297	Sep 25	3	2	NY	Hook
298	Sep 26	3	2	NY	Craig
1963 (44)					
299	Apr 11	7	0	NY	Rowe
300	Apr 19	8	1	at NY	Craig
301	Apr 21(1stG)	1	0	at NY	Hook
302	Apr 22	5	0	at LA	Drysdale
303	Apr 23	9	0	at LA	Perranoski
304	Apr 26	6	1	at SF	Stanek
305	Apr 28	9	0	at SF	Larsen
306	May 2	5	1	at Cin	Jay
307	May 3	5	2	Chi	Buhl
308	May 7	4	0	SF	Marichal
309	May 11	6	0	at Pha	Mahaffey
310	May 18	7	3	at Chi	McDaniel
311	May 19(1stG)	8	1	at Chi	Ellsworth
312	May 24	1	0	Pit	Friend
313	May 30	5	0	LA	Drysdale
314	May 31	6	1	Hou	K. Johnson
315	Jun 7	9	1	at Pit	Sisk
316	Jun 12	4	2	NY	Cisco
317	Jun 17	1	1	Pit	Cardwell
318	Jun 19	3	0	Pit	Francis
319	Jun 23	3	0	SF	Sanford
320	Jun 30	1	0	at LA	Willhite
321	Jul 3	6	1	at SF	Sanford
322	Jul 4	5	1	at SF	Fisher
323	Jul 11(1stG)	3	1	at StL	Broglio
324	Jul 13	1	2	at StL	Simmons
325	Jul 19	7	0	LA	Drysdale
326	Jul 21(1stG)	7	0	LA	Roebuck
327	Jul 28	4	1	Cin	Maloney
328	Jul 29	1	1	Cin	Tsitouris
329	Aug 2	3	2	NY	A. Jackson
330	Aug 14	7	3	LA	Drysdale
331	Aug 23	9	1	at LA	Sherry
332	Aug 26	8	1	at Hou	Brown
333	Aug 27	4	1	at Hou	Nottebart

HANK AARON'S HOME RUNS (Continued)

No.	Date	Inn	Base	Opp	Pitcher	No.	Date	Inn	Base	Opp	Pitcher
334	Sep 2	3	0	Pha	McLish	383	Jul 11	7	1 at	Cin	Ellis
335	Sep 6	3	0 at	Pha	McLish	384	Jul 19	1	0	NY	Fisher
336	Sep 7	3	0 at	Pha	Culp	385	Jul 20	7	2	NY	L. Miller
337	Sep 9	7	1 at	Cin	Jay	386	Jul 21	1	1 at	LA	Osteen
338	Sep 10	3	0 at	Cin	Tsitouris	387	Jul 22	1	2 at	LA	R. Miller
339	Sep 10	7	0 at	Cin	Tsitouris	388	Aug 4(1stG)	1	0	LA	Drysdale
340	Sep 15	7	1 at	StL	Burdette	389	Aug 4(2ndG)	7	0	LA	Osteen
341	Sep 25	3	1	Cin	O'Toole	390	Aug 11	3	0	StL	Washburn
342	Sep 29	1	0	Chi	Buhl	391	Aug 11	5	2	StL	Washburn
	1964 (24)					392	Aug 15	1	0 at	Chi	L. Jackson
343	Apr 16	3	2 at	Hou	Owens	393	Aug 17	5	1 at	StL	Stallard
344	May 10(1stG)	7	0 at	Pit	Friend	394	Aug 31(1stG)	3	0 at	Cin	Jay
345	May 23	8	0	StL	Taylor	395	Sep 8	6	0	Pha	Culp
346	May 24	8	0	StL	Shantz	396	Sep 17	1	0	SF	Marichal
347	May 30(1stG)	4	1	Chi	Buhl	397	Sep 17	3	1	SF	Marichal
348	Jun 7	5	1	Chi	Buhl	398	Sep 20	6	0	Pha	Culp
349	Jun 8	1	1 at	Hou	Brown		**1966 (44)**				
350	Jun 14(1stG)	9	1 at	LA	Perranoski	399	Apr 20	1	0 at	Pha	Culp
351	Jun 22	5	0	LA	Ortega	400	Apr 20	9	0 at	Pha	Belinsky
352	Jun 27	2	1	NY	Willey	401	Apr 25	5	1 at	SF	Priddy
353	Jun 28(2ndG)	5	2	NY	Lary	402	Apr 26	3	1 at	SF	Bolin
354	Jun 30	5	1 at	StL	Craig	403	Apr 27	9	0 at	LA	Sutton
355	Jul 16	1	0	SF	Perry	404	Apr 28	6	0 at	LA	Drysdale
356	Jul 26(1stG)	1	0 at	NY	A. Jackson	405	Apr 29	9	0	Hou	Sembera
357	Jul 26(2ndG)	9	2 at	NY	Hunter	406	May 1	9	0	Hou	Cuellar
358	Jul 31	9	2 at	Chi	McDaniel	407	May 8	1	0 at	Hou	Cuellar
359	Aug 1	8	0 at	Chi	Burdette	408	May 11	1	1	Cin	Ellis
360	Aug 6	6	2 at	Cin	Jay	409	May 11	5	2	Cin	Ellis
361	Aug 11	3	1	Hou	K. Johnson	410	May 17	5	0 at	StL	Simmons
362	Aug 11	6	2	Hou	Woodeshick	411	May 18	6	1 at	Pit	Law
363	Aug 16	4	1 at	SF	Duffalo	412	May 20	2	2	Chi	Faul
364	Aug 24	1	0	Pha	Bennett	413	May 21	7	0	Chi	Jenkins
365	Aug 30(2ndG)	8	2	SF	Herbel	414	May 27	2	0 at	Chi	Broglio
366	Sep 3	4	0 at	StL	Craig	415	Jun 1	6	1	SF	Herbel
	1965 (32)					416	Jun 3	9	0	StL	Gibson
367	Apr 29	8	0	StL	Taylor	417	Jun 8	1	0 at	NY	Fisher
368	May 2(2ndG)	5	0	Pha	Belinsky	418	Jun 8	3	3 at	NY	Fisher
369	May 4	6	0	Hou	Dierker	419	Jun 14	7	1 at	Pha	Craig
370	May 4	8	0	Hou	Coombs	420	Jun 18	8	1	Pit	Law
371	May 16	3	1 at	Pha	Short	421	Jun 19	8	0	Pit	Veale
372	May 30	5	1 at	Hou	Dierker	422	Jun 21	3	0	Pha	L. Jackson
373	Jun 1	8	0 at	Hou	Woodeshick	423	Jul 3	8	0 at	SF	Sadecki
374	Jun 8	10	1 at	Chi	Hendley	424	Jul 9	6	0 at	LA	Koufax
375	Jun 10	3	1 at	Chi	L. Jackson	425	Jul 17	7	1	Cin	Nottebart
376	Jun 12	1	0 at	StL	Gibson	426	Jul 21	7	0 at	StL	A. Jackson
377	Jun 19	5	1	StL	Sadecki	427	Jul 24(2ndG)	4	0 at	Cin	Ellis
378	Jun 20	6	0	StL	Purkey	428	Jul 26	7	0	StL	A. Jackson
379	Jun 29	9	0 at	NY	McGraw	429	Aug 2	5	0 at	Chi	Roberts
380	Jul 5	8	0	Hou	Farrell	430	Aug 13(2ndG)	9	0	Pha	Culp
381	Jul 7	7	0	Hou	Taylor	431	Aug 14	2	2	Pha	Buhl
382	Jul 8	1	0	Hou	Nottebart	432	Aug 22	6	1 at	LA	Drysdale

234

HANK AARON'S HOME RUNS (Continued)

No.	Date	Inn	Base	Opp	Pitcher
433	Aug 26	6	1	NY	McGraw
434	Aug 30	7	2	Chi	Holtzman
435	Sep 5(2ndG)	5	1	at Pit	Cardwell
436	Sep 13	1	1	at Chi	Holtzman
437	Sep 13	2	0	at Chi	Holtzman
438	Sep 22	4	2	Pit	Cardwell
439	Sep 25	4	0	Pit	Sisk
440	Sep 25	8	0	Pit	McBean
441	Sep 27	4	2	SF	Sadecki
442	Oct 1(2ndG)	8	1	at Cin	O'Toole

1967 (39)

No.	Date	Inn	Base	Opp	Pitcher
443	Apr 19	1	0	Hou	Giusti
444	Apr 19	4	0	Hou	Giusti
445	Apr 28	6	2	Pha	Ellsworth
446	Apr 30	6	0	Pha	Buhl
447	May 5	5	2	Cin	Ellis
448	May 10(1stG)	8	1	at Pha	Bunning
449	May 10(2ndG)	4	1	at Pha	L. Jackson
450	May 14	6	0	at Pit	Ribant
451	May 17	6	1	NY	Seaver
452	May 21	2	1	Pit	Blass
453	May 21	8	1	Pit	Mikkelsen
454	Jun 1	1	0	at StL	Washburn
455	Jun 2	9	1	at Cin	Ellis
456	Jun 3	1	0	at Cin	McCool
457	Jun 4	5	0	at Cin	Maloney
458	Jun 12	1	2	at Pha	Ellsworth
459	Jun 14	6	2	at Pha	Green
460	Jun 22(2ndG)	8	1	at SF	Linzy
461	Jun 27	3	3	Hou	Blasingame
462	Jun 27	8	1	Hou	Schneider
463	Jul 5	7	2	Chi	Hartenstein
464	Jul 9	8	0	at NY	Fisher
465	Jul 14	6	0	Pha	Wise
466	Jul 21	4	1	at StL	Briles
467	Jul 22	8	1	at StL	Hughes
468	Jul 27	1	1	Cin	Ellis
469	Aug 3	3	0	at Chi	Simmons
470	Aug 12(2ndG)	8	0	Hou	Cuellar
471	Aug 13	7	1	Hou	Sembera
472	Aug 16	3	2	SF	Bolin
473	Aug 19	5	1	at LA	Osteen
474	Aug 29	1	0	Pit	Sisk
475	Aug 31	8	0	LA	Osteen
476	Sep 3	7	1	LA	Drysdale
477	Sep 4(1stG)	1	1	Pha	Wise
478	Sep 12	3	0	NY	Fisher
479	Sep 14	4	1	NY	Frisella
480	Sep 20	5	1	Cin	Pappas
481	Sep 26	6	2	at Cin	Pappas

1968 (29)

No.	Date	Inn	Base	Opp	Pitcher
482	Apr 15	7	1	StL	Gibson
483	Apr 17	7	0	Chi	Hands
484	Apr 19	3	1	at Cin	Tsitouris
485	Apr 21	1	0	at Cin	Pappas
486	Apr 23	1	0	at Cin	Niekro
487	Apr 28	9	1	Pha	Wise
488	May 11	1	0	LA	Osteen
489	May 11	3	2	LA	Osteen
490	May 14	5	1	at Pha	L. Jackson
491	Jun 9(2ndG)	1	1	at Chi	Hands
492	Jun 12	3	1	StL	Briles
493	Jun 17	4	0	Cin	Maloney
494	Jun 21	8	0	at StL	Willis
495	Jun 27	1	0	Pha	Short
496	Jun 28	8	0	at LA	Kekich
497	Jul 5	3	1	Hou	Cuellar
498	Jul 7	4	0	Hou	Dierker
499	Jul 7	5	1	Hou	Dierker
500	Jul 14	3	2	SF	McCormick
501	Jul 26(1stG)	9	2	at Pha	G. Jackson
502	Aug 6	4	0	Chi	Niekro
503	Aug 21(2ndG)	3	1	at Chi	Nye
504	Aug 23	5	2	Pha	Wise
505	Aug 25	4	0	Pha	L. Jackson
506	Aug 28(2ndG)	6	0	at Pha	J. Johnson
507	Aug 29	1	0	at Pha	L. Jackson
508	Sep 11	3	1	SF	Marichal
509	Sep 22	1	0	at SF	Bolin
510	Sep 29	6	1	LA	Singer

1969 (44)

No.	Date	Inn	Base	Opp	Pitcher
511	Apr 12	4	0	Cin	Nolan
512	Apr 16	1	1	at Hou	Lemaster
513	Apr 28	3	2	Hou	Dierker
514	May 3	3	1	LA	Osteen
515	May 13	1	0	at NY	Gentry
516	May 15	3	0	at NY	Cardwell
517	May 15	7	0	at NY	Koonce
518	May 18	7	0	at Mtl	Face
519	May 22	1	1	NY	McGraw
520	May 31	1	0	at Chi	Jenkins
521	Jun 1	5	1	at Chi	Holtzman
522	Jun 2	8	0	at StL	Waslewski
523	Jun 3	6	0	at StL	Carlton
524	Jun 6	4	0	Pit	D. Ellis
525	Jun 8(1stG)	8	0	Pit	Hartenstein
526	Jun 11	5	0	Chi	Nye
527	Jun 12	8	2	Chi	Selma
528	Jun 17	9	0	Hou	Billingham
529	Jun 25	8	0	LA	Osteen
530	Jun 27	5	1	at Hou	Lemaster
531	Jun 30	3	2	Cin	Cloninger

235

HANK AARON'S HOME RUNS (Continued)

No.	Date	Inn	On Base	Opp	Pitcher	No.	Date	Inn	On Base	Opp	Pitcher
532	Jul 7	3	1	at LA	Foster	582	Jul 29	7	2	StL	Linzy
533	Jul 8(1stG)	1	0	at LA	Osteen	583	Aug 1	1	1	Pit	Dal Canton
534	Jul 15(1stG)	5	0	at Cin	Carroll	584	Aug 1	7	1	Pit	Pena
535	Jul 24	6	1	Mtl	Radatz	585	Aug 2	5	2	Pit	Ellis
536	Jul 25	7	0	Mtl	H. Reed	586	Aug 7(1stG)	6	1	at SD	Roberts
537	Jul 30(1stG)	3	0	at Pha	G. Jackson	587	Aug 9	8	0	at SD	Dobson
538	Jul 31(1stG)	6	0	at Pha	Palmer	588	Aug 12	2	1	Mtl	Stoneman
539	Aug 9	3	0	NY	Seaver	589	Aug 26	9	1	at NY	Gentry
540	Aug 13(1stG)	3	1	Pha	Boozer	590	Sep 3	3	2	LA	Foster
541	Aug 13(1stG)	5	0	Pha	Boozer	591	Sep 5(2ndG)	8	1	SF	Robertson
542	Aug 17	6	0	StL	Carlton	592	Oct 1	4	0	at Cin	Washburn
543	Aug 21	6	0	at Chi	Hands		**1971 (47)**				
544	Aug 24	14	2	at StL	Grant	593	Apr 7	7	0	at Cin	McGlothlin
545	Aug 28	1	2	at Pit	Blass	594	Apr 10	9	1	Pit	Blass
546	Aug 28	7	3	at Pit	Dal Canton	595	Apr 13	6	0	Cin	Gullett
547	Aug 30	7	0	Chi	K. Johnson	596	Apr 14	1	1	Cin	Cloninger
548	Sep 5	3	1	at Cin	Merritt	597	Apr 14	4	0	Cin	Cloninger
549	Sep 7	7	0	at Cin	Ribant	598	Apr 20	1	1	at Pit	Moose
550	Sep 10	4	0	SF	Bryant	599	Apr 25(1stG)	9	0	SD	Roberts
551	Sep 11	4	0	SF	McCormick	600	Apr 27	3	1	SF	Perry
552	Sep 17	12	0	at LA	Lamb	601	May 1	1	1	LA	Osteen
553	Sep 21	7	2	at SD	Dukes	602	May 1	8	1	LA	Mikkelson
554	Sep 26	4	0	SD	Corkins	603	May 2	8	0	LA	Brewer
	1970 (38)					604	May 8	8	2	at SF	J. Johnson
555	Apr 9	1	1	at SD	Kirby	605	May 18	1	1	NY	McAndrew
556	Apr 10	3	3	at Hou	Griffin	606	May 21	6	0	at NY	Ryan
557	Apr 13	1	1	SF	Reberger	607	May 27	6	0	at Mtl	McAnally
558	Apr 14	3	1	SF	Reberger	608	Jun 1	1	1	Hou	Blasingame
559	Apr 18	4	1	LA	Sutton	609	Jun 6	9	0	Chi	Hands
560	Apr 23	5	0	at Pit	Walker	610	Jun 8	1	1	StL	Carlton
561	Apr 28	1	0	at StL	Torrez	611	Jun 13	3	0	at Hou	Wilson
562	Apr 30	7	0	Chi	Cosman	612	Jun 21(1stG)	8	1	Mtl	Raymond
563	May 1	1	0	Chi	Decker	613	Jun 27	7	1	Cin	Nolan
564	May 5	2	1	Pit	Moose	614	Jun 27	9	1	Cin	Granger
565	May 6	1	1	Pit	Ellis	615	Jul 4	4	0	at NY	Seaver
566	May 8	6	2	StL	Gibson	616	Jul 10	7	0	at Pit	Blass
567	May 9	5	1	StL	Culver	617	Jul 17	3	0	LA	Alexander
568	May 11	10	0	at Chi	Reynolds	618	Jul 20	9	1	SD	Roberts
569	May 15	8	1	at Cin	Nolan	619	Jul 21(1stG)	1	1	SD	Arlin
570	May 17(2ndG)	3	1	at Cin	Simpson	620	Jul 21(1stG)	3	0	SD	Arlin
571	Jun 2	7	1	NY	Gentry	621	Jul 24	6	0	at LA	Osteen
572	Jun 18	5	1	at Mtl	Renko	622	Jul 31	8	0	at SD	Norman
573	Jun 19(2ndG)	5	1	Hou	Lemaster	623	Aug 3	7	0	at Pha	Short
574	Jun 20	4	0	Hou	Griffin	624	Aug 15	6	0	Hou	Forsch
575	Jun 21	1	1	Hou	Dierker	625	Aug 20	1	0	StL	Cleveland
576	Jun 21	4	1	Hou	Dierker	626	Aug 21	6	1	StL	Carlton
577	Jun 30	1	1	at Cin	McGlothlin	627	Aug 21	7	2	StL	Carlton
578	Jul 3(2ndG)	2	1	SD	Dobson	628	Aug 23(1stG)	6	0	Pit	Blass
579	Jul 17	6	1	at StL	Briles	629	Aug 24	4	0	Pit	Veale
580	Jul 25	6	1	at Chi	Jenkins	630	Aug 25	1	1	Pit	Kison
581	Jul 29	3	1	StL	Torrez	631	Aug 29	1	1	at Chi	Pizarro

HANK AARON'S HOME RUNS (Continued)

No.	Date	Inn	On Base	Opp	Pitcher	No.	Date	Inn	On Base	Opp	Pitcher
						672	Sep 27	1	0	at Cin	Grimsley
632	Sep 10	11	2	SF	J. Johnson	673	Oct 3	9	2	LA	Sutton
633	Sep 11	1	1	SF	Carrithers		**1973 (40)**				
634	Sep 14	1	2	at Cin	Gullett	674	Apr 11	6	2	at SD	Troedson
635	Sep 14	5	1	at Cin	Gullett	675	Apr 12	6	0	at SD	Norman
636	Sep 15	5	0	at Hou	Billingham	676	Apr 15	7	0	at LA	Downing
637	Sep 17	8	0	at LA	Osteen	677	Apr 20	3	1	at Cin	Gullett
638	Sep 21	1	0	SD	Franklin	678	Apr 27	4	0	NY	Seaver
639	Sep 26	5	0	LA	Osteen	679	May 1	3	1	Mtl	Moore
	1972 (34)					680	May 1	7	0	Mtl	Strohmayer
640	Apr 22	3	2	Cin	Gullett	681	May 5	1	0	at Pha	Carlton
641	Apr 23	8	0	Cin	Billingham	682	May 13(1stG)	9	1	SD	Greif
642	Apr 25	2	1	StL	Gibson	683	May 13(2ndG)	3	0	SD	Norman
643	Apr 26	1	0	StL	Wise	684	May 16	6	0	at Hou	Reuss
644	May 5	1	1	at StL	Gibson	685	May 22	6	0	SF	Marichal
645	May 6	8	0	at StL	Wise	686	May 27	1	1	at StL	Cleveland
646	May 26	4	1	SF	Marichal	687	Jun 9	3	0	StL	Spinks
647	May 28(1stG)	6	0	SF	Bryant	688	Jun 9	5	0	StL	Andrews
648	May 31	1	0	SD	Norman	689	Jun 11	4	2	Pit	Rooker
649	Jun 10	6	3	at Pha	Twitchell	690	Jun 15	4	0	Chi	Bonham
650	Jun 13	10	0	NY	Frisella	691	Jun 16	6	0	Chi	Reuschel
651	Jun 14	4	0	NY	Matlack	692	Jun 22	2	0	at SD	Jones
652	Jun 24(2ndG)	8	0	at LA	Brewer	693	Jun 29	6	1	LA	Downing
653	Jun 28(1stG)	9	1	at SD	Corkins	694	Jul 2	6	1	SF	Barr
654	Jun 29	6	0	at SD	Caldwell	695	Jul 8	4	0	at NY	Stone
655	Jul 2	1	1	at Hou	Roberts	696	Jul 8	6	1	at NY	Stone
656	Jul 3	7	2	at Hou	York	697	Jul 13	5	2	Mtl	Stoneman
657	Jul 9	4	0	Pit	Briles	698	Jul 17	6	0	NY	McGraw
658	Jul 11	7	2	at StL	Santorini	699	Jul 20	7	2	Pha	Twitchell
659	Jul 19	1	0	at Pit	Briles	700	Jul 21	3	1	Pha	Brett
660	Aug 6	4	0	at Cin	Simpson	701	Jul 31	9	0	Cin	Borbon
661	Aug 6	10	0	at Cin	Gullett	702	Aug 16	8	2	at Chi	Aker
662	Aug 9	1	1	Hou	Reuss	703	Aug 17	6	0	at Mtl	Renko
663	Aug 13	3	1	Cin	Hall	704	Aug 18	8	0	at Mtl	Rogers
664	Aug 16	8	0	at NY	Gentry	705	Aug 22	6	0	StL	Cleveland
665	Aug 29	5	0	Mtl	Moore	706	Aug 28	1	2	Chi	Pappas
666	Sep 2	1	1	Pha	Brandon	707	Sep 3	3	1	SD	Kirby
667	Sep 2	7	1	Pha	Scarce	708	Sep 3	5	0	SD	Romo
668	Sep 13	7	0	Cin	Hall	709	Sep 8	7	0	Cin	Billingham
669	Sep 13	9	0	Cin	Hall	710	Sep 10	3	1	SF	Carrithers
670	Sep 17	3	1	SF	Bryant	711	Sep 17	8	0	SD	Ross
671	Sep 26	1	0	at Cin	Gullett	712	Sep 22	6	2	Hou	Roberts
						713	Sep 29	5	2	Hou	Reuss

No.	Date	Inning	On Base	Opp.	Pitcher
714	_____	_____	_____	_____	_____
715	_____	_____	_____	_____	_____